VOICES FROM A TRUNK
The Lost Lives of the Quaker Eddisons 1805–1867

VOICES
FROM
A TRUNK

The Lost Lives of the Quaker Eddisons 1805–1867

Sara Woodall

Blackthorn Press, Blackthorn House
Middleton Road, Pickering YO18 8AL
United Kingdom
www.blackthornpress.com

ISBN 978 1 906259 42 6

Contents

CONTENTS

I do believe that maybe there is some kind of incredible network, a connection, a sort of spider web, or many spider webs that connect things, places, events. I think that everything has cause and effect, that we don't live long enough to see the relationship between events and the connections. But they are there, and they are magical.

Isabel Allende

Acknowledgements

This book could not have been written without the enthusiasm, encouragement and advice of my husband who put up with my unhealthily close relationship with the dead relatives. I thank Simon Creedy who allowed me to search the Bedale attics; my mother and Martin Eddison for the portraits; Sydney Eddison for her constant encouragement; Dan Woodall for educating me about steam engines; Sue Bradbury OBE, Editor-in-Chief of the Folio Society who gave invaluable help over the structure of the book; Henry Machin for extensive information about Gateford and for finding Arthur Young's description of John Eddison's farming methods; Aubrey Bowden, Booth Eddison's descendant who gave me information and pictures of Booth's family; my half-brother Andrew Hellicar who transcribed the murdered man's diary, gave me the little watercolour of Gateford House and made so many useful suggestions; Jenny Eddison for her information about Thomas Hardy; Robert Eddison; Lady Eyre for offering up the Eddison album on the internet; Lida and her late husband David Kindersley for involving me in publishing, and to Graham Beck for his useful advice; Philip Moore for photography; Phil Treble for the book design; Julia and Jeremy Lewis for much helpful advice; Hon. Richard Seebohm for researching the pencil drawing of George Fox; Oliver Pickering of Leeds University for information on the Leeds Quakers; Arabella Ainslie; Geoffrey Elliott; my good friend Gillie Coutts for her meticulous edit of the final draft; Duncan Robinson Director of the Fitzwilliam Museum and Master of Magdalene College, Cambridge, who came to look at Benjamin Eddison's portrait; Sir Roy Calne FRS and Andrew Crawshaw who commented on the Pain document; Professor Paul Israel, Editor of the Thomas Edison Papers at Rutgers University who was interested in my research. Lastly but not least my neighbour Adrian Bridgewater for his unflagging support and suggestions over the many drafts of the manuscript. And I cannot forget the Bedale ghosts whose benign presence appeared to overlook my every move. They seemed to generate many coincidences and without them this book could never have materialised.

Notes on the text

The Spellings of Eddison and other surnames were erratic as late as the eighteenth century so to save confusion I have in most places kept to a single spelling.

Money values are notoriously difficult to establish, so for simplicity I have multiplied 19th century values by a factor of fifty, being aware that this leaves many jagged assumptions.

Family Tree

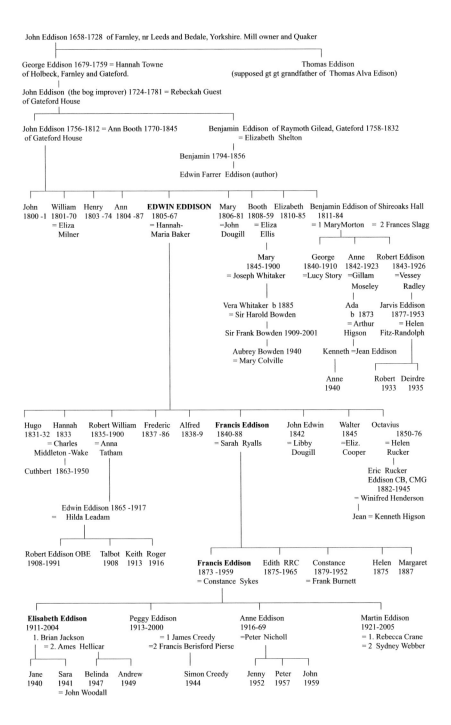

John Eddison 1658-1728 of Farnley, nr Leeds and Bedale, Yorkshire. Mill owner and Quaker

George Eddison 1679-1759 = Hannah Towne
of Holbeck, Farnley and Gateford.

Thomas Eddison
(supposed gt gt grandfather of Thomas Alva Edison)

John Eddison (the bog improver) 1724-1781 = Rebeckah Guest
of Gateford House

John Eddison 1756-1812 = Ann Booth 1770-1845
of Gateford House

Benjamin Eddison of Raymoth Gilead, Gateford 1758-1832
= Elizabeth Shelton

Benjamin 1794-1856

Edwin Farrer Eddison (author)

John	William	Henry	Ann	**EDWIN EDDISON**	Mary	Booth	Elizabeth	Benjamin Eddison of Shireoaks Hall
1800 -1	1801-70	1803 -74	1804 -87	1805-67	1806-81	1808-59	1810-85	1811-84
	= Eliza			= Hannah-	=John	= Eliza		= 1 MaryMorton = 2 Frances Slagg
	Milner			Maria Baker	Dougill	Ellis		

Mary
1845-1900
= Joseph Whitaker

George
1840-1910
=Lucy Story

Anne
1842-1923
=Gillam
Moseley

Robert Eddison
1843-1926
=Vessey
Radley

Vera Whitaker b 1885
= Sir Harold Bowden

Sir Frank Bowden 1909-2001

Aubrey Bowden 1940
= Mary Colville

Ada
b 1873
= Arthur
Higson

Jarvis Eddison
1877-1953
= Helen
Fitz-Randolph

Kenneth =Jean Eddison

Anne
1940

Robert   Deirdre
1933   1935

Hugo	Hannah	Robert	William	Frederic	Alfred	**Francis Eddison**	John Edwin	Walter	Octavius
1831-32	1833	1835-1900		1837 -86	1838-9	1840-88	1842	1845	1850-76
	= Charles	= Anna				= Sarah Ryalls	= Libby	=Eliz.	= Helen
	Middleton -Wake	Tatham					Dougill	Cooper	Rucker

Cuthbert 1863-1950

Eric Rucker
Eddison CB, CMG
1882-1945
= Winifred Henderson

Jean = Kenneth Higson

Edwin Eddison 1865 -1917
=   Hilda Leadam

Robert Eddison OBE	Talbot	Keith	Roger
1908-1991	1908	1913	1916

Francis Eddison	Edith RRC	Constance	Helen	Margaret
1873 -1959	1875-1965	1879-1952	1875	1887
= Constance Sykes		= Frank Burnett		

Elisabeth Eddison	Peggy Eddison	Anne Eddison	Martin Eddison
1911-2004	1913-2000	1916-69	1921-2005
1. Brian Jackson		=Peter Nicholl	= 1. Rebecca Crane
= 2. Ames Hellicar	= 1 James Creedy		= 2 Sydney Webber
	=2 Francis Berisford Pierse		

Jane	Sara	Belinda	Andrew	Simon Creedy	Jenny	Peter	John
1940	1941	1947	1949	1944	1952	1957	1959
		= John Woodall					

Abbreviated Eddison Family Tree

Showing a possible connection to Thomas Alva Edison

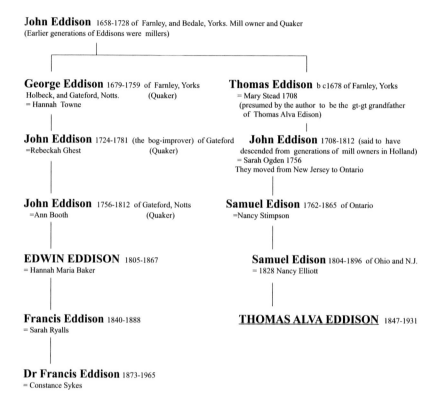

John Eddison 1658-1728 of Farnley, and Bedale, Yorks. Mill owner and Quaker
(Earlier generations of Eddisons were millers)

George Eddison 1679-1759 of Farnley, Yorks
Holbeck, and Gateford, Notts. (Quaker)
= Hannah Towne

Thomas Eddison b c1678 of Farnley, Yorks
= Mary Stead 1708
(presumed by the author to be the gt-gt grandfather
of Thomas Alva Edison)

John Eddison 1724-1781 (the bog-improver) of Gateford
=Rebeckah Ghest (Quaker)

John Eddison 1708-1812 (said to have
descended from generations of mill owners in Holland)
= Sarah Ogden 1756
They moved from New Jersey to Ontario

John Eddison 1756-1812 of Gateford, Notts
=Ann Booth (Quaker)

Samuel Edison 1762-1865 of Ontario
=Nancy Stimpson

EDWIN EDDISON 1805-1867
= Hannah Maria Baker

Samuel Edison 1804-1896 of Ohio and N.J.
= 1828 Nancy Elliott

Francis Eddison 1840-1888
= Sarah Ryalls

THOMAS ALVA EDDISON 1847-1931

Dr Francis Eddison 1873-1965
= Constance Sykes

To John and Dan Woodall,
and to Sydney Eddison.

Prologue

Twelve years ago in the chaos of my grandparents' attics I opened a black trunk and found on the top, a sixteen page document dated 1829 which appeared to be the rantings of an unnamed hypochondriac but in the end turned out to be descriptions of the agonies of my great-great grandfather, Edwin Eddison 1805–1867. The document begins ominously:

> *The first time that I recollect feeling my pain was after playing Football at Gateford when I was about 11 years old … and whenever I played with much exertion I invariably had Bloody Urine …*

Like many others, I was ignorant about this generation of the family but here was thrilling evidence of their existence. On the threshold of destruction and jumbled under mounds of moth-eaten clothes were everyday Georgian documents: house inventories, clothes lists, Quaker marriage certificates, frail genealogical charts, farming notes that impressed the agriculturalist Arthur Young, lists of horses with lovely Georgian names, secret messages in shorthand, laboured poems, undertakers' invoices and even a grocer's receipt for nasty tasting funeral biscuits. Pulsating letters gave apoplectic accounts of a bigamous marriage and a ship's diary told of the last days of a murdered man. This delicious cacophony of bygone chatter echoing across history plunged me into a forgotten world and drew me inexorably into Edwin Eddison's life. Reading of his miseries and studying old medical books, my eyes were opened to the quackery of the age.

The early Eddisons of Yorkshire and Nottinghamshire belonged to the Society of Friends with links to George Fox, and the family were part of the close community of Quakers involved in key moments of the Industrial Revolution. The letters reveal the family's connection with the invention of the steam plough, anti-slavery protests, legal battles to save children from sweeping chimneys and the birth of the railways when money poured into Quaker banks. There is an account of the crash of the great Quaker Overend and Gurney bank in 1866, the year Edwin took his family to America to visit rich relations and the letters sent home from this trip give a vivid description of the country recovering from the civil war.

I found a scrap of paper written by my grandfather which said that one Joseph Eddison (born in 1754), was thought to be an ancestor of Thomas Alva Edison the inventor of the light bulb and the phonograph and said to be the most prolific inventor in history. Joseph had left England aged twenty-three to fight for the British in the American War of Independence, which for a Quaker was against the rules. He was never heard of again. But Joseph could not have been the link.

Thomas Alva Edison looked astonishingly like my grandfather and the great-aunts always said there was a connection. This led me to scour fourteen generations of Eddison family trees and further research was simplified because in earlier days the name Eddison was uncommon in Yorkshire. I eventually came up with a theory, which though impossible to prove, made more sense than the Joseph Eddison story. I also discovered the fact that Thomas Alva Edison was from Quaker stock which is not mentioned in his biographies.

Quaker achievements run through the book, but this is a tale about the vibrant life of a comparatively rich and successful family at the threshold of the Industrial Revolution and before the discovery of significant medicines. Edwin Eddison and his agonies are at the centre of the story.

I
Anonymous Portraits

Can a ghost laugh, or shake his gaunt sides,
when you are pleasant with him?

Charles Lamb

On a wet afternoon my great-aunt Edith Eddison was killing slugs in her mossy greenhouse and as I watched her wield her slug scissors I had a feeling that the past was slipping by but was too young to ask her questions that later needed answers. She was the last of the spinster great-aunts who lived at the Old Manor, a dark house full of treasures in the small Nottinghamshire village of Epperstone. After she died my mother chose, among other family possessions, a painting of a beautiful man which now belongs to me.

Many years later, my mother turned up at my house and, dumping three portraits in the hall, said tersely, 'these are for you'. She had just come from her childhood home, St Gregory's House in Bedale, which had been inherited along with all its contents by her younger sister Peggy with whom her relationship was thorny. The unloved paintings had languished for years in the damp attics and Mother felt for some reason that I ought to look after them.

Then in the autumn of 2001 when visiting my uncle and aunt, Martin and Sydney Eddison in their old clap-board house in Echo Valley Road, Newtown, deep in Connecticut woods, I was given two more family portraits and a Victorian photograph album. But no facts.

Every time I passed the portraits on my walls I felt an uneasy kinship as they stared bleakly down. Who were they? Where had they lived? My mother, when asked, merely shrugged her shoulders and made disparaging remarks about their looks. No one knew until something happened that pulled me into their world and made my head reverberate with their chatter and the most private details of their lives. Quite by chance and guided, I tell myself, by ghosts, their life stories unravelled and words were to fall from their mouths like voices from a distant phonograph.

In one portrait a middle-aged woman wears a neatly goffered ruff and has a letter in her hand. She has watchful eyes and her black curls peep from an

[1]

elaborately pleated bonnet. The second painting is of a red faced man in a brown jacket and the third is of a humorous fellow with a likeness to Robert Eddison OBE, a twentieth century actor cousin. The portrait that belonged to the Epperstone aunts is of a handsome man with Regency locks and a high collar. His name, Uncle Henry, had been whispered in low voices by the great aunts.

As a child I had felt a fascination for the nineteenth century and often drew imaginary family groups with mournful faces and drooping whiskers. I loved old photograph albums and was insatiably inquisitive about relations – so I suppose it wasn't surprising that I felt compelled to race the two hundred miles up to Yorkshire when I heard that my grandparents' house was to be sold.

St Gregory's House had been built near the church at the far end of the North Yorkshire market town of Bedale. A low wall stood at the top of the path leading to the front door and with its pleasing symmetry and prim beauty the house looked out commandingly towards the little town.

In 1698 Richard Peirse Esq. presented Francis Pemberton to the Rector-ship of Bedale. Two years later Pemberton built St Gregory's House for his mother, the first brick house to be built in the area after The Great Fire of London and subsequent stipulations that only stone and brick houses were allowed. The house sits perfectly in its surroundings because its bricks were made on the neighbouring site of the Union House beside Bedale Beck. Robert Hird, a local historian said of the house 'its mode of architecture is the most fanciful of any in Bedale'.[1]

My grandfather, Dr Francis Eddison, having rented the house since 1912, bought it from Sir Henry Berisford-Peirse in 1929. My Aunt Peggy, (who in her sixties married Francis Berisford-Peirse, a cousin of the present bar-onet) was the last Eddison to live there. She died in an overheated home for the elderly in 2000 and the last time I saw her she was an emaciated, weakly creature, trussed in sheets and able only to move one alarmingly lively eye. A ghastly end to her life enforced by society and well-meaning doctors, nurses,

1   *Hird's Annals of Bedale* (1975) edited by Lesley Lewis.
    (Robert Hird 1768–1841)

carers and officials - fearful of litigation. In her father's day she would have had her own death.

As I arrived the house was being cleared by the auctioneers who had already removed the main furniture and were shortly to gather up the contents of the top rooms and the cellars for a later sale. There had to be family documents amongst the chaos. I did not know what to expect but was comforted by the fact that my grandparents were supreme hoarders and I was drawn on by an excitement I could not ignore.

Four musty rooms awaited me at the top of the dark staircase. They were heaped high with a lifetime's litter and the air was alive with disturbed ghosts. The grandparents were hopelessly untidy and these haunted rooms were the memorial to their indecisions – a fragmented epitaph of their long occupancy of the house. Wallpaper sagged and near the windows a leaf-mould of dead flies littered the floor. All around were mounds of junk and in one attic I could see the dismal sight of my grandfather's fine library strewn across the floor, soaking up the damp from leaking windows. There were ancient medical and historical volumes, their lovely old covers stuck to the floor – books on the husbandry of mules and horses in the First World War muddled up with Thoresby Society publications, theological books, old Leeds maps, biographies and leather bound copies of Punch from the very first issue. Here and there, tattered thrillers and American novels from the fifties were scattered around, their uncongenial covers cheering the gloom.

About ninety years earlier my mother had slept nervously in one of the attic rooms when the rest of the house was full. She had heard the ghosts and shuddered at the memories. Three of the rooms were large, the walls covered with once-pretty sprigged wallpaper. They had been for maids, but after the first World War only Ellen the kindly cook remained and, for her own determined reasons, she insisted on sleeping next to her warm sweaty kitchen in the basement amongst the warren of store rooms and cheese-smelling larders.

So the task ahead was formidable as I only had a few hours for my search. The chaos was mind-blowing. Simon Jenkins had written about his love of attics saying that they contain the souls of buildings and are the true resting places of household gods. He describes them as spaces glowing with promise, where downstairs order would rule, but upstairs would be anarchy, and in anarchy lay imagination.

Almost at once the ghosts took charge and although I know it is quite ordinary to expect them to interfere when dead lives are being disturbed (even Henry James imagined he saw the ghost of his brother at his elbow when writing *Notes of a Son and Brother*), but my experience was strange. As I entered the first attic, a black trunk, swathed in moth-infested clothes was in front of me and close beside it was a red suitcase of brittle imitation leather.

Lying on the floor, half-hidden by the red suitcase and threatened by a tottering pile of books, was a frontispiece torn from a book. It showed an oval engraving of a man in a pigtailed wig. Something made me pick it up. The page was attached to part of the blue cardboard cover and under the portrait was written:

MR ABRAHAM BOOTH,
Minister of the Gospel, London.
Engraved by Mackenzie from a Miniature
in the Possession of Mr Isaac Booth.

I opened the red suitcase. Inside were a few letters written with spidery handwriting. The first one was dated 1797. The signature was Abraham Booth. This was an exciting start as these few old letters would put flesh on the bare names of unknown people on the family tree. Little did I know that a steady stream of stifled voices would later pour from the old trunk.

Michael Holroyd has said 'By recreating the past we are calling on the same magic as our forebears did with stories of their ancestors round the fires under the night skies. The need to do this, to keep death in its place, lies deep in human nature.'[2] These feelings are ignored at one's peril. They are profound and it would have been unbearably rude to toss away all trace of these dead people as rubbish. Instead of tales round fires some sort of story, no matter how ordinary, had to be told – to bring them alive and to halt their obliteration for a while. Time was short and as so much family history was about to disappear, I worked feverishly for the few remaining hours. At the end of the day I felt the ghostly applause as I wound my way down the wide oak staircase.

2   Michael Holroyd, *Works on Paper*, Little Brown 2002.

Mr ABRAHAM BOOTH,

Minister of the Gospel, London.

Engraved by Mackenzie from a Miniature
in the Possession of Mr Isaac Booth.

2
Opening the boxes

There are ghosts in the air and ghostly echoes on paper
And the thunder of calls and notes.

Dylan Thomas

Many enthralling family histories begin with old deed boxes and trunks and I was grateful to the ghosts for parting the mess and arranging Abraham Booth's stray portrait beside the red suitcase containing his letters which I had almost fallen over.

Inside the suitcase was a box file with a rusty spring clip. It contained a badly typed family tree, the sheets stuck together with rough white-gummed tape which transposed me to a particular day when I was ten years old. I remembered wandering into the library to find my grandfather, Dr Francis Eddison, sitting at his partners' desk which was piled with a profusion of papers. The church bells started up next door and their companionable chimes seeded into my memory.

My grandfather was a large man with bushy eyebrows and his kindly face was alive with his interest in fellow beings. The room smelt of tobacco, old wooden tennis racquets and dogs and the walls were lined with books lovingly handed down from generation to generation. Grandfather treasured them and would have agreed with Professor George Steiner who said, 'books – the best antidote against the marsh-gas of boredom and vacuity.' How could the fastidious Francis Berisford-Peirse have later banished them to the attics?

Francis Eddison qualified as a doctor in 1905 and practised well into his eighties and even then, when his wobbly old legs prevented him from climbing stairs, he would shout up helpful advice to his ill patients in their beds from down below. He was also a coroner with an extensive knowledge of the law and in recognition of his work his coffin was borne into St Gregory's church by eight perspiring policemen.

Sometimes he used his library to see patients, but his main surgery was in a lower room reached by narrow wooden stairs. Before his marriage, after riding miles to visit sick people on his horse, Mrs Freedom, he would fall asleep in

Francis and Constance Eddison by the front door at St Gregory's House, Bedale

W. H. Auden and his wife

*Constance Eddison with her daughters
Elisabeth and Peggy*

Adventures
with a
Typewriter

In every age Man has equipped himself with that whereby to live—the warrior his sword, the knight his steed, the craftsman his tools, and now the modern girl—her typewriter.

When you start an adventure it is always wise to start right, not only in what you do but in what you think. Maybe you have just enrolled in a Business Training College, or have a typewriter at home and mean to teach yourself. In either case you are seated before a typewriter, and this book is in your hand—you are ready for the Adventure.

Perhaps you look something like this ·

a vast scarred leather chair, leaving his housekeeping sister Helen to her high jinks with the curates.

The day that I had wandered into the library as a child, he was battling with a hefty typewriter. He delightedly showed me how he could type both red and black letters and unrolled the family tree from a spring-clip box file, pointing out my name at the bottom. Now, fifty years later here I was, opening the same box file, miraculously saved from the attic compost.

Inside there was an instruction book *Adventures with a Typewriter* with a jolly girl on the cover and the caption 'Ready for the Adventure.' Overleaf was another picture of a girl in a tie and bobbed hair, coyly looking over her shoulder, saying 'Perhaps you look something like this?' Grandfather wasn't as keen as these eager girls and his typing remained atrocious.

There were also letters from Dr George Auden, grandfather's greatest friend. They had studied medicine and served together in the RAMC in the First World War. Both had married tall difficult women called Constance and the three Auden boys would come to stay at Bedale from time to time. In one of the letters I read:

> *The three boys are married. The Youngest Wystan has, as I dare say you have seen, achieved a success as a writer and critic.*

Mystified by this, I later bought W. H. Auden's biography which confirmed the three boys' marriages and related that in 1934 Christopher Isherwood wrote to ask Auden if he would marry Thomas Mann's thirty-year old lesbian daughter Erika to provide her with a passport. She was a journalist, rally driver and ran a satirical cabaret in Amsterdam performing anti-Nazi sketches. Isherwood was to portray her in his book *Goodbye to Berlin* which later became the musical *Cabaret*. Auden wired back 'DELIGHTED'.

The wedding in the registry office was hilarious. Auden did not know any of the answers to the Registrar's questions –

'Her name?'

'Well, she has been married and divorced – I don't know.'

'It doesn't matter, tell me later. Her age? – Never mind.'

They emerged into the sunshine and Auden said, 'He would have married me to the poker.'

Grandfather would have appreciated this story.

The black trunk was the greatest find and would make the silenced mouths of my portraits speak volumes. It held papers untouched for two hundred years. Attached to its handle was a faded label saying:

FAMILY Papers
See Also Old Calf Books etc.
Dr Eddison, Bedale, Yorks.

I lifted the lid. This was exciting as here was a time-capsule which would transport me into a Georgian world. I found worn leather folders, rolls tied with faded pink ribbons, meticulous farm accounts, poems, a wine-stained ship's journal dated 1830 (sent back from Australia with a mystery), old Quaker marriage documents, a 1767 Gretna Green marriage certificate, frail genealogical lists, maps of Leeds at the beginning of the Industrial Revolution, letters, wills and a stud list of seventy-six horses with lovely Georgian names,: Jolly, Molly, Bashful, Bounce, and the unfortunate Polley Farter. The writer of this list was John Eddison, born in 1724, and a friend of the celebrated agriculturalist Arthur Young.

Later, in another attic room, piled high with frayed Edwardian clothes, coroners' reports, pointed flapper shoes, bags, pith helmets, medical instruments, dangerous looking smears on medical slides, all heaped in wild abandon, I found the box of the old Eddison calf-bound books.

I picked up a document lying defiantly on top of all the others inside the trunk. There was something odd about this sheaf of foolscap papers fastened with a rusty pin. The sixteen pages were filled with large, clear handwriting – every now and then mistakes corrected by a scratchy Georgian nib. Solemnly the title proclaimed:

Memorandum respecting the **Pain** in my Side
10 Albion Street, Leeds, 17th September 1829

Whoever would want to write sixteen pages about their pain? Why was it on top of all the other documents? What was wrong with the man? As there was no signature I had no idea who he was. But he was to become the centre of the story and once I had discovered his identity, he seemed to take charge, driving me on and urging me not to waste time. How else could I have endured two years researching and reading the letters, spending hours with a magnifying glass, puzzling over maddening cross-written pages? It became

Memorandums respecting the
Pain in my Side

10 Albion St. Leeds 17th Sep: 1829

The first time that I recollect feeling
any pain was after playing at Football
at Gateford when I was about 14 years
old (1816). I am not certain at
what time it was exactly but I
know it was before I was 12 years
old – It might be before I was 10.

I am not sure that I had never
had bloody urine nor that I had
never felt any pain before the
above mentioned playing at football
But my urine was certainly
bloody then & I think for 2 days.
I do not recollect that I had
much pain. I think I had very
little. I have played at football
many times since then but
never since I was about 15 years
old; and whenever I played with

1.

an obsession and at times it was almost unbearable to read of his pain and the medical treatment he endured. In his case Voltaire's comment, 'doctors entertain the patient while nature performs a cure' seemed only too true.

As I read the letters, my affection for these unknown Quaker Eddisons grew and I began to think that ancestors were more fun than living relations. Dead relatives like budgerigars, were entertaining, uncritical and did not answer back, but I bore in mind Virginia Woolf's comment that biographers are like miners' canaries 'testing the atmosphere, detecting falsity, unreality and the presence of obsolete conventions'– a warning here to be cautious with all assumptions.

Why was it quite so fascinating? All families are interesting, all lives full of dramas, but sadly evidence is usually destroyed. It would have been so easy to throw away the threadbare greying tablecloth with family initials dating from 1735, the scrap of paper with George Stephenson's anecdotes, the ephemera, and the children's letters that shine with the enchantment of Constable's landscapes and the poetry of John Clare. To have stuffed these treasures into dustbin bags would have left just sterile names and dates on the family trees.

Much was ordinary in the letters, but rows, revenge, ripostes were hidden among respectful remarks; here and there secret episodes and suspected dramas could be imagined but embarrassing facts had surely been sifted out. Now with the portraits, photograph albums and visits to houses, their lives could be reconstructed creating an useful umbilical connection to the present.

This story, aside from the medical mystery, is a search for echoes, associations and feelings – the lost moments of history and the magical sense of continuity. It is a silent communication with the dead, which I hope will be useful to future generations.

The letters revealed the identity of Edwin Eddison my great-great grandfather, the man who had written about his pain. He was born at Gateford House in Nottinghamshire in 1805 and his life drew me deeply into his era and into the dreadful world of nineteenth century medicine.

3
Living with Pain

Give me a doctor, partridge plump,
Short in the leg and broad in the rump,
An endomorph with gentle hands
Who'll never make absurd demands.

W. H. Auden

Having discovered that Edwin Eddison had written the sixteen page document dated 1829 entitled *Memorandum respecting the **Pain** in my side* I sat down at the kitchen table to read the pages again more carefully. Edwin, a young lawyer of twenty-four was about to consult England's leading surgeon, Mr Abernethy. Perhaps he wrote the account to clarify his mind. He was obviously extremely worried.

> *The first time that I recollect feeling any pain was after playing at football at Gateford when I was about eleven years old. I am not sure that I had never had bloody urine nor that I had never felt any pain before the above mentioned playing at football. But my urine was certainly bloody then and I think for 2 days. I do not recollect that I had much pain. I think I had very little. I have played at football many times since then, but never since I was about 15 years old; and whenever I played with much exertion I invariably had Bloody Urine. I omitted to say before that I attribute the first Bloody Urine to my having both feet kicked from under me and my falling on the right side on a small Hillock.*

On the second page a drawing of a torso shows the pain radiating from a small brown dot representing the navel.

At his desk in his house in Leeds, the weakened Edwin scratches away with a steel nib. Already he has seen nine doctors who have brightly said that he will get better, but his bones tell him otherwise. He feels he is incurable and that their awful treatments were doing no good. He is right.

The pain is now intolerable which has made him even more determined to consult the celebrated John Abernethy, FRS, a humorous, cynical fellow and one of the richest and busiest doctors of the day with a reputation for being

John Abernethy FRS, a humorous, cynical fellow and one of the richest and busiest doctors of the day

Grimaldi by George Cruikshank

The pain is always on the right side & has always been in the same place to the best of my recollection.

If a tape were put round the body about half an inch than inch above the navel it would pass over the seat of the pain 6 inches from my navel & 11 from my back bone. I feel a difficulty in saying how near I think it is to the surface of the Belly but I guess it to be at least 2 inches or an inch & a half.

The site of Edwin's pain

blunt and at times even cruel. Edwin enters his surgery clutching his sixteen foolscap sheets. He was nervous as the surgeon was notorious.

An anatomist, physiologist and surgeon, Abernethy was founder of St. Bartholomew's Hospital Medical School in 1790. His lectures were so popular that they were taken down by fast writers and published in the Lancet – its publishers promptly sued by Abernethy.

Like his great colleague John Hunter, Abernethy only operated when absolutely necessary and had downed instruments in 1827 the year before Edwin's visit. Two years later at sixty-seven he died.

When asked by an indolent patient for a cure for gout, Abernethy replied 'Live upon sixpence a day and earn it'. He invented 'Botanical Pills' 'for irritation of the kidneys and diseases of a delicate nature' along with other pills and ointments – mixtures mainly of petroleum, which made him a certain amount of money. Edwin was intuitively suspicious of the prescription that Abernethy dashed off after his consultation.

The doctor was interested in diets and is thought to have invented the hard and rather dull Abernethy biscuit. Nutritional biscuits were not a new idea; Dr William Oliver of Bath had invented his 'Bath Olivers' as a diet for wealthy, over-fed patients a century earlier. The Abernethy biscuit was basically a plain Captain's biscuit with sugar and caraway seeds added, presumably, because they were thought good for digestive disorders.

There are many anecdotes about the great doctor.

A rich woman with a nervous complaint irritated him by describing her frivolous troubles with too much detail. He interrupted by holding out his hand for the fee. She gave him a £1 note and a shilling which he rudely returned saying 'There, Ma'am! Go and buy a skipping rope, that is all you want'.

A titled gentleman who consulted the doctor was received with the rudeness for which he was notorious. The patient lost his temper and told Abernethy that he would make him 'eat his words'. 'It will be of no use', the doctor replied, 'for they will be sure to come up again'.

There is a well known story about a patient who went to his surgery complaining of melancholy. After an examination the doctor exclaimed, 'You need amusement. Go and hear the comedian Grimaldi. He will make you laugh and that will be better for you than any drugs'. Said the patient quietly – 'I am Grimaldi'.

The Pain document continues:

The pain is what I call an aching pain. I can compare it to nothing better than this. Put the finger in the mouth and bite gently at the root of the nail and now and then bite keenly to imitate the twinges and throbbings. In walking I have generally found partial relief from putting my right arm behind me across the loins or small of my back and sometimes by putting my umbrella across my loins and holding it there as I walked along by hanging both my elbows upon it and bringing my hands forward.

Edwin details all the possible causes of the pain describing various methods of relief, preferring a horse-hair mattress to a more comfortable feather one, hot flannels and a bladder (an early form of hot water bottle) and, surprisingly, mentions that he 'once had a warm bath'. He also has an insatiable urge to jump hedges – an antic he shares with Jonathan Swift who had the same wild desire to 'run like a buck across country; gates, stiles and quicksets he no more valued than if they had been so many straws.' Cut by hand in those days, hedges fortunately were fairly low.

In the month of March or April last, thinking myself quite recovered having had no pain for at least 6 month or perhaps 12 months, I had a mind to try my skill at jumping and exercise of which I have been almost madly fond from childhood and having within a short time before often jumped over styles and low gates without feeling any injury I tried at a Hedge with a ditch on both sides and I suppose I jumped in height 4 feet and a few inches and in length about 4 yards. I just caught the tip of one foot on a fast Briar in the Hedge and fell on my hands and feet on the other side. I did not feel much shaken but the next morning I noticed that my urine was very bloody.

Now some unpleasant details:

I recollected the night before noticing the sound of the running of the urine being dead and frothy but did not look at it particularly. The sediment was very dark coloured; almost black. It was not like coagulated Blood but more like what I fancy blood would be if it were dried and finely powdered and then mixed with a little water to make it liquid.

… and an embarrassing fall in front of a coach party …

*Soon after this I was out at a tea party and in coming away (certainly not drunk
for I think I had had neither wine nor spirits) it was in the dark and I forgot
that there were 5 steps at the door. The coach and party were waiting of me and
I went quickly out of the door setting my left foot on the threshold and expecting
to set my right foot on the same level in an oblique direction from the door and
missed all the steps except just the corner of one and fell flatly on my right buttock
and right hand. I sprained my right foot and for several days felt pain in my side
but my urine was not very Bloody. I omitted to say that the jumping was in the
morning (8 o'clock) and that though I did not notice my urine to be bloody that
day yet it might have been bloody every time of voiding (emptying) after the jump
as I always went to the water closet which is rather dark. The urine which I first
noticed was what I voided on the evening of the day of jumping and I forgot to say
it was covered over with a fat flake, like hot tallow dropped from a Burning candle
into cold water. On the 6th of July last I first consulted Mr Thackrah a Surgeon at
Leeds and at his recommendation I put 6 or 7 Leeches on, the 7th July.*

This was the doctor Edwin most respected. Charles Thackrah 1795–1833, a
founder member of the Leeds Medical school in 1831, who also had a life
dogged by ill health, despite which he wrote books on industrial diseases,
addressing the postural deformities in child mill workers and dust diseases in
miners. His work influenced the passing of the Factory Act 1833 prohibit-
ing the employment of children under nine in the textile mills. Sir John Simon considered his contribution to preventive medicine as comparable to the
work of Jenner on smallpox.

Now Edwin attempts some cures:

*I have been Bled many times lately with Leeches but have not found so much
benefit at any time as the first. The first time I was bled was when I was about 12
years old. I had 6 and felt very much relieved from them. Mr Langley a Surgeon
at Worksop then attended me and he had previously recommended a Lotion which
frothed when I rubbed it on the side and smelled of Camphor. I do not recollect that
I felt benefit from it. I think it was useful in making me think I was not well and I
was therefore induced to take more care of myself.*

Foolishly he went for a brisk fourteen mile walk, suppressing, he said, 'a
mad urge to jump' and was almost sick with pain. Not daring to go back to
Mr Thackrah, he boarded the coach to Doncaster clutching a box of quiver-
ing leeches. It was a distance of 45 miles (two day's journey) and from there he

Edwin was nervous of trying 'emollient clysters'.
Engraving from Juke's book on Indigestion.

took a jolting gig to Gateford. Once home, twelve leeches were applied and
then two days later a dozen more. Then seventeen fresh ones four days later,
then nineteen more. He was so confident this time that the blood letting had
done the trick that he decided to venture out with a party to Chatsworth,
Matlock, Bakewell, Buxton, Castleton, Middleton, Buslow and Chesterfield.

This was asking for trouble. Proudly he insisted that he had walked further than any of the others but, descending the High Tor at Matlock, he fell
and was soon in constant pain. Reaching home, white faced and perilously
short of blood, sixteen more bloodthirsty little leeches were attached to his
pale skin. But the pain still hammered away. Mr Thackrah now ordered a
blister plaster to be put on for ten days. This was excruciating and Edwin
thrashed about trying to get some relief. Why were the plasters so horrible?
Anti-Hysteric Plasters, described in the late 18th century Buchan's *Family
Physician*, were made by melting galbanum, tacamahaca powder, yellow wax,
Venice turpentine, powdered cumin and afafoetida. This useless unguent was
spread on a piece of soft leather and applied to the skin and then forty drops
of laudanum rubbed on the surface of the plaster helped to dull the excruciating itch. That night Edwin suffered further intense agony when his left testicle
became drawn up. Blinded by pain and swathed in hot flannels, he took an

anodyne draught made from Peruvian bark [3]. The blister plaster did not work so another torture was tried

> *After it I had an Antinvonial Powder Plaster (I think it was called). It was also painful at times and I think I had as much loss as profit from it, for when it itched I rubbed or scratched the side and it being at all times very soon injured from pressure, I think I hurt it with the rubbing. It was on about a week.*

This was probably an Antimony Powder Plaster, the worse kind of treatment for Edwin's particular complaint. Antimony compounds were used to cause skin eruptions, diarrhoea and vomiting in the belief that the diseased area was responding by being brought to the surface. Its use caused reactions similar to arsenic poisoning, damaging the kidneys and the violent vomiting tended to lead to death in a few days.

Fortunately Edwin refuses to have any more blistering or plastering 'unless the medical advisers were very obstinate'. But the pain returns even more severely. He tries very hot poultices and then one of his rare hot baths. Nothing seems to work. He is nervous about trying 'emollient clysters' (enemas) a favourite torture recommended in a little book, *Indigestion* by Edward Jukes [4] (which something made me pick up from the attic floor!). Edwin has now been holed up in his room for twenty days so he tries some weird postures

> *I find most relief when the pain is very severe by propping my back with a round sofa pillow and putting my right leg under my left thigh in a tailor like manner.*

According to Dr Buchan a likely cause of the pain was damage to the kidney or an ulcer somewhere in the urinary passage. Buchan's treatment for inflammation of the kidneys was bleeding ten or twelve ounces from the arm or foot every twenty-four hours and leeches applied, eye-wateringly, to the haemorrhoidal veins.

Edwin paid a great deal of money for Abernethy's diagnosis which was in the end humiliating. He prescribed a teaspoon of castor oil in a dessert spoon of peppermint water – a very ordinary treatment for constipation. He also

---

3   First advertised in England in 1658. Distantly related to
    the aspirin.
4   *Indigestion and Costiveness*, Edward Jukes published 1831

wrote an almost illegible prescription for a blue pill. Edwin writes disparagingly

> *I have not tried the Pills. Castor Oil seems to suit me better than anything that I have tried. I think salts make me worse.'*

In Edwin's copy of *Indigestion*, Edward Jukes writes sneeringly about Abernethy's blue pill containing mercury which he considered dangerous. Jukes writes 'It is much to be regretted that the name of Abernethy should be associated with such insufferable quackery'. A younger contemporary of Abernethy's, John Elliotson, said that even if Abernethy had lived a hundred years and did good all the time, he would not overcome the mischief he caused by his blue pills. Yet Elliotson offered to replace these heavy little pills with colocynth and bitter lemon, a purgative so powerful that he was accused of poisoning his patients.

At the end of the sixteen pages of misery Edwin writes an indignant paragraph giving a worrying insight into his childhood:

> *My father was a farmer and when I was a boy, (i.e. from about 10 years old to 14) they used to call me idle because I did not like to work even as a sort of amusement, either in favours by most boys. This charge galled me to the very marrow and under irritated feeling I have often let my wounded pride get the better of my reason and have often at such times worked for a short time very hard so that at night or the next morning my urine would be as much like blood as wine. I have sometimes when the pain has been severe complained but not often. I thought it was quite derogatory to my character. At this time of my life I used at some seasons of the year to go to bed with my stockings as often wet as dry and have often put them on wet the next morning.*

The last sentence was written after he had heard one of Mr Abernethy's more dubious pronouncements: 'wet feet are some of the most effective agents death has in the field. It has peopled more graves than all the gory engines of war. Those who neglect to keep their feet dry are suicides'.

Did the pain ever go away? How did Edwin cope with life? How long did he live? Obviously he married and had children but I was curious to to know more and so it was necessary to read through the huge number of letters that were in the black trunk.

Edwin Eddison, standing awkwardly to relieve the pain

I showed the 'Pain' document to two medical friends — one, Andrew Craw-shaw, thought that Edwin might have had a disease of the right kidney. Of course he could not diagnose the disease but imagined it was caused by an accident and then complicated by infection. The second, Professor Sir Roy Calne FRS, who performed the world's first liver, heart and lung transplant, agreed that the recurring pain in the left loin with blood in the urine was ag-gravated by activity. As it started after the football game in 1816 and recurred with colic on and off up to 1829, he felt that as it was a chronic condition, TB was unlikely as Edwin seems to have been too well and the condition did not spread. He thought it could have been a stone or malformation of blood vessels in the kidney and that the treatment he received would not have helped: the leech bleeding would probably have made him worse. Of course Sir Roy could not say what treatment he would have given.

Diagnosis is impossible but these two professionals' views seem more than likely to explain the cause of Edwin's pain and one can only be amazed and impressed that he managed to tolerate it and survive a full life. I suspect Dr Abernethy's biscuits would have been far better for him than all the dubious treatments he undertook during his lifetime.

4
Edwin's Birthplace

Respectable means rich, and decent means poor.
I should die if I heard my family called decent.
Thomas Love Peacock, *Crotchet Castle*

Many years ago my brother gave me a primitive watercolour in a stout wooden frame of a house which he had found in my parents' attics. On its back someone had written: *GATEFORD HOUSE. Home of the respectable family Eddison.*

This had to be Edwin's childhood home, so I needed to find out if it still existed. I was not optimistic as coal mining had riddled the district and the painting itself was unclear. Driving through the village of Gateford in Nottinghamshire my husband turned the car round in the Old Gateford Road and glancing to my right I noticed a tall red brick house separated from the road by a small lawn and hedge. Surely it had been too easy to find? We left the car, held the picture up, counted the windows and were amazed that this 280 year-old house looked as fresh as the day it was built. There was a garden at the side surrounded by a wall and at the back there was a courtyard flanked by old farm buildings.

Gateford House is described in Nikolaus Pevsner's The Buildings of England: '… an 18th century double-pile brick house of two-and-a-half storeys. The earlier part is the gabled rear range of *c.* 1700 to which a front range with hipped roof and pedimented doorcase was added in *c.* 1720–40'.

The first Eddison to live in the house was George Eddison 1679–1759, a Quaker of Farnley and Holbeck near Leeds, Yorkshire. George was a successful clothier in Holbeck. He died at Gateford House but it is unclear when he went to live there with his wife Hannah and six children. It is thought that he bought a farmhouse and small-holding at Gateford and then converted it to a gentleman's residence by building on the new front and wings in about 1720. He acquired the tenancy of Gateford Farm and possibly also rented Gateford Hall Farm.

There are records of George Eddison attending various Quaker meetings, paying for Friends Meeting House repairs and subscribing to William

Gateford House, Nottinghamshire

Penn's works in 1724. A branch of Eddisons from the Adel area near Leeds had emigrated to America in 1696 so links with the new country were strong and George Eddison's son, another George, sent money across the Atlantic to Quaker Friends in America. This, and other hearsay stories, from my great-aunts,[5] led me to believe that there was a connection with the inventor, Thomas Alva Edison[6], whose great-grandfather is unknown. The biographies say that Thomas Alva was of Dutch ancestry but my grandfather thought the link was George Eddison's grandson Joseph (b. 1754) who appalled his Quaker relations by enlisting to fight for the English in 1777 in the American War of Independence and was never heard of again. As Thomas Alva's grandfather

5 Edwin's grand-daughters Edith, Margaret and Helen Eddison who lived at The Old Manor, Epperstone, Nottinghamshire.

6 Thomas Alva Edison 1847–1931 the prolific American inventor and businessman, among whose inventions were the phonograph, the carbon microphone used in all telephones and a practical light bulb. He applied the principles of mass production and large scale teamwork to the process of invention.

Samuel was born in 1767, Joseph could not have been the connection. My theory is that a more likely connection was Thomas Eddison (who later disappeared from the records), brother of George Eddison the first inhabitant of Gateford House. This theory is described in Chapter 6.

Before he took over Gateford House, George Eddison married Hannah Towne of Holbeck in 1718 at a Quaker ceremony in Leeds and there was a pencilled list of witnesses to their marriage among the papers. In those days Quaker weddings were not recognised by the Church so Quaker children were often deemed illegitimate. Later judgements in the civil courts considered the marriages good as long as they were open and before many witnesses.

The first Leeds Quaker Meeting House was in Water Lane, Holbeck near where George Eddison had lived, but as the town prospered Holbeck soon became engulfed by smoky factories. This may have been why George moved to Nottinghamshire to live among the huge houses of the Dukeries. Even before the Norman Conquest Carlton-in-Lindrick had six resident Thanes or Earls and in the Eddisons' day Dukes abounded: Norfolk, Newcastle, Portland, Kingston and Leeds all lived cheek by jowl in their vast houses. The woollen industry had been profitable in Leeds, so probably George made money and thought farming would be a more respectable way of life. Perhaps he wanted to live near Quaker Friends.

George knew the Rodes family who were in the inner circle of the Quakers of the day and who had lived since the time of James I at Barlborough Hall, a house about six miles from Gateford which was said to have been built by Robert Smythson. A note among the papers describes a pleasant evening George spent with the Rodes, which suggests that the Society of Friends was their link.

Sir Francis Rodes, 3rd Baronet of Barlborough was a friend of the Quaker William Penn (1644–1718) who founded Pennsylvania. His daughter Frances Rodes married Gilbert Heathcote in 1690 and as her shy brother, Sir John Rodes 4th Baronet did not marry, her grandson Gilbert Heathcote took the name Rodes and inherited the estate.

A surprising Quaker link with the slave trade is recorded: Gilbert's brother John Heathcote, in partnership with Dodshon Foster, another Quaker, had two small ships, *The Barlborough*, 40 tons and *The Bold*, 70 tons, which sailed from Lancaster in the 1750's to the Guinea coast to pick up slaves to take to Barbados and Jamaica. In total the two ships transported 650 slaves in five voyages.

Exploration of the Rodes's family history revealed another Eddison link with the early settlers in America. In 1681, after the death of her husband Sir Francis Rodes 3rd Baronet in 1675, Dame Martha Rodes, deeply in debt, had to mortgage a third of the manor of Gateford to her bailiff, Samuel Barker for £360, who also managed the Rodes's coal business.

The enterprising Samuel Barker, also a Quaker, was able to buy 1000 acres in Pennsylvania from William Penn. He was one of the first settlers in Burlington, New Jersey along with a posse of closely knit Quakers – several connected by marriage to the Eddisons: the Farnsworths, Fretwells, Revells and the Stacys of Ballifield Hall. Mahlon Stacy (a cousin of Samuel Barker) was an influential member of the group and was related to the Aldams of Warmsworth who were prominent early Quakers and cousins of the Eddisons. Perhaps Mahlon Edison, the uncle of Thomas Alva Edison, was named after this early settler? Could George Eddison's mysterious brother, Thomas have travelled with a brave band of Quaker settlers? Unfortunately passenger lists are not complete.

When old George Eddison died at Gateford House in 1759 his son John (1724–1781) took over. John was a successful wool merchant who farmed at Gateford with zeal. In 1748 he married Rebekah Ghest whose aunt Elizabeth was married to John Aldam [7] and the Aldam cousins dart in and out of Gateford House in the letters.

It is said that Quakers preferred to rent rather than buy property because 'it was thought the heart would be more firmly fixed on things eternal if living between hired walls and be less likely to glory in earthly possessions'. A quizzical note in the trunk, stated that George Eddison's son John 'bought Gateford – or did his trustees? – from Mr Rodes of Barlborough Hall.' It is not clear whether Gateford House was owned or rented, even though it is legally documented that John owned some of the land and rented 314 acres in 1778. There are notes that John bought the live-stock on 1 August 1760, the year after his father George had died .

John was a passionate farmer and on two frail sheets dated 1768, his strong hand records the names, ages and values of his 41 horses, including the aptly

---

7   His grandfather Thomas Aldam 1616–1660, known as the First Friend, frequently entertained George Fox (founder of the Quaker movement) at Warmsworth, Doncaster.

John Eddison's 1768 list of horses and farming costs

named Polley Farter, valued at £7.7s. Better horses were valued at £42. There were also 24 cows, 43 sheep and other farm paraphernalia and the the stock was valued at £967. All seemed to be going well, but one day while trawling the internet I was shocked to find an announcement from the Leeds Intelligencer stating: 'John Eddison of Gateford shot himself in his own garden 7 August 1781.' Nothing more.

Arthur Young FRS, agricultural reformer and writer who admired John Eddison's farming methods

The agriculturalist Robert Bakewell of Dishley

Illustration from Arthur Young's book The Farmer's Tour Through the East of England, *1771, showing John Eddison's whin mill and hay barn*

Things must have been going badly wrong. I found a note saying that John had a lawsuit with the local landowner the Duke of Norfolk, the expenses of which caused the sale of Gateford. A further note said 'Received 17 May 1780 of Mr John Eddison 7 shillings for advertising twice in the Nottingham paper, goods and estate to be sold'.

John Eddison was a man of intelligence. He was an excellent farmer and friend of the leading agriculturalist of the day, Arthur Young, FRS [8], who wrote about John's curious way of improving bog-land by an original manipulation of twitch grass [9]. There were descriptions of John's farming methods in Young's book, *The Farmer's Tour Through the East of England* which was published in 1771. In the preface Young wrote: 'I am indebted to friend Eddison of Gateford for a very curious account of improving a bog, and other particulars. He is an excellent farmer.' Fifteen pages of the book describe John's farming, with lists of stock and his expenses. There is an illustration of 'Mr Eddison's Whin Mill at Gateford,' the text explaining that after being bruised in this mill, the young shoots of gorse (whin) grown on poor land, could be used in the winter for the horses who preferred squashed whin to corn and hay. There is also a drawing of Eddison's unique barn with projecting roofs and racks filled with foodstuffs from inside the barn, sheltering the heads of horses and the food from the rain, although today's vets would disapprove of the the high racks which would cause hay seeds and dust to enter the animal's lungs.

Arthur Young writes glowingly of John's methods of improving forest wasteland at Gateford and his other successful farming ideas, describing how his breed of long-horned cattle improved the average milk yield. Young writes 'The average quantity of milk per cow 3 gallons. Mr Eddison has had some that gave 9 gallons a day.' Today's average yield is around six gallons a day.

Young says: 'Mr Eddison has gained a very good and profitable breed of sheep by hiring a tup of the agriculturalist Mr Bakewell of Dishley'. Robert Bakewell 1725–1795 (a rotund individual whose magnificent portrait on an appropriately robust horse hangs in the National Portrait Gallery), revolutionised English sheep and cattle breeding. He was the first to establish trade in ram-letting on a large scale and one year made 1,200 guineas from the letting of an energetic single ram. His methods transformed the quality of Britain's cattle, horses and sheep, so John Eddison spent his money well, hiring one of these wildly expensive rams.

---

8   Arthur Young, *The Farmer's Tour Through the East of England*, 1771

9   Twitch grass sown into the bog takes root and forms a matted net-work of roots so that it is bound into a firm surface on which a carpet of white clover and other valuable grasses take over and the twitch grass disappears.

John Eddison's unexpected suicide at Gateford in 1781 was a blow to the family. His twenty-five year old son, John, (1756–1812) took over the lease of the house and land and rather late in life, at the age of forty-three, married Ann Booth of Kirkby Woodhouse. There may have been debts as John seemed in a scramble to make money, becoming a corn and seed merchant and a partner with Benjamin Jefford and George Phipps trading as Jefford Eddison & Co, Woolstaplers. As well as all this he was farming land round Gateford.

Woolstaplers, key figures in the textile world, were business men of capital. They organised the supply of wool from the farmers and their pack-horse trains trudged over the countryside. The wool was sorted, scoured, then handed out to the wool combers. 'Tops' of the combed wool were then distributed to the hand-spinners and in fine weather women and children could be seen everywhere spinning outside cottage doors. The collected spun yarn was passed to hand-loom weavers who specialised in weaving different types of cloth: camlets, tammies, russels, serges and calimancoes. The woolstaplers' warehouses would be filled with the finished pieces of cloth for display on market days. Later they described themselves as stuff makers or woollen cloth makers.

Riots broke out in Nottingham in 1789 over the high price of food. By July 1800 wheat cost almost three times as much as in early 1799. Soup houses were set up but many people died of hunger, so a royal proclamation urged the reduction of flour in each household and soon each person was restricted to one meagre loaf a week. The Nottingham riots lasted three days, then the army was called in. Fortunately the Eddisons were a safe twenty miles away at Gateford.

There is a letter to John Eddison from his wife Ann, at Gateford House dated 12 February 1802. John is in London staying with his wife's uncle the famous preacher the Reverend Abraham Booth who is not well. In the letter Ann asks her husband to buy a fashionable straw bonnet, 'if you do not think it too trifling', leaving the style to his superior judgement but being a strong Quaker John probably bought something disappointingly drab. She tells him various sacks of malt have been ordered, the sheep are doing well, that the two children are tolerable and that she has not quite weaned nine months old William. She poignantly adds of the first-born – 'John is not very well. He continues to remember his father. He was dreaming one night saying 'now dear Father'.

The baby's death later that year was followed by the death of Uncle Abraham Booth in January 1806. Ann and John Eddison could not attend the funeral as the journey from Nottingham in winter months was too grim. The lesser roads, impassable in foul weather, were mere beaten earth tracks with holes filled in with brushwood and loose stones. Travel on the main roads was fraught with difficulties: the soundest harnesses were liable to snap, a wheeler go lame, a horse stumble, or the cock-horse fail to appear at the bottom of a hill to help the coaches climb up. Such trials were intensified by the boggy roads in winter and, recovering from the birth of her fifth child at that time, Ann would have been in no state to travel.

Nine children were born at Gateford House in the space of twelve years. Then disaster struck. Just a few months after their son Benjamin was born, John had felt an urge to write his will and died a fortnight later in February 1812 at the age of fifty-six, just one year younger than his suicide father. No reason is given for his death, but Ann, now in her early forties, had to cope with the farm, mortgages, running the house and dealing with eight children under the age of eleven. She was lucky to have the support of her brother-in-law Benjamin Eddison, who lived across the fields at Raymoth Gilead Farm. Her unmarried brother, Robert Booth living in Nottingham was a helpful co-guardian to the children.

Ann was capable and conscientious. She was tiny, a fraction over five foot and weighed seven stone. We know this from the meticulous records of her fourth son Edwin who listed the heights, weights and ages of all the family. Sometimes, if they would stand still for a moment, he even measured their feet. Ann stares out knowingly from her portrait [10], her dark eyes on the verge of a twinkle and she holds a folded letter, perhaps from one of her sons at Joseph Tatham's Quaker school in Leeds. This small lady lived through the American and French Revolutions, the Napoleonic Wars, the birth pangs of the Industrial Revolution and the reigns of George III, George IV, William IV and the first eight years of Queen Victoria.

A glowing description of Ann appears in a letter that her great nephew James Granger wrote in 1909 to Dr John Edwin Eddison:

I remember her well. I always had a very high opinion of her and considered her to be prettiest old lady I knew. I saw and spoke to her on several occasions. In my young days I remember hearing remarks made, and greatly to her credit, respecting her mode of training her large family after the death of your grandfather, when

10   Owned by the author.

I think the oldest child living was under eleven years of age… eight children, a large number to look after, and a very onerous duty on her part, most excellently carried out.

Ann Eddison (1770–1845).
One of five known portraits

In a red Moroccan-leather ledger fastened with a brass clasp Ann scrupulously entered her accounts in a confident hand. She lent money to family members and was a mortgagee to several properties — a usual source of income when stocks and shares were not commonly held. From 1837 to 1846 she paid £5,428 rent to the local landowner, Henry Machin Esq. of Gateford Hill.

Knowing that the Machins had been friends with the Eddisons from Georgian times, I contacted Henry Machin who lives at Keeper's Castle, Gateford. He was most helpful providing me with precise details and maps showing the land the Eddisons owned and charmingly ended his first letter:

It seems that relations between John Machin and the Eddisons deteriorated somewhat during the latter half of the 19th Century. Henry Eddison was given notice to quit in 1860 and George Eddison, who seems to have suffered from a severe drink problem was given notice in 1876. Sadly the very long-standing friendship and association of the Machins, Vesseys and Eddisons seems to have ended on a sour note, and I am very pleased that after an interval of 125 years diplomatic relations have now been restored

The earliest recorded owners of the Gateford estate were the de Gaitfords in the early fourteenth Century. It later passed to various families through marriages and bequests including the Knights, the Townleys and eventually the Rodes family of Barlborough, of whom the Vesseys and Eddisons were long standing tenants. The Rodes family title to the land was contested in the latter part of the eighteenth century and as a result their estates were divided. Shortly after this Cornelius Heathcote Rodes began to dispose of his interests at Gateford.

The following details were given to me by Henry Machin about land around Gateford. An area once Gateford Forest, still unenclosed at the end of the eighteenth century, was let jointly for grazing to John Eddison (the bog-land improver), Elizabeth Vessey and Thomas Nelson. This land and more nearby was sold by Cornelius Heathcote Rodes of Barlborough Hall to Thomas Woodcock in 1795, Woodcock then sold about 192 acres to John Eddison's son, Benjamin of Raymoth Gilead who built the farm buildings that are there today. The Ash Tavern, a haunt of Robin Hood, stood on the site at the time Benjamin bought the farm and may have been incorporated into his farm buildings. The main barn is now the Gateford Three Legged Stool pub.

In 1820 Benjamin Eddison bought a further 64 acres and a farmstead from Cornelius Heathcote Rodes. Twenty years later Benjamin's son, another Benjamin, who ran the racing stud at Raymoth Gilead Farm, sold the farm and land to Henry Machin for £20,657. This younger Benjamin born in 1794 (known to Edwin as his 'sporting cousin') used to enjoy Newmarket and other racecourses which was unseemly behaviour for a Quaker. There may have been colossal racing debts but the reason for the sale may have been tied up with a scandal described in Chapter 12.

Old Benjamin had a grandson, Dr John Eddison (1821–1910) who lived in Worksop. A caricature of this eccentric character by James Baldock shows a grumpy old man in a tall hat who was said to have been unqualified and 'walked the hospitals.' He had passed through Guy's Hospital and eventually became a member of the Royal College of Surgeons. Dr John had a great liking for old garments: he was the last man in Worksop habitually to wear a tall hat and black frock coat and was frequently mistaken for the Duke of Portland.

Dr John Eddison's extreme dislike of medicine caused him to refuse to practice

His extreme dislike of medicine caused him to refuse to practice to the exasperation of his father who in the end was forced to give him an annuity. He loathed women and went so far as to say that his dislike for his profession arose from the fact that it brought him into considerable contact with them. He and his cousin Benjamin did good service during the cholera epidemic in the 1850's when the Local Board decided to give Benjamin £10 and John only £5, probably because he reeled away from contact with the female cholera victims.

Henry Machin told me that in 1808 the Rodes sold Henry Vessey an area which included Gateford Hall and the farm buildings but he was not exactly sure when the Eddisons first occupied the area which included Gateford Farm and Gateford House. He said that in 1820 Ann Eddison, her brother Robert Booth and her brother-in-law Benjamin Eddison appear to have been on the verge of buying the freehold of Gateford House. The Machin's draft deed of release has a note on it which states that Benjamin Eddison and Robert Booth contracted for the sale of the estate and should be made parties to this deed and the presents should be conveyed to Mr Machin. A letter from the Eddisons to Henry Machin offers a deal which would involve him in buying the freehold together with the land now occupied by Gateford Rise and Dawber Street. This was owned by Ann Eddison and appears to have been offered at a premium price. She may have felt that money was needed to educate her eight children and provide additional capital after their father's bequests when they came of age.

Gateford House and the farm were eventually bought by Henry Machin for £15,000 in 1820 with the condition that the Eddisons could have a further thirteen years' lease and that Henry Machin could have twenty acres to build himself a house in return for leasing a further twenty acres of Gateford Hall Farm to the Eddisons. The Machins' fine new house Gateford Hill went up in 1823 built of the stone from the ancient Roche Abbey and also Lindrick stone from the nearby quarry.[11] The writer, Edwin Eddison (Benjamin's grandson) in his book on Worksop[12] talks of 'the Machins in their modern Hall.' Gateford Hill a handsome late Georgian house, now a nursing home, was said to be the inspiration for D. H. Lawrence's Wragby in 'Lady Chatterley's Lover' but other houses in the area have also made this claim. Edwin's book contains

11   Lindrick quarry supplied the stone for the Houses of Parliament.
12   Edwin Eddison, Worksop 'The Dukery' and Sherwood Forest, published 1875

fascinating local insights. No doubt there was a copy on the floor of the Bedale attics, but I managed to buy a first edition on the internet for £65 and by a weird coincidence the book had belonged to my great-grandfather. He had inscribed this copy: Francis Eddison, Syward Lodge, Dorchester. The ghosties were at work again!

Two days before Christmas 2002 a parcel fell onto the doormat. It was a cardboard roll from Henry Machin containing a print of Gateford House by the topographical artist, Samuel Heironymus Grimm (1733–1794). Henry had written that the original watercolour had been bought by his brother, Judge John Vessey Machin of Normanton Hall who had discovered it quite by chance at an exhibition in London.

The painter, a friend of Cornelius Heathcote Rodes, spent several months in the summer of 1785 staying at Barlborough. The Machins suggested that the commissioner could have been Sir Richard Kaye who is recorded in the Oxford Companion to Art as having employed Grimm to make drawings in Nottinghamshire and Derbyshire.

Looking closely at the picture, Gateford Hall (bought by Henry Vessey in 1795) is shown on the extreme left. The buildings on the extreme right are those bought by Benjamin Eddison in 1820 when he added 64 acres to Raymoth Gilead Farm. Gateford House in the centre towers over the farm buildings and five cheerful farmhands are having a picnic near some stacked sheaves of corn. On the very far left a man is riding towards Gateford Hall. Is this John Eddison, the bog-land improver visiting the Machins on one of his gorse-fed horses?

On a later visit to Nottinghamshire it was extraordinary to walk through the front door of Gateford House holding a green-checked note-book labelled: *1852 Inventory of Ann Eddison's Furniture, Silver-plate etc* written by William Eddison after his wayward brother Henry had been evicted from the house. All had seemed hopeful when Henry moved in after his mother's death in 1845. He needed to print his identity on the house but, room by room, the list of contents were puzzling. In the White Bed Room, probably his mother's room, there was no bed, nor were there beds in the other bedrooms, just the usual bedroom furniture. But in the south east attic, which he may have chosen for his bedroom, there was a grand sounding four poster bed, bought the year his

Gateford House by Samuel Heironymous Grimm (1733–1794)

The Quaker William Penn, founder of Pennsylvania, was a friend of Sir Francis Rodes of Barlborough

Barlborough Hall, Derbyshire by Samuel Heironymous Grimm

Dodsham Foster, a Quaker owner of slave ships

[35]

mother died, which had crimson moreen [13] hangings, a feather mattress, bolster and pillows, a double mahogany chest of drawers, a night chair and a mahogany towel horse. In the North East Attic was '½ share of Shower Bath' with a pencilled 'Eliz Eddison belongs the other half.'

It was surprising to read that my portrait of Robert Booth (Ann's unmarried brother) had hung in the drawing room since Quakers were not supposed to have their portraits painted, let alone display them. In 1837 Edwin enthusiastically describes the painting: 'My uncle Robert's is without exception the most correct portraiture of life that I ever saw, one might suppose the very hairs of his head had been numbered.' Also in this room was a valuable painting of birds by the Dutch painter, Melchior Hondecoeter, 1636–1695 which may well have ignited William Eddison's passion for taxidermy.

In the dining room there were sixteen hair-seated mahogany chairs. Henry must have removed the dining room table. There was a Broadwood semi-cabinet pianoforte which cost £50 in 1839 which would have been disapproved of by fervent Quakers. An antique jug mentioned in the inventory (valued at 5s) caught my eye. Could this have been my own brown Nottingham-ware loving-cup made for Ann Eddison's grandmother Elizabeth Booth and inscribed to mark the christening in 1734 of her famous son, Reverend Abraham Booth? It had been carefully passed down to my grandfather by Constance Moseley, granddaughter of Edwin's brother Benjamin Eddison of Shireoaks Hall and given to me by my cousin Simon. Also on the list was a 'dessert dish, slave pattern' which must have been the now rare dish made by Wedgwood, an abolitionist, who with his keen marketing skills was eager to appeal to Quaker households.

A '½ share of Phaeton with Elizabeth' which cost £10 in 1848 was on the list. The phaeton was the sports car of the age; perhaps the dashing Henry splashed out after his mother died? There was also '½ share of carriage foot warmer, a gophering frame with rods and gophering irons.' Very necessary with all those bonnets.

Wandering from room to room with the inventory in my hand, I was drawn further into the Eddisons' lives and the letters were later to make more sense. Light from an elegant Venetian window fell on the stairs leading to the

13   Stout corded fabric, cotton or woollen, sometimes watered.

bedrooms and on the next floor, the attics, bigger than those at Bedale, seemed too generous for maids. The family who showed us round were interested in the inventory and particularly by the grand bed in the attic. They were sure that there were ghosts in the house and described a grey haired woman wearing a light blue-grey dress with a frilly collar who had been seen laughing at the end of a bed in the south east attic. She was said to reach out her hand in a friendly way. The room had a chill about it and people refused to sleep there.

The symmetry of Gateford House which had been occupied by five generations of Eddisons is similar to the structure of St Gregory's House, Bedale where my grandfather Francis Eddison lived; his son Martin bought an old clap-board house in the Connecticut woods that has the same symmetrical beauty. My own house has matching windows and prudish respectability and I fantasise that after long family occupancy the shapes of their houses somehow become wired into the family DNA.

Ann Eddison would have been horrified at the ending of the Eddison occupancy of Gateford House. Widowed at the age of forty-two, she had managed the farm and the staff and had scrupulously looked after the family money. After she died somebody had to take over. Her eldest son William was settled elsewhere; Edwin was a successful lawyer in Leeds; Booth was rising in the world of medicine and Benjamin was already farming at Shireoaks. So that left Gateford House in the hands of the handsome, amusing Henry. How did it all go wrong? He took over with such enthusiasm and the family held its breath. But seven years later, now hopelessly alcoholic, Henry became an embarrassment and the long suffering Machins had to give him notice. He was packed off to live with his married sister, Mary Dougill at Finthorpe House, Almondbury but his behaviour shocked everybody there, so he was moved on and ended his days aged seventy-one at Lightridge, a nursing home not too far from his sister Ann who lived at Toothill Hall near Huddersfield.

I found the copy of a letter dated 16 August 1860 dealing with Henry's eviction in which John Vessey Machin wrote with well oiled tact to Henry's youngest brother Benjamin who lived at Shireoaks Hall:

My dear Sir,
I assure you that I greatly regretted having to give your brother a discharge. I should have done so a long time since had I not a very sincere regard for you all, but as it is now done and I am comparatively a young man I hope that whoever becomes my tenant may remain so for a permanency, and I wish therefore to have things put into such form that it may cause but little of any future trouble. Much

*as I value the friendship of you and your family I cannot promise you the farm, for
I consider it absolutely necessary that the tenant should be permanently resident. I
am sorry I could not consider your letter sooner but this is a country where letters
travel slowly especially on a Sunday. Let me express a hope that the kind feeling
which has existed between our respective families may still remain and believe
me no one regrets your brother Henry's state more than I do as I think no man
promised to do better than he did.   In haste your very truly, J. Vessey Machin*

Two days later came Benjamin's reply:

*Sir, My sister informed me last evening that you had sent a notice to my brother
Henry to quit the Gateford farm. I beg respectfully to apply first for myself as
a Home for my sisters or if you prefer they maybe Tenants themselves … For
them. I shall be grieved for the Home of my Ancestors and the place of my birth
to go out of the Family and I think to have you to be into consideration the good
understanding and mutual friendship that has existed for generations with your
family and ours you will not allow it to pass into other hands. I can assure you my
brother Henry has caused us deep anxiety and deep concern for some time past,
and I am sorry to see he is now so affected that I could not urge him to continue
the Farm. I should have preferred a personal interview, but when I called this
morning upon Mrs Machin to inquire your address, I ascertained by her reply that
you return on Tuesday or Wednesday next I thought that I had better defer seeing
you until then.
With kind regards, I am dear sir, your very truly, Benjamin Eddison*

Respectability and wholesome honesty were vital elements of Quaker life as
exemplified by the inscription on the back of my little watercolour of Gateford House. But just sixteen years later the respectability of the family was to
be upset by another blow. In his letter dated 15 October 1876, the same John
Vessey Machin of Gateford Hill, wrote to his father Henry Vessey Machin:

*I have given George Eddison [14] notice to leave his farm. His father has been to me
and tells me I am treating him very harshly and so people say… I am very sorry
to have felt forced to give him notice, but when he had drunk himself into such a
state of delirium his wife had to leave him. I only put off serving the notice in May*

14   George Eddison 1840–1910, Edwin's nephew.

*because his father asked me and the man was so excited it was perhaps as well.
The family have been here so long I am very sorry, but it has been such a gross
case I dare not keep him – I fear that wicked Vicar of Worksop has set a very bad
example that too many follow.*

It was shocking that another inebriated Eddison was being ejected from his
farm but it seems that the Vicar of Worksop had much to answer for. This hard
drinking George Eddison was the son of Edwin's younger brother Benjamin
who lived nearby at Shireoaks Hall, a multilated building that needs some
description.

Shireoaks Hall

The beautiful, battered Shireoaks Hall lies just a mile across the fields from
Gateford House; its name deriving from an immense oak that grew at a point
where the three counties of Nottingham, Derby and York met and over which
many of its branches fell. John Evelyn in *Sylva* (1664) described the great oak
as 'a tree of remarkable size standing in the grounds of the late Sir Thomas Hewitt, about a mile from Worksop Park, which drops into three shires

*Shireoaks Hall c. 1910 at the time
of George Eddison's death*

Shireoaks Hall today

and the distance from bough-end to bough-end is thirty yards, sufficient to shade 233 horses.'

The vast house, built between 1610 and 1617, may have been designed by John Smythson rather than his father Robert, whose work includes Longleat and Hardwick. He also did plans for Barlborough for Francis Rodes. Mark Girouard[15] writes: 'Hardwick, Bolsover, Manor Lodge, Barlborough and Shireoaks, five houses that are within a few miles of each other which are collectively strange, exciting and original as any group of buildings in England or Europe'.

Edwin's youngest brother
Benjamin Eddison of Shireoaks

Describing Shireoaks he writes: 'A mile and a half from Manor Lodge, on a tree surrounded rise in a loop of the river Ryton, is the mutilated fragment of a house rather larger here than Manor Lodge but similar in many respects...'

Edwin's youngest brother Benjamin lived and farmed 836 acres at Shireoaks. He was fascinated by farming as a child and when he had just turned eight he writes to Edwin in September 1819:

> *We finished harvest a month since next Wednesday the stack yard is full there are two wheat stacks and a blend corn next to it a barley stack 20 yards long, it leans into the lane sadly, they have propt it with four of the trees that were at the top hovel, there are 4 barley stacks on the other side of the yard and an oat stack in Narkins croft ... We were very busy whilst harvest lasted we began on 9th August so thou must reckon how many days we were over it. Elizabeth and I cocked the rackings in the low eight acres... We want rain very much indeed the turnips are dying both at top and bottom we sold some sheep yesterday. I think this is a long letter. I am quite tires... (sic)*

Another letter in November ends with a little drawing of a cat:

15   Mark Girouard, *Robert Smythson and The Elizabethan Country House*, Yale 1985

Robert and Vessey Eddison

Dear Brother, We have got the oat stack in ... there were only four mice in so it does not signify a deal Margaret Casson came to our house last week. She and sister Ann helped them to get the stack in but they did not say any thing about footing them I wish they had I'll assure thee Booth says he is not going to have a kitten ... I hav sown some wheat on the croft hill it is all come up ... turnips are in a very porstate.
With love to thee brother, Benjamin Eddison.

The exact date when Benjamin Eddison took over the lease of Shireoaks Hall is not known. In January 1841 Robert Booth of Nottingham wrote to his sister Ann Eddison of Gateford House describing how Benjamin was getting on:

I am glad to hear Benjamin has got a farm more to his mind and liking. If he should be in want of money it is probable I can furnish as much as may be necessary. But I should prefer it being lent, to you, as others of my nephews might expect the same accommodation which might not be convenient to me to supply, and if it goes from you it alters the appearance. I should charge 4% ... When he was here last he told me he wished to have taken Mr Horncastle's Farm which was as large as the Shireoaks Farm, but he was too late in his application. I said it was a large farm and would have taken a deal of money ...

Benjamin married twice, firstly to Mary Morton by whom he had three children, George, Ann and Robert and then secondly to Frances Slagg of Mosborough Hall with whom he had five more children, one of whom, Charles became a Manhattan banker and lived in a haunting Gothic mansion called Strawberry Hill which had been built in 1855 on the bank of the River Hudson and was described, along with others nearby, as 'castles for robber barons and industrial giants.'

Benjamin's second son Robert Eddison, born at Shireoaks in 1843, married Elizabeth Vessey Radley (known as Vessey) who was extremely pretty and who used to go on holidays with my great-grandmother, Sarah Eddison, Edwin's daughter-in-law. In a little red notebook I found a description of a trip they made to Scotland in 1890 where they saw Queen Victoria and her children in Craithie Church, Balmoral and bumped into John Brown's brother in the woods who showed them the walking stick given to him by the old Queen. They were thrilled and went on to look at John Brown's grave.

One day I was astonished to find for sale on the internet an album of Eddison photographs belonging to a Lady Eyre whose mother had obtained it at an auction in the 1950's. It had belonged to Benjamin Eddison's daughter Anne who was born at Shireoaks in 1842 and after I bought it, several more genealogical clues emerged.

When Benjamin Eddison died in January 1884, his eldest son George went to live at the extraordinary Shireoaks Hall. At the time of his ejection from his farm, George and his wife Lucy had seven children. Nine more were to follow and three were to die young. Seven sons were bachelors and three daughters spinsters. John, one of the three boys who got married, left Shireoaks and found a future in Canada.

Even though much of the house had been pulled down by the time George took over there was plenty of room for the thirteen children who were taught by an appropriately named governess, Emily Spurr. There are two albumen photographs of their mother Lucy: in one, taken when she was newly married, she has a disappointed look and in the other, after having given birth to twelve children and with four more to go, she looks impassive and has grown stout. She died suddenly aged sixty-two. Writing a letter she fell back, saying 'Oh! My head!' and according to an obituary her death was caused by apoplexy. Her grave was comfortingly filled with moss and flowers and George's wreath bore a card to his 'loving and devoted wife.'

George died at Shireoaks at the age of sixty-nine in 1910. An appreciative obituary states that he was sometime tenant of Fanfield and Deepcar farms and managed the Shireoaks Colliery farms, Clowne, Darfoulds and Holme

Carr. In all he farmed 480 acres employing six men and six boys and was also a considerable miller. It is cheering to read:

> Mr Eddison was a born farmer. He took the greatest pride and pleasure in his crops … there were few agriculturists better known in the district … he was a warm supporter of the Labourers' Friend Society. Mr Eddison was a keen sportsman. In his younger days he was a bold rider to hounds a sure shot, and an expert angler … it was his fondness for outdoor sport and the fresh air that accounted for his robust constitution and healthy vigorous life.

Coal was found at Shireoaks. The Duke of Newcastle who owned the mineral rights sank the original shaft in 1860 and Benjamin's son, Robert Eddison J. P. who lived at Mount Vernon, Retford became the colliery manager.

On a dismal March day my husband John and I drove up past the water-meadows and found Shireoaks Hall. Exploring its dilapidated remains we could see they had once been part of a colossal mansion surrounded by parkland, with avenues, water gardens, terraces, and thirty-four cascades. There had been a banqueting house with murals and marble walls in nearby Scratta Wood over which young Eddisons scrambled when they went 'a- nutting' in the autumn. Shireoaks was less of a shambles in those days and George Eddison's glowing obituary of 1884 describes his knowledge of it:

> He was well versed in the history of Shireoaks Hall, and on the occasion of a ramble in the grounds by the Worksop school-teachers some years ago, he related some interesting anecdotes concerning the eccentric Hewitts, into whose possession the old Hall came about 1559. It was a descendant of this family, Sir Thomas Hewitt, who had had the Cascades constructed and he built the banqueting house in Scratta wood, a portion of the cellars of which still remain. This house represented Sir Thomas's rather lax notions of Heaven, his intention being to erect a mausoleum close by as depicting his idea of Hell. Mr Eddison used to point to the hollow trunk of an old tree close to the Hall as a 'cover' from which in olden days the door used to be shut as they fleeted past. The Cascades are still existent, though minus their pristine glory and crayfish are still found in the water.

We walked up to a crumbling building beside the house to see if it was occupied and met the man, Mr Godlewski, who lived in the only habitable part of the house. He very helpfully showed us around some of the magnificent rooms and the old staircase and told us that he was still in touch with Benjamin's grandchildren in Canada.

John Woodall and Leo Godslewski in one of Benjamin Eddison's barns

We visited Shireoaks some years later to take photographs of the house which was now owned by Mr Godlewski's son Leo, an architectural historian, whose praises are sung by Mark Girouard in *Robert Smythson and The Elizabethan Country House*, where he thanks his fellow enthusiast, Leo Godslewski, 'who rescued Shireoaks from decay and probably from demolition, for his help, suggestions and plans.'

Leo was interested by the descriptions of the place in the Eddison letters and by one to my grandfather dated 6 February 1947 from Vera Whitaker, Edwin Eddison's great niece, born in 1885 describing memories of having boiled beef at Shireoaks and fishing for crayfish in a lovely cascade that flowed down a hill into a lake in front of the Hall.

We were shown the large dovecote and the farm buildings which were already ancient in Benjamin's day. Preserved by Leo Godlewski, the barns are long and solidly built and there is a mill where oxen would have trundled round a central pillar grinding the grain. Could there once have been a whin mill? [16]

Much of the land the Eddisons farmed, particularly around Gateford, is now built over but roads still bear their names: Eddison Road, Eddison Park Avenue, Eddison Close and Eddison Plantation off the Carlton Road.

Having explored the surroundings of Edwin's youth I was now able to absorb the time-capsule of childhood letters which echoed enthusiasms, life at Gateford and also Edwin's insecurities and ill health.

---

16   Invented by his grandfather John Eddison and illustrated in Arthur Young's
       book *The Farmers tour Through the East of England*. 1771.

5
Childhood –
First Episode Of Pain

Pleasure is oft a visitant; but pain
Clings cruelly to us.

John Keats, *Enymion*

There was much fear in England in 1805, the year Edwin was born at Gateford House. Napoleon had swept across Europe winning victories over the Russians and Austrians at Austerlitz and the English were nervous that he would be turning his attention to England as his troops were known to be massing at Boulogne. Some even thought that he might be building a tunnel under the Channel.

John and Ann Eddison were settled at Gateford House and there were three, possibly four, children in nappies that year: four year-old William, two year-old Henry and one year-old Ann, who turned out to be prettiest of the three girls and although she never married, left a surprisingly large fortune when she died.

It is not known if Ann Eddison farmed out her children. In those days of high infant mortality it was normal to have babies in quick succession so her nine pregnancies in eleven years were not unusual. But on 29 February 1812 her life was shattered when her husband John died – just five months after Benjamin's birth.

This was a terrible blow. Eight children under the age of eleven was responsibility enough but now Ann had to cope with running the farm and family finances. With the help of her brother, Robert Booth and brother-in-law, Benjamin Eddison of Raymoth Gilead Farm, she took a firm grip. A glowing comment about her in the obituary of her fifth son in the British Medical Journal states: 'Mr Booth Eddison's mother, who has been dead some years, was remarkable for her ability in bringing up her large family, and fitting them for responsible and useful situations in life.' [17]

There was another death in the family that year. Ann's seventy-six year old father Robert Booth the elder died in the village of Kirkby Woodhouse, and her brother, William Booth left a blunt account of the events in his 1812 diary:

February 12	*Went to Gateford, John Eddison poorly. Bought of Benjamin Eddison a drench for the old horse 8d.*
February 29	*John Eddison died at noon today*
Mar 17	*Went to Gateford to take an account for John Eddison's effects. Robert was there.*
Mar 23	*We returned from Gateford – I fancied to be beset in an highway-man coming from Mansfield.*
Jun 20	*Went to Nottingham to administer to J. Eddison's Will.*
Aug 14	*My Father died between 9 and 10 o'clock this morning.*

The tiny widowed Ann Eddison coped well. But money was tight and schooling had to be paid for. Fortunately the guardian uncles, Benjamin Eddison and Robert Booth, were on hand for advice and they decided that the respected Quaker boarding school in Leeds, founded by Joseph Tatham in 1756, was the best place for the boys. So as soon as they were eight or nine the young Eddisons were packed off with their trunks and tuck boxes piled high on the top of the coach, clutching little paper wraps of sweetmeats for the journey.

The Quakers, Joseph and Mary Tatham, had moved from Kendal to Leeds in 1756 to start up the school which had grown quickly and had become well known, catering for the children of wealthier Friends. The curriculum included Latin, Greek and, usefully, 'merchant's accompts'. The school was then taken over by a nephew of the founder, another Joseph Tatham (1767–1843).

---

17   *British Medical Journal* 23 April 1859

At **LEEDS**, in *YORKSHIRE*,

(An agreeable and airy Situation)

Y O U T H

Are BOARDED, and carefully inftructed in

ENGLISH, LATIN, GREEK, FRENCH,

AND OTHER MODERN LANGUAGES;

Alfo, in Writing, Arithmetic, Merchants Accompts, Geometry, Trigono-
metry, Navigation, Geography, the Ufe of the Globes, &c.

By *J O S E P H   T A T H A M,*

WITH PROPER ASSISTANTS.

N.B. JOSEPH TATHAM being lately removed into a new Houfe, purpofely erected for the
agreeable Accommodation of a large Family, is enabled to offer his Services more extenfively
than heretofore; and, by a fteady Attention to the Improvement, Health, and Behaviour of the
Youth under his Care,—by taking every convenient Opportunity to imprefs on their tender
Minds a juft Senfe of their moral and religious Obligations, he hopes (through Divine Affiftance)
to difcharge fo important a Truft to the Satisfaction of his Friends.

The T E R M S are,

BOARD, exclufive of WASHING, per Annum - - - - - - £14 0 0
LATIN, ENGLISH, and WRITING, - - - - - - - - - - 1 10 0
Ditto, with ARITHMETIC, MERCHANTS ACCOMPTS, &c. - - 2 0 0
FRENCH or GREEK 2l. 2s. or with any of the above, - - - - 3 10 0
ITALIAN, &c. with or without the above, - - - - - - - 4 4 0

LONDON: Printed by Frys, Couchman, and Collier, in Queen-Street, near Upper-Moorfields.

Pupils included the well-known botanist and missionary, James Backhouse
and several Peases – members of the railway and banking family of Darlington. Other pupils included the Heldens, Fothergills, Fryers, Hodgsons, Jow-
itts, Lloyds, Luptons, Paynes and Edwin's future uncle-in-law, George North
Tatham, who was later to be mayor of Leeds three times and owned the
Adel estate.

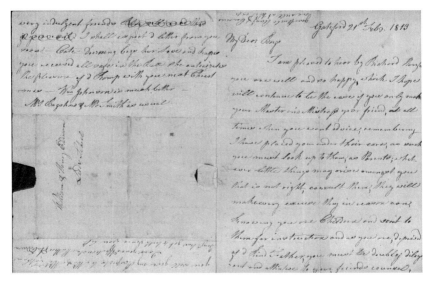

One of Ann Eddison's letters to her boys at Tatham's school.

In February 1813, Ann Eddison wrote a chatty letter to her two older boys. In the folded document addressed simply to William and Henry Eddison, Leeds School, she urges them to look upon Mr and Mrs Tatham as parents and friends and to consult them if they have worries. She is concerned about William's breathing and Henry's bitten finger nails and describes the bustling life on the farm. She ends with the news that Benjamin has grown four teeth since they left.

More motherly letters full of the happenings at Gateford are trundled by coach to the school. Ann bemoans ruinous carriage costs of parcels of books and apples and tells the boys little details she knows will interest them: the breeding of the chickens and rabbits, news of the uncles and cousins and reports that Mr Tatham says they are being good boys.

Just as I was about to leave the Bedale attics something made me pull out a book bound in burgundy leather from under a pile of thirties' clothes. It was by Richard E. Tatham and had been privately printed in 1856 with a 13 foot genealogical chart and fifteen pages of notes. The author was only eighteen when he finished it and its accuracy was particularly remarkable as there was no easy access to genealogical material in those days. The Tathams were descended from John and Grace Tatham both born around 1580 in Tatham in Lancashire and the family were Quakers from the early times of the Movement.

In the summer of 1814, nine year-old Edwin was sent to join his two elder brothers at Tatham's school. A letter home in August of that year contains the first mention of his pain:

> *Dear Mother*
> *There are only 6 boarders I like the school very well for a sckool but I do not find it better than I expected Mrs asked me if I had any pain in my side please to tell Booth to take care of Venter [the dog] and the pigeons this letter is unknown to the master so it is but very short*
> *I am your affectionate son E. Eddison*

I found a red notebook among the papers entitled: 'Regular Management of the Seminary kept by Joseph Tatham, Camp Lane Court, Leeds, 1818'. Here are a few rules that Edwin had to obey:

The first mention of Edwin's pain

Rule I   That the bell ring for the boys to rise precisely at six o'clock in summer; and that all be in the school-room half an hour afterwards, with hands and face washed clean, hair combed and clothes in decent order.

Rule V   That each boy endeavour, to the best of his abilities to speak upon all occasions with a full and distinct articulation – to avoid everything unnatural or provincial in his dialect, and to attend to grammatical propriety.

Rule IV   That no boy sleep out of or change the bed appointed for him by the master or mistress without express permission.

At the end of the nineteenth century pronunciation based on Court English was considered to be a sign of education. Wordsworth and Keats both spoke

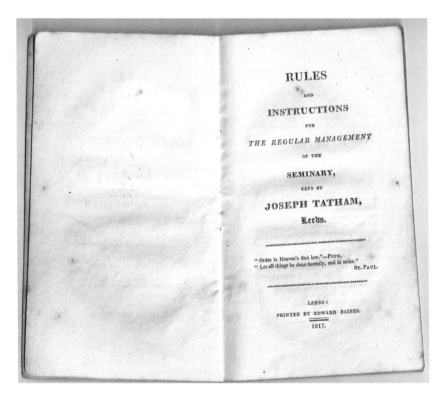

Tatham's school rule book

with accents, the former had a northern burr and the latter a West Country inflection. Interestingly the Eton-educated Gladstone, much the same age as Edwin, retained traces of his Lancashire accent which can be heard on the 1888 paraffin wax cylinder recording of his conversation with Thomas Alva Edison.

Bed sharing was common practice even in the most expensive and famous boys' public schools. Sir Philip Francis, contemplating his son going to Harrow in 1776, specified that he must have a bed to himself, writing: ' I insist upon his lying alone. His learning may take its fate … but his health and morals require all our care.' Nearly everyone at that period shared beds from time to time: women shared beds with women servants, with children or with friends. Men often shared with total strangers at inns.

In Nottingham there were great rejoicings over the victories against the French in November 1813. Two bullocks and twenty sheep were roasted to the sound of fireworks, which must have momentarily cheered the poor who were suffering from high rates of unemployment and hunger as food prices were being kept artificially high by the Corn Laws. Another hard winter was ahead, the second winter of the Great Frost, when deep-piled snow lay frozen on the ground from January to March. The last year of the river fairs was held in February 1814 on the frozen Thames, with booths and stalls; whole oxen were roasted and a book was printed at a stall on the ice. Later the demolition of old London Bridge increased the flow of the Thames, preventing ice from forming so readily. It was said in the cold winter of 1813 that men's moustaches froze as hard as rapiers and fashionable women shivering in low cut dresses quickly adopted a new trend of buttoned-up gowns.

Gateford House, with roaring fires in most rooms, would have been a haven for the young Eddisons, but with babies coming thick and fast, the children were packed off to the village school at the first possible moment. A naive poem written by Edwin in later life describes this part of his childhood. His earliest memories were of lying in the mown grass watching the workmen make hay and he remembers his hurt feelings when he was supplanted by his mother's 'nurslings springing fast.' At his first school about a mile from the famous Shire Tree at Shireoaks, he was 'taught his ABC, aided by twigs of the birchen tree' and writes of the hefty schoolmistress lifting her brawny arm 'an inch or two above her head shrieking "spare the rod and spoil the child".'

But a catastrophe of immeasurable proportions, now almost forgotten, was imminent and would profoundly effect the world's climate for the next three years. Two months before the Battle of Waterloo, on 10 April 1815, a volcanic

St James's Church, Tatham, from a drawing by Thomas Tatham, 1850

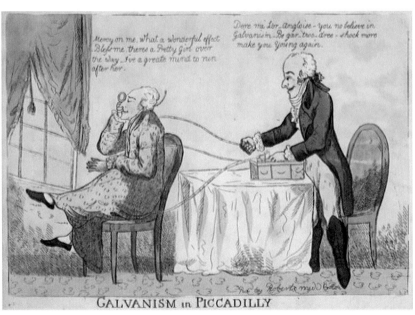

An affluent man receiving galvanic electric therapy from a quack doctor

eruption on the Island of Tambora in Indonesia was the most violent ever re-corded. It was six times more powerful than Krakatoa and Vesuvius combined. The eruption blew 4,000ft off the top of the mountain creating a crater five miles wide and killing an estimated 120,000 people. The eruption was linked to a subsequent drop in global temperature recorded in ships' logs in the summer of 1816, when crops failed across Europe and many died of starvation. In his poem 'Darkness' Byron described the nightmare weather of 1816 'the bright sun was extinguished … morn came and came / and brought no day.'

That year without a summer was a black year. Average summer temperatures fell to 56 degrees Fahrenheit, the lowest since the little ice age of the late seventeenth century. Fog smothered London and fires burned in households right through what should have been the warm months. The harvest was appalling as the wheat would not ripen. There is no record of how it affected Gateford as there is only one letter that year. It is from eleven year-old Edwin writing to William in May. His punctuation has not improved:

> *… we have a heifer calved and she is like a mad thing she would have killed it in a short time but we stopped her she got Daniel up in a corner and she made him look sharp or else she would have forked him soon we have 218 lambs tell me when you mean to come home. I am Dear Brother Your Affectionate brother E. Eddison   It is writs shameful do not let it be seen if you do.*

There was another ferociously cold winter in 1818. Nine year-old Booth Eddison writes a beautifully neat letter to Edwin using the formal Quaker 'thees' and 'thous'. He describes the pigeons he was breeding, the two men put in prison for stealing coal and ducks adding that brother William has shot twenty-six little birds and a crow. William loved shooting, and would happily shoot from five to seven in the evening and the birds were useful for his passion for taxidermy. As the game laws of 1816 limited hunting of game to landowners and the punishment for poaching was transportation for seven years, game-keepers were often shot by poachers to avoid this dreadful sentence. Henry moans about the strictness of Lord Surrey, a spoilsport, who even discouraged Mr Vessey, a neighbouring landowner, from shooting game.

After leaving Tatham's school, William and Henry were apprenticed to a cloth manufacturer, John Wood of Dalton near Sheffield. They are now seriously bored and are appalled at the thought of the apprenticeship stretching five or seven years ahead. In his spare time William makes an electrical machine for Edwin. Was this machine a toy or was it something he thought might cure his pain? In 1752 Benjamin Franklin had flown kites into thunderstorms to show that the electric current stored in a tin-lined glass jar was the same as the flashes of lightning which lit up the heavens. John Wesley [18] proposed that electricity might be a good treatment for a variety of medical conditions. He was impressed by how the human body gave off sparks when exposed to an electric charge and wrote 'who can comprehend how this ethereal fire issues out of my fingers?' He bought an electrical appliance for the treatment of those who came to him seeking medical help which produced, he claimed, 'an immediate cure in ailments including rheumatism, sciatica, epilepsy, contraction of the limbs and melancholia. His machine generated only a slight electric charge, so 'no one has received any hurt thereby' he wrote, but for thousands it had done 'unspeakable good'. Nothing more is heard about Edwin's electrical machine.

In the summer Ann fusses around Gateford looking for clean hampers. She sends chaotic parcels of black currants and raspberries by coach which arrive in an embarrassing squelchy mess. Henry is crestfallen when he finds that a nightshirt she has included in a parcel of asparagus is damp and far too small. Poor little Edwin is still struggling at school. He is not very well and writes worryingly:

Dear Mother,
I am sorry Esq Rhodes is so poorly Mr Horsfall told me he was poorly. Henry tells me you are beginning to build a new shed and a dove coat over it which I am glad to hear.

I am much as usual in health I do not think I am any different from when at home Mr [Tatham] told you in the last letter I wrote that I was better but that was of his own composing for he asked me and I told him I was much as usual for I was not very well that week. I do not think I am any worse but I cannot run about and you must think it is not very pleasant to me to see them run about so much … it is very different being here from being at home though the Ms [Tatham] may be a Motherly woman it is not like being with a Mother. I have generally the pain in my bowels in a morning and I have had boiled milk to my supper for the last fortnight … I hope this will find you in good health.   I remain your aff. Son. E. Eddison

18   John Wesley, *The Desideratum or Electricity made Plain and Useful,* 1760

He writes a long letter to sister Ann, saying that he is staying at school over Christmas (not unusual for Quakers). He likes the grown up expression 'dare say':

... Tell Benjamin and Elizabeth I am much obliged to them for their Wallnuts and I will crack them on Christmas Day tell them they must write to me and I will write to them I would like to see them. Dare say they would be as glad to see me. Tell them I have had three pretty little mice. One had no hair upon it I dare say they would have liked to have seen it ... I hope mother and yourself are in good health I dare say you think it very fine weather love to mother accept the same yourself. I remain your truly affectionate brother, E. Eddison

Eight year-old sister Elizabeth wants to see his hairless mouse:

My dear Brother,
As I cannot see you I am determined to write to you I would have done before but nobody would hold my hand. I should like to have seen your mice one would look very curious without hair I think. Miss Vessey has had her clothes hedge robbed they catched the woman and took her to Southwell house of correction, she was a tramp. Mrs Savile is coming to live with us. Mother desires you will send word whether your stockings fit. I get grammar every day and can nearly say my multiplication table ... your affectionate sister Elizabeth Eddison.

Edwin now writes again to his mother and the letter reverberates with anxieties:

... Master wishes me to write to inform thee that my side has for this last week been much worse than usual and they wish thee ask William Langleys advice about it, and to write back as soon thou canst to let them know who he thinks would be best. I am in general very well in health except the pain in my sides. I am Dear Mother, thy ever Affectionate Son, E.Eddison
I am sure I never can be comfortable at school so long as I have the pain in my side.

There is a calming note from the headmaster Joseph Tatham on the back of the letter, and presumably Ann Eddison has agreed to medical intervention:

Ann Eddison, Esteemed Friend,
Edwin has written on the other side mentioning that the pain in his side has

latterly been worse than usual … We have attended (I think I may say) to all the means which thou mentioned as likely to relieve him, and one or other has in part at least conduced to afford him ease. We have not consulted any medical person in his case here, it would therefore be pleasant to me to receive such instructions from the Physician or surgeon who has attended him at home … Or if it be thought advisable for us to consult our usual medical attendant, R. Battye whom we have good reason to look upon as well skilled in his profession … Edwin's appetite is in general very good, he looks well in the face, and has, I think, grown stouter than he was when he first came. Perhaps the little exercise he has taken comparatively with other boys, may have in part contributed to his growth. We shall be pleased to await your instructions; in the meantime I am very respectfully thy friend, Joseph Tatham

Things may have improved as the pain is not mentioned for a while. Meanwhile ten year-old brother Booth, the most academic of the children with the prospect of a glowing medical career, writes beautiful neat letters full of the delights of farming at Gateford, nearly always mentioning Venter the dog and his pigeons which he enjoys breeding. Perhaps he was already interested in their medicinal use. Doctors at the time prescribed pigeons as efficacious against dysentery, 'take an infusion of the dried and powdered stomach of a pigeon … For bloodshot eyes: apply fresh pigeon blood and for melancholy sadness: apply half a freshly killed pigeon to the head and the soles of the feet.'

A raucous harvest supper at old Uncle Benjamin Eddison's farm is hated by Edwin's quiet sister Elizabeth. She much prefers the excitement of going 'a-nutting' with her friends, a romantic amusement mentioned in the diaries of the Bermudian Fanny Palmer, Jane Austen's sister-in-law. In one letter Booth describes going a-nutting in Scratter Wood and scrambling near the remains of the old banqueting house in the grounds of Shireoaks Hall, the partly-demolished great house where his younger brother Benjamin would be living one day.

Booth is still obsessed with his pigeons:

Dear Brother,
It is my birthday but I have not had a holyday … thy awry necked billy is dead…
Venter is very well I have not been into the Pigeon coat lately but when I was in there was two or three nests and one had an egg in there are many Pigeons now … The fat Beasts sold for 24£ each … I am in the Single Rule of Three direct in accounts. We have sold Beauty to Mr Aldam. Thy ever affect. Brother Booth Eddison

Four members of the family wrote to Edwin on one particular day in
November 1819 so he must have been ill again. Mary, struggling to keep up
with the brighter Booth who is also at Mr Tyzacks school in Park Street,
Worksop, writes:

Dear Brother,
I am not so far in accounts as Booth. I am only in questions in Reductions but
I shall soon be in the Rule of Three. Mr Tyzack has bought the House that Mr
Tompson used to live in up Street and we are to have a school there but it will not
be ready while after Midsummer holidays Mr Nailor says we are to have a very
grand ball there. Trinket has got six pups this morning. This is all I have to say at
present so remain thy affectionate sister, Mary Eddison

In December exhausted Brother William writes:

… I have of late been quite thrown preserving birds, having preserved 12 during
the last three weeks, many of which are kingfishers. The last I have done is a
moorback, or a red grouse which I have done in a first rate style and intend to
present it to Mr Casson.

He advises Edwin to rear goldfinches, saying they are the best singers; he
has an eye on their beautiful plumage. Meanwhile the weakly Edwin battles
on. His illness seems to be turning him into a hypochondriac and this long,
anxiety-ridden list was amongst the family papers:

MAXIMS FOR MY OWN USE … 1819
Never spend more than 6 hours in sleep
Never speak on any subject whilst in a passion
Be determined assiduously to persevere in every good occupation
Instantly banish all carnal and libidinous desires from the mind by turning the
attention to some other object; as the conjugation of a Latin verb or any similar
employment.
Never, or very seldom drink wine spirits or ale unless for the promotion of health
and then be certain that it is for that solely and not for the gratification of luxurious
propensities.
Never give way to idle postures in sitting
Be civil to all and intimate with few
Neither be led or driven a single step by profligates or libertines.

Be not censorious but rather be ready to praise laudable endeavours and actions. Etc
etc. including: Never be intimate with servants.
Seldom or never attend theatres or public balls
Never retire before the cloth is drawn
Never be afraid of being ridiculed for dressing plainly
Never blow your nose or sniff at table or in company if avoidable
Never wipe your mouth with the table cloth
Never appear confounded at having made a mistake
Never glory in your misconduct as that is the emblem of a fool
Guard against entering on scientific subjects; rather keep to what is called tea table
or small talk. (I recant 1822) Etc.etc.

His sister Ann aged thirteen writes bossily to twelve year-old Edwin, saying that their mother 'desires him to clean his teeth well and to stand straight.' She fusses about a new cheese she has sent in a hamper to cheer him up after his disappointment at a parcel of rotten pears and says she will be sending some winter stockings.

Edwin grinds out another Christmas at school and William tactlessly describes the fun of shooting with the Aldams at Gateford on Christmas Day. He is good at presents and sends Edwin a balloon with instructions to fill it with brown paper and ignite:

> *... I hope you will receive the balloon? Safe. We intended to have set it up here for a trial but have never had an opportunity ... you must fix another wire cross wise to fasten the spring. The Balloon should be first filled with brown paper and when completely filled, light the spring? Dipped in spirits of wine and it will ascend.*

Sixteen year old Henry writes about the dazzling gas lighting being installed in Sheffield shops and asks Edwin if he has any plans about his future. He suggests something in the wool business, which he was thinking of changing to himself as he was becoming bored by his apprenticeship in the drapery trade. He adores living at Gateford and thinks that buying and selling wool could combine well with farming. Writing to Edwin he says darkly: 'I would not advise you to be placed behind a counter by any Means'.

Henry Eddison was the tallest of the boys. His mother must have found him the most beautiful of her children and the artist she chose for his portrait was a good one. But Henry had expensive tastes and hankered after a grander lifestyle and bristled at his mother's parsimony The tedium of the drapery

Henry Eddison (1803–1874) was rather too fond of fashionable life

business drove him to seek distractions in Sheffield but his later foray into the wine business did him no good at all.

It is odd that the two elder Eddisons went into trade, but their mother and the guardian uncles worried that the farm could not possibly provide liveli-hoods for all five boys. Arthur Young's *The Farmer's Calendar 1809* proclaims the joys, profitability and satisfaction of farming and says successful farmers could live as gentlemen which would have suited Henry. Young said rich shop-keepers often retired for pleasure from the counter to a farm and that no rich farmer ever went for amusement from his fields to a shop and went on to discuss occupations that connected well with farming:

> … there are not many branches of trade that combine well with a large farm. Upon account of the manure which is raised, an inn is admissible, if a man can bring himself to relish the employment. A manufacture of potash for the same reason, may be very beneficial. Considerable carriers are usually great farmers. Malting unites very well with a farm … some great farmers in Norfolk have built ships in the nearest sea ports for carrying their corn to London and they have also employed them in bringing oil-cake and other manures …

At Tatham's school fourteen year-old Edwin is having worries about his career. Uncle Robert Booth, realising the boy was bright, suggests medicine or the law. His mother writes to Edwin in October telling him of her own problems: she is menopausal and now it is her turn to complain of a pain in her side. The doctor finds many unfavourable symptoms: one of them being the dreaded pleurisy which had killed far too many Booths on her side of the family. He plunges her into the worst possible treatment with enthusiastic bleeding which of course makes her even more anaemic. But tiny Ann is tough and recovers; she has to concentrate her attention on Edwin's future.

By now the young boy had courageously worked out his own ideas realizing that the seriousness of his pain limited his choice. He explained to his mother that a legal career would suit him best, as he 'would not have to move around too much.' At one point he considers studying medicine. You can feel the tension in the letter written in October 1820:

Dear Mother,
It is with sincere pleasure I congratulate you on your recovery from your late illnesses … I hope you are now able as usual to attend to household affairs … I begin to feel rather desirous of getting a situation as I expect I must stay 7 years when I will, and at about 22 or 23 years old (if I live till then) I shall wish to be released from apprenticeship. As I have heard a good deal said about Mr Richard Payne and have no objections to him but like his appearance very well, I think if Uncle were to write to him it might be as well, perhaps. Mr Horsfall told me he thought he was in want of an apprentice. If Uncle wished, he might write to

Master, and he could speak to him as he is very well acquainted with him …
I remain your affect. Son, E. Eddison
My Brown Trowsers are almost worn out. I shall want another pair if you think
not, say. I expect I may as well get them at our Tailors without troubling Mr
Horsfall as it will make little or no difference in the price. I think the coat and
Waistcoat will do for a few months.

The next month he writes an exceedingly neat letter to his uncle Robert
Booth:

Dear Uncle,
Master wishes me to write to inform thee that he called at Richard Ecroyd Paynes
office after the receipt of thy letter. He took with him a specimen of my writing and
gave such an account of my progress in other studies and of my general character,
as made R. E. P. regret that he was circumstanced as he is. He had been in treaty
for some months, about a young man, and had just fully agreed to take him, so
that at present he has no opening for me. His present terms are 50 Guineas the
Premium, the young man, finding his own board, and lodgings. He told Master
if his business increased as it was doing at present it was probable he might want
another in a short time. It is a situation that I think I should have liked very well,
better than where much more business is done. Master desire his love to thee, to
Aunt and Mother. Accept the same from me, I am, Dear Uncle, Thy Afft. Nephew,
E. Eddison

Although he was advised to become a barrister, he finally decides to be an
attorney and sees the need to be apprenticed to an eminent person, even
though the premium would be higher. He joins the aptly named Richard
Ecroyd Payne, Attorney of Cundalls Yard, Briggate, Leeds, as an articled clerk.
The Paynes are Quakers and distant relatives of the Eddisons.

6

Earlier Eddisons and Connections to Thomas Alva Edison

Inventors must be poets so that they may have imagination
Thomas Alva Edison, 1925

In his photographs the inventor, Thomas Alva Edison looks startlingly like my grandfather, Dr Francis Eddison. Their faces, shapes, their stance and even their clothes are uncannily similar. If only the Epperstone aunts had still been alive I could have probed their memories; however some significant discoveries about a possible family connection with the inventor were soon to be made.

Shortly after our visit to Bedale my cousin Simon Creedy brought me a large leather trunk containing a jumble of papers. There were old invitations, chatty letters from the thirties, Christmas cards, crumpled handkerchiefs, Bedale Hunt Ball dance programmes with scribbled lists of eager partners, a bag of pre-war icing sugar and even a disintegrating lollipop leaching stickiness into wasted wads of writing paper headed simply 'Bedale, Yorkshire, Telephone 17.'

Kipling once described biography as higher cannibalisation, which partly describes my voracity in untying limp ribbons and sorting the letters, inventories, farm accounts, obituaries and wills. Sometimes little scribbled notes fell out, meaningless at the time but useful later in the general jigsaw of history. Drawings and silhouette portraits in black tissue paper would emerge and many small oblong family trees fastened with white boot laces and two hundred year-old pins. Some had helpful hearsay notes such as: 'he remembered George I' or 'born a boute 3 o'clock' or 'he taught me to make hay'.

The earliest letters in the trunk were written on high quality rag paper, folded into three, sealed with wax and addressed on the outside. There were no envelopes. Recipients were charged by the sheet, weight, plus the distance

Early Eddison Family Tree

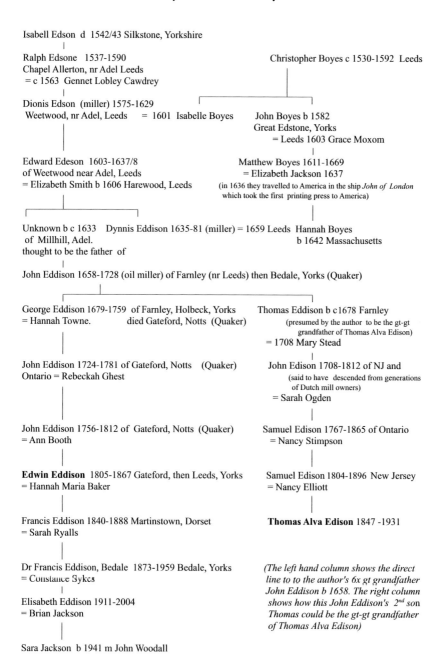

Isabell Edson d 1542/43 Silkstone, Yorkshire

Ralph Edsone 1537-1590
Chapel Allerton, nr Adel Leeds
= c 1563 Gennet Lobley Cawdrey

Christopher Boyes c 1530-1592 Leeds

Dionis Edson (miller) 1575-1629
Weetwood, nr Adel, Leeds = 1601 Isabelle Boyes

John Boyes b 1582
Great Edstone, Yorks
= Leeds 1603 Grace Moxom

Edward Edeson 1603-1637/8
of Weetwood near Adel, Leeds
= Elizabeth Smith b 1606 Harewood, Leeds

Matthew Boyes 1611-1669
= Elizabeth Jackson 1637
(in 1636 they travelled to America in the ship *John of London*
which took the first printing press to America)

Unknown b c 1633   Dynnis Eddison 1635-81 (miller) = 1659 Leeds Hannah Boyes
of Millhill, Adel.   b 1642 Massachusetts
thought to be the father of

John Eddison 1658-1728 (oil miller) of Farnley (nr Leeds) then Bedale, Yorks (Quaker)

George Eddison 1679-1759 of Farnley, Holbeck, Yorks
= Hannah Towne.   died Gateford, Notts (Quaker)

Thomas Eddison b c1678 Farnley
(presumed by the author to be the gt-gt
grandfather of Thomas Alva Edison)
= 1708 Mary Stead

John Eddison 1724-1781 of Gateford, Notts (Quaker)
Ontario = Rebeckah Ghest

John Edison 1708-1812 of NJ and
(said to have descended from generations
of Dutch mill owners)
= Sarah Ogden

John Eddison 1756-1812 of Gateford, Notts (Quaker)
= Ann Booth

Samuel Edison 1767-1865 of Ontario
= Nancy Stimpson

Edwin Eddison 1805-1867 Gateford, then Leeds, Yorks
= Hannah Maria Baker

Samuel Edison 1804-1896 New Jersey
= Nancy Elliott

Francis Eddison 1840-1888 Martinstown, Dorset
= Sarah Ryalls

Thomas Alva Edison 1847 -1931

Dr Francis Eddison, Bedale 1873-1959 Bedale, Yorks
= Constance Sykes

Elisabeth Eddison 1911-2004
= Brian Jackson

Sara Jackson b 1941 m John Woodall

*(The left hand column shows the direct
line to to the author's 6x gt grandfather
John Eddison b 1658. The right column
shows how this John Eddison's 2nd son
Thomas could be the gt-gt grandfather
of Thomas Alva Edison)*

and addresses were brief: just 'Mrs Eddison Gateford' or 'Benjamin Eddison Shireoaks.' Some were closely cross-written without paragraphs and when the news was particularly incontinent the writing veered madly round the tops of pages.

The Edson/Edeson/Edsone/Edesons who were millers living around Adel, near Leeds between 1500 and 1630 are very likely linked to the earliest of our Eddisons on the family tree, the oil-miller John Eddison (1658–1728) of Bedale, later of Farnley near Leeds, Yorkshire. To anchor all the names and dates in the papers, I consulted the family tree done in 1968 by Lt. Colonel George Stephenson a descendent of Edwin's brother, William Eddison the taxidermist. Edwin, who was born in 1805, was interested in genealogy and, perhaps fearing an early death, had meticulously written up his research on foolscap sheets when he was quite young. Double checking with other sources, the International Genealogical Index lists, Thoresby Society Volumes and old wills, I found no inaccuracies.

According to George Stephenson, the earliest form of the name was from Edstone [19] in North Yorkshire but I found nothing further to connect the place with the family. The surname de Edstone was in use during the thirteenth and early fourteenth centuries, changing latterly to Edstone, Edeson, Eddeson and Edson. As late as the eighteenth century the spellings of the surname Eddison were erratic, changing sometimes to Eddinson.

Stephenson found a de Edstone of Edstone (1234) and after a gap, a Simon de Edstone of Edstone. His son William de Edston (1286) was from Tyvington. [20] The tree continues with Walter (1301) Henry (1344), Robert (1373), then John Edston (1385) from Dodworth near Silkstone. There is a note in the Yorkshire Deeds that John leased five bovates of land, meadow, wood and 6 acres: about 71 acres altogether. Then there is a gap of two generations until the reign of Henry VIII when Isabell Edson, from Silkstone, a village between Sheffield and Leeds, appears.

Isabell signed her will on 4 October 1542, the year Catherine Howard was beheaded, and her son James was the executor of the will. She left her sister

---

19   Great Edstone, near Salton in Yorkshire was the birthplace of John Boyes, b. 1575 whose sister Isabelle married Dionis Edson and whose granddaughter Hannah married Dynnis Edison in 1601.

20   Now probably a village called Tivydale next to the village of Silkstone.

Alice six pence, her daughter Jennit, among other unreadable items, her dresses and her best hat was left to Ann Woodson. In those days clothes marked obvious social contrasts and since only a small section of the population could afford to buy starched ruffs, padded doublets and farthingales, those of the Edson's standing would probably have treasured anything that had been expensively made. Poorer yeomen would have had rough, scratchy home-made clothes, so Isabell's will gives the impression that the Edsons had money.

Isabell's son, James of Silkstone left a very lengthy will in 1593 and must have been successful to afford the legal fees. He left his house and contents jointly to his wife Agnes and his son John, but only 'so long as the two wives can agree, or else John Edson's wife to depart the house.' He also left to his wife and son 'all his wagons, plows, horses teams and harrows to be divided between them with promise that James Edson my son shall have my widows moiety after her decease. The residue of all my goods shall be divided into three parts.'

Ralph Edsone, (thought to be James's brother) was born about 1537, and lived at Weetwood near Adel, not far from Leeds. He married Jennit Lobley and owned a house at Meanwood where he died in 1590. He was the first of a line of millers and seems also to have farmed. There is a rather curious link or echo in that Edwin Eddison's wife inherited an estate at Adel, not far from Meanwood in the nineteenth century, so Edwin's family would have trodden the same fields as Ralph and his descendants.

Two of Ralph Edsone's sons, William and Dionis were millers. The latter owned and leased property around Adel and also owned a wood mill. Millers were influential in towns and villages and were often the richest men in the area so this is probably how the Edsones acquired land. It is impossible

In 1636 the Boyes family sailed in the ship 'The John of London' which took the first printing press to America.

to tell exactly how much land Dionis (born in 1575) owned and leased but he is recorded as selling twelve messuages, eight cottages and other pieces of land. On page 75 in the Subsidy Roll of 1627 he is named as the only man in Chapeltown who had sufficient wealth to be taxed.

The adventurous Boyes family married twice into the Eidson family (as spelt in his will, but Edson in the parish register). At the end of the reign of Queen Elizabeth, in 1602, Dionis Eidson married Isabelle Boyes whose nephew Matthew and his family were early settlers in America.

Matthew Boyes, a clothier of Leeds sailed with his wife Elizabeth from Rowley, Yorkshire to Salem, Massachusetts in 1636 (just sixteen years after the Mayflower) with the Rev Ezekiel Rogers and a group of 20 families who were suffering from the religious persecution of the times. Sailing on the ship 'The John of London', they took the first printing press to America and were among the first people in the western world to start making cloth. This little group named their settlement Rowley and Elizabeth Boyes bore twelve children there under terrifying circumstances.

But the Boyes family did not end their days in Massachusetts. Matthew appears to have hopped back and forth with tedious, treacherous journeys in cramped little ships. On a return visit in 1646 to discuss trade in cloth with William Sykes of Hull, he must have been horrified by the changes that had taken place. He might not have known about the bubonic plague that had struck Leeds in 1644 killing 1,300 people out of a population of 6,500, even though the infected poor were hastily bundled into plague cabins built at Quarry Hill on the outskirts of the town.

In *Pilgrims: New World Settlers and the Call of Home*, Susan Hardman Moore [21] writes that after the first significant wave of English migrants (about 21,000 in the 1630's) many came home for good and she concludes that after 1640 more people left New England than arrived: in all about a quarter of the settlers remained. They had, it seems, lost heart and 'dropped out of the onward march of American history'. The Boyes, mentioned in her book, were in this category.

She describes how most of the migrants left England in mutually supportive groups led by gentry and clergy. Until the 1630's, the typical migrant had

21   S. H. Moore, *Pilgrims: New World Settlers and the Call of Home*,
     Yale University Press 2007

been an unskilled adolescent working his ticket to the Virginian plantations. The New England pioneers were different. They were more literate and of higher social standing than the earlier unskilled migrants and, migrating with their entire family, they tended to have greater expectations.

Worried about the dangers of life in America, Matthew Boyes brought his family home to Yorkshire in the early 1650's when his eldest daughter Hannah, who had been born in the fierce heat of a Massachusetts summer, was only four years old. At eighteen, she married her cousin, Dynnis Edison, the miller of Millhill, near Adel, (son of Edward, grandson of Dionis, whose wife was Isabelle Boyes). Hannah may have been sentimental about America, remembering the freedom and the good times playing with friendly Indians in the hot sun and her stories may have encouraged her husband to visit the new land. We know that she and Dynnis Edison travelled to Dublin where their son Edward was born in 1680 and it is possible that the whole family were en-route to a new life in America. We know that Dynnis's son Edward died in Richmond, Virginia in 1732 and that his descendants are numerous in America today.

The 1629 will of Dynnis's grandfather (the Elizabethan Dionis Edison, the miller of Weetwood near Adel who was born in 1575) implies that he was an independent businessman owning property and working for himself. Items mentioned are: leather britches, a 'lether dublytt', hat and shoes, along with his cottages, land and list of horses, which gives the impression he was a higher yeoman. During Elizabeth's reign, the sumptuary laws were still in effect. No man below the degree of a knight's eldest son could wear velvet jerkin, doublet nor satin, damask, taffeta or grosgrain, while women below the degree of a knight's wife could not wear velvet or embroidery with silk. As a concession to the growing middle classes, however, the laws were amended 1579–80. There is no sign in the will that Dionis lived above his station. A 'lether dublytt' was quite respectable. Reading Dionis's will one imagines that his grandson Robert Dawson was pleased to have been left a pair of leather britches, the leather doublet, a hat and a pair of shoes. Thomas Oldfield, in the same will was left another pair of leather britches and a doublet of canvas. Dionis also left 'one pound or my best suit of apparel whether hee will choose' to William Cautharie of Adel. Clothes were expensive as even for a plain linen shirt the material would go through twenty different processes and would then be bleached in the sun for seven months. So a linen shirt would be passed from person to person and received as an honour.[22]

In the will there is no mention of a carriage. A yeomen rode on horseback with his wife behind him. Horses were an indication of wealth and Dionis Eidson's will includes five horses; 'a dun fole, a dun fillie, a grey mare, and a little black hobbie.' (Hobby horses were strong, active horses used for amusement, generally too small to be working horses. Charles II raced his hobbies at Newmarket). 'A bay fillie' was left to Christopher Boyes, presumably his wife's nephew. Dionis gave his daughter Elizabeth one of his best cows and 40 shillings. The daughters, Jennit, Grace and Jane were left £10, £30 and £20 respectively and Jane was also left the rent of one house 'where John Harrison now dwelleth.' Jennit was left a cow at the time of her marriage to Richard Kirk who was from a well to-do family of nearby Millhill. Her brother-in-law was Thomas Kirk of Cookerigg, so she was great-aunt to Thomas Kirk FRS, (1650–1706) friend of Ralph Thoresby FRS, diarist, author and widely credited with being the first historian of Leeds.

An interesting question is the value of a testator's estate. This is not easily answered as the yeoman's land, his greatest asset, would not be mentioned in his will as most of it was only leased and merely passed by custom to the eldest son.

Dionis Edeson's will states that he 'owned and leased the farm where he dwelt, the new close in Meanwood, Tongue Royde close and appurtances, as well as the house where John Harrison lived.' He leased the Mill, a close called Dog Croft near Adel Churchyard and the 'Park in Meanwood of my lease of William Tottie.' Dionis left his wife Isabelle 'the reversion of the wood mill, the farmhouse where they lived and the reversion of Daniel Foxcroft's close.' He also had quite a number of debts owing to him (possibly mortgages), so altogether Dionis would have been considered wealthy amongst contemporary yeomen. An indication that he was high ranking as a yeoman is that in an earlier will he leaves a small amount of money to every one of his servants and his maid Mary Abbot receives a bequest of 12 pennies. There is also a tragic note recording that on 15 September 1628 his servant William Linsett was 'slayne by a milne wheel.' Dionis himself died a year later during harvest time aged fifty-four, leaving six children, Edward, Ann, Jennit, Jane, Elizabeth, and Grace.

---

22   Anna Reynolds, *The Art of Tudor and Stuart Fashion*,
        Royal Collection Trust 2013

Soon after Dionis's death in 1629 the tranquil growth of Leeds was disturbed by religious and political dissent. The Civil War which erupted in 1642 caused special problems for Leeds which was on the side of the King. The commercial class including all those in the cloth industry, were strongly against the war but Sir Thomas Fairfax, with a powerful Parliamentary force, captured the town in 1643.

Dionis and Isabelle's only son Edward born in 1603, seems to have lived at Chapel Allerton, near Adel. He inherited a considerable amount of property from his father but this seems to have disappeared during the turbulence of the Civil War. He married Elizabeth Smith of Harewood, a village about eight miles away and they are listed as having four children, Elizabeth, Frances, William and Dynnis. There may have been others, but the records were frequently incomplete due to the political upheavals.

John Eddison (sometimes written as Eddinson or Edeson) was without doubt Edwin's ancestor. An oil-miller of Bedale, he was born just after Christmas 1658, two years before Charles II was back on the throne. Edwin records that John went on to live at Church Street, Leeds and later lived at Farnley a village six miles from Adel (three miles from Leeds), where he died in 1728. We can only assume that John's father (born approximately 1633) was a brother of Dynnis the miller of Millhill who was born in 1635. Three reasons strengthen the assertion that John Eddison of Bedale was related to the milling Edesons of Adel area. First, the name was at that time uncommon in the area, second Farnley is near Adel and third, both families had milling backgrounds.

The great plague had carried off a fifth of the population in Leeds in 1644 and Church records were frequently vandalised and often ceased during the Civil War, so that genealogical research is almost impossible for this period. Matters became worse in 1653 when the government assumed control of all church registers and appointed civil officers in each parish to keep custody of the books. They were the only people allowed to make entries in the registers, charging a fee of one shilling for each entry to be made, so many people did not even bother to record births. During 1654 the solemnising of marriages became the sole responsibility of Justices of the Peace rather than the clergy. Couples not wishing to offend their beliefs chose not to have a formal marriage and some risked marrying secretly in a church ceremony. When Charles II came back to the throne in 1660, church records restarted.

John Eddison the oil-miller, my great (×6) grandfather settled in the small town of Bedale thirty miles from Leeds. Tanners and skinners plied their foe-

Bedale, c. 1820

tid trades on the banks of the Bedale beck and this fast-flowing stream powered the corn mill at Aiskew, built in 1680 which can still be seen today.

One February afternoon my cousin Simon showed us the site where John
Eddison would have milled linseed, grown locally from flax plants or from
seeds shipped from the Baltic to Hull, to be crushed for cattle cakes and fer-
tiliser. Various oils were used for paints and a compound based on linseed oil
was used for caulking ships' decks and for weatherproofing the seamens' crude
canvas smocks made from the remains of wind-torn sails. Linseed oil was also
used for protecting farm implements.

In Bedale there is another curious Eddison echo. Unaware that his ancestor
had lived here, my grandfather chose to spend his married life in St Gregory's
House built by the church in 1700 at the far end of the market town. John Eddison the oil-miller of Bedale might well have seen the house's construction
but it is unlikely that he would have foreseen that his great (×4) grandson Dr
Francis Eddison would live there or that Francis's grand-daughter would find
the family papers in the attics.

John Eddison the oil-miller lived through two years of the Commonwealth and the reigns of Charles II, James II, William and Mary, Anne, George
I and George II but he was only seventy when he died in 1728. He was the
first Quaker in the family and one can imagine George Fox, the founder of
the movement, casting his piercing eyes on the young miller when he came to

Bedale 1890. St Gregory's House is next to the church, partly hidden by trees

preach in Bedale on a raw February day in 1677. At that time Fox's dream was to form a colony of Friends in America based on ideas drawn up by William Penn and Robert Barclay. He would have been on a recruiting drive, urging Yorkshire Friends to sail to New Jersey and later that year a band of brave Quaker families from Yorkshire and London crossed the Atlantic in three tubby little ships to find a new life in America.

In my search for possible links between a member of the Yorkshire branch of Eddisons and the famous American inventor, Thomas Alva Edison, supposedly of Dutch ancestry, some clues emerged. Although his great-great grandfather is unknown, the inventor's great-grandfather, John is said to have arrived in America from Holland as a child with his widowed mother.

Scanning all the names and dates on my family tree and also those of the Eddisons from the Adel area who were early settlers in America, nothing seemed to fit, until I came across a note scribbled by Edwin Eddison in 1823 saying that his father's cousin, George Eddison of Holbeck, Leeds (born in 1750) told him that his (George's) grandfather John, (born in 1658, the oil-miller of Bedale and Farnley) had another son, Thomas (born around 1683 at Farnley, Leeds).

I found that Thomas Eddison of Farnley had married Mary Stead on 11 July 1708 and that they had a son John, but then the trail went cold. From the dates it would make sense for this son John to have been the English great-grandfather of Thomas Alva Edison.

[71]

Thomas's great aunt Hannah Edeson (*née* Boyes) was born in Massachusetts in 1659; his father's cousin Edward (who chose to spell his name Eidson) had settled in Virginia around 1696 – so there would have been added incentive for a voyage to the New World. But none of the names or dates on Edward Eidson's well-documented family tree connect in any way to the inventor's great-grandfather 'Tory' John Edison.[23]

There is no further mention of the Yorkshire Thomas Eddison, son of the oil-miller John of Bedale in the papers which I have archived. Could this Thomas Eddison of Farn-

Dr Francis Eddison of Bedale

ley have gone to Holland, the haven for persecuted Quakers? Did he sail to America with his wife and small son John? Did he die before or during the journey, as his wife was said to arrive as a widow? Other Eddisons and their Quaker connections already in the new land would, no doubt, have been welcoming and helpful.

I had a strong feeling that there could be a link with the inventor whose ancestors were also oil-millers, so I persevered for many more hours, spurred on by the fact that my grandfather Dr Francis Eddison looked astoundingly like Thomas Alva. Even as children their expressions and bone structures are similar. In later life their gaze and posture in the photographs are like those of

---

23 He is known as 'Tory' John in the text as he was later a Tory exile to Canada. Several accounts have Thomas as his father. The Roseland Historical Society, N.J states: 'The Edisons were mill owners ... Thomas Edison, the great-great grandfather of the inventor came from Holland to New York City and established a bank there. Thomas did not take part against the revolutionists in the struggle for independence. His son John, however was a major in the British Army.'

The inventor Thomas Alva Edison

Constance Eddison who breakfasted on
claret and tinned tongue

brothers. I then discovered that the Epperstone aunts, my grandfather's sisters, had told their niece Rachel Mainwaring-Burton that there was a connection.

As well as the photographic likeness, Francis Eddison and Thomas Alva shared several family traits: untidiness, height, kindliness and humour. At the end of his life the inventor suffered from diabetes and Brights disease; both illnesses found in members of my own Eddison family.

Like my grandfather, Thomas Alva was eccentric. Both enjoyed camping. In the early days of his marriage my grandfather would camp in a simple tent in the wilds of Yorkshire where he revelled in being mistaken for a gypsy. My grandmother who was glamorous would take among other necessary things, thirteen cushions and a bedroom looking-glass and they would breakfast on claret and tinned tongue. Thomas Alva went on yearly camping trips with Henry Ford, Harvey Firestone the rubber tyre manufacturer and President Harding. While Henry Ford chopped wood, Edison would obtain food from farms and would hand out chocolate bars to children who immediately recognised him as 'Mr Gramophone!'

Thomas Alva Edison was a colossal figure among inventors with 1,093 patents issued in his name. His own favourite invention was the phonograph, created in 1877 which recorded sound on tinfoil cylinders by using two needles, one for recording and one for playback. My grandfather Francis Ed-

[73]

dison would have been seventeen in 1890 when it was discovered that many veterans of the Charge of the Light Brigade in the Crimean War were destitute. Edison's representative in Britain arranged to make three wax cylinder recordings to be sold to support the Light Brigade Relief Fund: Alfred Lord Tennyson reading his *The Charge of the Light Brigade*; Florence Nightingale's message to the veterans and a trumpeter sounding the charge at Balaclava.

Alexander Graham Bell invented the telephone with a magneto type receiver but Edison, with whom he had been working, made it commercial in 1878 by producing the carbon transmitter which made the sound much clearer. It was said that Edison originated the salutation 'Hello' over the telephone. When the first telephones came into use, people were accustomed to ring a bell on the box and then say, ponderously, 'Are you there? Are you ready to talk?' Edison did away with that when he caught up the receiver one day and yelled into the transmitter one word – 'HELLO!'

More signs of a possible family connection soon began to emerge. Biographies of the inventor say that Thomas Alva Edison was of Dutch ancestry but none say that he was from Quaker stock. I found evidence that 'Tory' John Edison was a Quaker in an account by Robert W. Moore [24] which describes how Samuel Moore's neighbour Henry Edison (said in the account to be 'Tory' John Edison's brother) was tarred and feathered for his Quaker beliefs. The torture was extreme, causing Henry's death and his widow, warned that the rebels [25] would be back to burn the house, prepared to move in with her brother-in-law 'Tory' John Edison. The Moores and the Edisons then fled from New Jersey to the shores of Lake Fundy, Nova Scotia. [26] A footnote in Moore's account states categorically that this Quaker 'Tory' John Edison was the great-grandfather of Thomas Alva Edison and the biographies of the inventor all state that Thomas Alva's great-grandfather, the Tory rebel John Edison fled with his family from New Jersey to the Bay of Fundy as casualties of the Revolution.

24   Robert W. Moore, *The Trials and Travels of Samuel Moore, born Rahway, New Jersey 1742*, 2007

25   Those speaking out against the British.

26   In his book *Edison His Life, His Work, His Genius*, Allen & Unwin 1935, W. A. Simonds describes the Edison family leaving New Jersey and settling on the shores of Lake Fundy, Nova Scotia.

There is a mystery about 'Tory' John Edison's father. Some biographers say he was Thomas Edison a patriot banker but this is dismissed in W. A. Simonds' book *Edison, his Work his Genius* who thinks that the banker Thomas might have been a brother or a cousin.

The possible connection with English Eddisons is shown below:

ENGLISH EDDISONS   AMERICAN EDISONS

John Eddison 1658-1728 of Farnley, nr Leeds and Bedale, Yorkshire
Mill owner (Earlier generations of Eddisons were millers)
(Quaker)

George Eddison 1679-1759 of Farnley, Yorks, later of
Holbeck, then Gateford, Notts = Hannah Towne
(Quaker)

                                 Thomas Eddison b c 1678 of
                                 = Mary Stead 1708 (Quakers)
                                 presumed by the author to be the
                                 gt gt grandparents of Thomas Alva Edison)

John Eddison 1724-1781 (the bog-improver)
of Gateford, Notts = Rebeckah Ghest
(Quaker)

                               (Tory) **John Eddison** 1708-1812
                        (Quaker) said to have descended from generations of
                        mill owners in Holland)
                        = 1756 Sarah Ogden. They moved from New Jersey
                        to Ontario

John Eddison 1756-1812 of Gateford, Notts
=Ann Booth
(Quaker)

                               Samuel Edison 1767-1865
                               = 1792 Nancy Stimpson

EDWIN EDDISON 1805-1867 of Gateford and
Headingley, Leeds = Hannah Maria Baker

                             Samuel Edison 1804-1896 of Ohio and NJ
                             = 1828 Nancy Elliott

Francis Eddison 1840-1888 of Martinstown,
Dorset = Sarah Ryalls

                             THOMAS ALVA EDISON
                             1847-1931

Dr Francis Eddison 1873-1959 of Bedale, Yorks
(who looked like the inventor) = Constance Sykes

Elisabeth Eddison 1911-2004
= Brian Jackson

Sara Jackson 1941 = John Woodall

Continuing my research I scanned the passenger lists of early merchant ships bound for New Jersey but found no Eddisons. Then one day I came across a group of familiar names on board three little ships sailing in 1677 under the plan of George Fox and William Penn to transport Quakers from Yorkshire and Nottinghamshire to Burlington, New Jersey. Many were Quaker relations and connections of the Eddisons.

On the ship The Kent bound for West New Jersey there were 230 Quakers including Thomas Farnsworth and Robert Stacey – both connected by marriage to the Gateford Eddisons. Another ship *The Fly Boat Martha*[27] from Hull arrived in Burlington, West New Jersey a month later with the family of Robert Stacey (various spellings) on board. (George Eddison's daughter-in-law was a Stacey and the Staceys lived at Ballifield Hall, Handsworth, near Sheffield, not far from the Aldams and Eddisons living at Gateford).

A third ship, *The Shield*, sailed from Hull to Burlington with Susannah Farnsworth, Thomas Revel, Mahlon Stacey, and John and Peter Fretwell on board, all Quaker connections with the Eddisons.

Did Thomas Eddison, born around 1678 of Farnley, Yorkshire and who married in 1708, decide to join this band of Friends and travel on a later ship from Holland? In some of the biographies of the inventor, 'Tory' John Edison is said to have arrived as a child with his widowed mother. Perhaps his father died during a hellish journey across the Atlantic and perhaps his wife was not listed, as women and children were not normally accounted for. Ships' passenger lists at that time were often incomplete.

Robert Moore's account includes a further link when he mentions that in the late summer of 1780 when the Moores boarded the British ship heading for the Bay of Funday, Nova Scotia, they travelled with 'many of their New Jersey neighbours like the Edisons and the Bowlbys.' John Bowlby, a miller and one of the earliest settlers in New Jersey,[28] was christened in 1703 at Barlborough, six miles from Gateford. He would have been much the same age as 'Tory' John Edison. The Rodes family of Barlborough Hall were friends of William Penn and the Gateford Eddisons knew the Rodes well. So these facts make it more than likely that the inventor's great-grandfather 'Tory' John Edi-

---

27   Out of 114 passengers, only 23 were named.
28   His grandfather was Samuel Barker the Rode's bailiff of Barlborough and
       one of the first settlers in Burlington, New Jersey, who bought 1,000 acres in
       Pennsylvania from William Penn.

son was related to the Eddisons of Gateford, particularly if it can be established that the family at that time were Quakers.

Quakers did not believe in christening their children. Names for babies were very carefully chosen by the parents and then approved by the community. In keeping with their belief in equality, they named the first son for the wife's father and the first daughter for the husband's mother, then reversed the process for the next son and daughter. This seems to be what happened to 'Tory' John Edison's family, which further strengthens my theory that his father was a Quaker and was called Thomas. 'Tory' John Edison in America named his children as follows:

Samuel (after his maternal grandfather Samuel Ogden)

Mary (after Mary Stead of Farnley, her possible English paternal grandmother)

Phoebe who died young [29] (after Phoebe Baldwin her maternal grandmother)

Thomas (after Thomas Edison, his possible English paternal grandfather)

My assumption that Thomas Eddison of Farnley born circa 1678 could be the great-great grandfather of the inventor rests on 1) family hearsay, 2) Quaker naming rituals, 3) similar milling ancestry, 4) the date [30] of Thomas Eddison of Farnley's marriage to Mary Stead in 1708, 5) the birth of their son John in 1708 and 6) the physical likeness to my grandfather.

There is some doubt about 'Tory' John Edison's birth, but 1708 is clearly inked on the extensive family tree sent to me by one of 'Tory' John Edison's descendants, Austin Edison of Wilmington, North Carolina and this date works with my theory that Thomas Eddison of Farnley was his father. It was said that there was exceptional longevity in the family: 'Tory' John was said to have died in 1812 at the age of 104 (which makes his date of birth exactly

29 According to W. A. Simonds in his book *Eddison His Life, His Work, His Genius* published 1935.

30 Vol XIII Part I *Thoresby Society, Leeds Parish Registers*, p 116.

1708) and his son Samuel died at 103 [31] both remarkable achievements that would have been noted by the family and handed down. Samuel's son died at 92; Thomas Alva at 84 and my grandfather Francis Eddison at 86.

I sent my researches to Professor Paul Israel, the Director and General Editor of the Thomas Alva Edison Papers at Rutgers University who agreed to meet me and was interested in my theories. He is the author of a book on the inventor and has commissioned one of his researchers to archive a treasure trove of letters from the inventor's daughter Madeleine Sloane which were housed in the Edison Birthplace Museum. The Curator of this museum, Lawrence Russell, who worked for the inventor's daughter

John Woodall and Professor Paul Israel
of Rutgers University

for nine years, told me that Mrs Sloane had told him that she thought that the family left England for religious reasons and that they had settled in Holland temporarily; she did not think that the Edisons were Dutch, although the widow Edison and her son John were said to have come to New Jersey from Holland.

31 A photograph of Samuel Edison's gravestone clearly marks 103 as his age at death.

7
Strong And Damp Quakers

The first step to peace is to stand still in the Light.
George Fox, *Quaker pamphlet, 1653*

Somebody once said that they were maddened by the aggressive humble-ness of Quakers and this captures the effect they often had on people out-side their group. As the Eddisons were involved with the Society of Friends since the movement began, I needed to know more about the organisation. My research was continually exposing Quaker involvements and connections; even Edwin's new boss, Richard Ecroyd Payne was related and was from old Quaker stock: in 1708 Edwin's great-grandfather had married Anne Aldam, the granddaughter of Thomas Aldam, a close friend of George Fox, the Move-ment's founder.

From the papers in the Bedale trunk a complicated mosaic began to un-ravel which links the Eddisons to many prominent Quaker families – the Backhouses, Barclays, Peases, Farnsworths, Vipons, Paynes, Biltons, Ecroyds, Fieldens, Frys, Firths, Gurneys and the Jowetts. Inbreeding was inevitable as the Quaker rule was that if the son of a Quaker married outside the Society his family could not attend the wedding and the errant child would be cast out in disgrace. Generations of social isolation and persecution had created strong clan feeling but there were many advantages in their closeness, par-ticularly in the mutual support in business and banking worlds. But Edwin Eddison broke away from the Society of Friends just before his marriage for reasons that are not clear.

George Fox was said to be a large bulky man with a powerful voice, fiercely piercing eyes and with a divine fire pouring through his veins. A small pencil drawing of Fox handed down through my family may not be a true likeness of the founder of the Society of Friends as no fully authenticated portrait of the preacher was painted or drawn in his lifetime. Richard Seebohm, a sixth gen-eration Quaker and the Brussels Representative of the Quaker Council for European affairs, was interested in this drawing and consulted Joanna Clark at the Friends House Library in Euston Road. She thought it was copied from

*The pencil drawing, handed down through the family, of George Fox,
founder of the Quaker Movement*

an engraving made by 'Sawyer junior' and published by T. Rodd; the engraving was thought to have been drawn from a lost painting by Sir Peter Lely, a contemporary of Fox. But this presumed painting by Lely was purchased in a London antique shop in 1858 and its authenticity has since been questioned.[32]

Until the mid 19th century Quakers officially shunned portraits as they thought that they might flatter and 'exalt the creature'. However, if family portraits were painted before the movement began in 1648 they tended to be hidden, hanging upstairs when they would not be seen by guests. The Eddisons cannot have been particularly obedient Friends and Ann Eddison, who

32   This painting is in Swathmore College, Pennsylvania.

anyway had not been born a Quaker, thought that portraits were essential and hung them defiantly downstairs.

A note pencilled on the back of my drawing of George Fox says: 'given to E. D. Eddison [33] by Emily Mewburn in 1890. See the little satin wood tea caddy made from the tree under which George Fox preached'. Alas, the tea caddy has long since disappeared but the Mewburn name provides another link: Emily's father, a friend of the Eddisons, was a key character in the founding of the railways. This episode is described in Chapter 11 when Edwin, judging by a scribbled note of a conversation with George Stephenson, was very likely present at the first steam passenger railway journey: an epoch-making Quaker enterprise which took place in 1825.

As we have seen, Edwin's great-great grandfather, the oil-miller John Eddison, born in 1658, was said to be the first Eddison Quaker. At the age of nineteen he may have been mesmerized by the blazing blue eyes of George Fox who came to preach by the Bedale market cross in February 1677 while recruiting Yorkshire Friends to sail to America to take up William Penn's offer to 'buy' tracts of land from the Indians in exchange for articles known to be irresistible to them. John Eddison's name was found on the Register of Friends in Leeds and his son George Eddison of Gateford House was also a Quaker. [34]

Descriptions of the travels of George Fox are enthralling. In 1672 he dashed off to America and raced around Maryland, Long Island, East Jersey, Virginia and Carolina. In 1677 the year he visited Bedale, he also visited 151 other places, including a speedy trip around numerous towns in Holland and Germany with Robert Barclay and William Penn. By the age of 67 he was dead.

The fall of the established Church during the Commonwealth allowed independent sects to flourish, and the ready availability of the translation of the Bible into English caused many to question the roots of religious authority at a time when people were intensely disturbed by the execution of the King. Thousands were dissatisfied with the Elizabethan Settlement and

---

33 Elizabeth Dougill Eddison, b. 1841, daughter of Mary Eddison and John Dougill. She married her first cousin Dr John Edwin Eddison, of The Lodge, Adel, son of Edwin Eddison. She was known as Aunt Libby. They had no children.

34 George Eddison's marriage certificate signed by many Quaker witnesses (SW archive).

attached themselves to emerging religious groups. George Fox's Journals give a vivid picture of the intellectual crisis in the Church; with the established and Roman Catholic church on the one hand and on the other, those who questioned whether the true word of God lay in these authoritarian establishments.

In his journal George Fox disparages the churches as 'steeple houses'. He writes: 'I was moved to open to the people that the steeple-house and the ground whereon it stood, were no more holy than that mountain; and that those temples, which they called the dreadful houses of God, were not set up by the command of God and Christ'. He insisted that you did not need the dressing up, the ceremonial and the architecture to understand the word of God, as these trappings and rituals hid the true meaning of Christianity. George Fox pronounced 'The Light within is the Light of Christ'.

Voltaire admired the Friends' simplicity and lack of rigid dogma. He wrote at length in his *Lettres Philosophiques* about the sect, gently mocking their eccentricities but praising their tolerance. He admired their freedom of thought, which was closest to his own view of man's right to his own opinion on the likelihood of the existence of a supernatural being. No amount of reasoning, he argued, could prove if there was a God, and therefore nobody had the right to force anyone to subscribe to one specific belief, or indeed to any dogmatic belief at all.

An epidemic of dissenting groups emerged including the Anabaptists, Brownists, Barrowists, Diggers, Levellers, Fifth Monarchy Men, Muggletonians, Behmenists and others. In the Peak district Fox came across some Ranters [35] who fell about swearing – an abomination for Quakers whose refusal to be bound by oaths caused many to be imprisoned. Quakers counted any swearing as breaking the commandment against taking God's name in vain. The Ranters insisted that in the Bible the prophets and even all the angels swore. After his brush with the Ranters Fox rode to Cambridge where he was nearly pulled off his horse by the the scholars whom he found exceedingly rude.

George Fox had come on the scene at just the right time. His great oratory, startling eyes and tremendous personality captivated the spiritually jaded. He believed that Christ spoke to him through a light from heaven, like Paul on the road to Damascus, and felt the light was in everyone and was the source

---

35   A radical sect associated with liberal sexuality.

of salvation. He did not force the Bible on his flock. His doctrine was that people should bring the light of God into their lives by sitting quietly and contemplatively speaking only when the spirit of God moved them. This was the point at which they quaked or trembled.

The judge who sentenced Fox to jail in 1650 was Justice Bennet of Derby, who was 'the first that called us Quakers, because I bid them tremble at the word of the Lord.' The shaking and trembling that went on was formidable. The first mention of a shake was when Fox went to Mansfield in 1648 'and the Lord's power was so great, that the house seemed to be shaken.' In 1651, priests, when told 'the man in leathern breeches is come', ran away and hid under hedges, terrified the Lord's power would make them tremble.

George Fox went to listen to a sermon at a 'steeple house' in Ulverstone in 1652 and when the poor priest had finished Fox spoke out so fiercely that afterwards the church shook (according to the journal) and, having issued a few confused words, the priest ran out fearful that the church should fall on his head.

Fox's preaching was so powerful that, standing at the market cross in Carlisle in 1653, he was threatened by the magistrates who sent in their sergeants to arrest him. The magistrates' wives threatened to pluck off the hair from his head, but they could not penetrate the ring of soldiers. Undaunted, Fox carried on. The people trembled; they too thought the steeple house shook and feared it would fall on their heads. When Fox was threatened with execution the priests who were sent up to his gaol 'were exceedingly rude and devilish, as well as a company of bitter Scotch ministers – Presbyterians, made up of envy and malice, who were not fit to speak of the things of God, they were so foul-mouthed'.[36]

Fox was later put in the dungeons among the moss-troopers, harlots, thieves and murderers, where he was appalled by the filth and horrified by a woman almost eaten alive by lice. He began to convert the other prisoners and was beaten up by the gaolers. Then he began to sing. The gaolers raged all the more and brought in a fiddler to drown the singing. Fox's loud voice drowned the fiddler, but after much campaigning by influential Friends, the noisy prisoner was released.

The persecutions were terrible and prisons were filled with Friends. Letters were intercepted, gatherings interrupted and people were beaten for us-

---

36   George Fox, *A Journal, Vol 1* first published in 1694

ing 'thee' and 'thou.' Angry men would say 'What! You ill-bred clown, do you THOU me?' and then proceed to beat the Friend, sometimes to death.

Quaker meetings were prohibited in 1661 and within five weeks 400 Friends had been arrested in Yorkshire alone; several were killed, the terror causing many to flee for a new life in America. But sadly, even in the New World the persecution did not stop. The Puritan New Englanders found the Friends objectionable and persecuted them cruelly.

Quakers continued to exasperate many but Robert Barclay and William Penn did much to counteract the often wild and inaccurate rantings of Quaker enthusiasts. Fox found these highly educated young men invaluable allies and Barclay's book, *An Apology* [37] made sense of some of the Quakers' more inconsistent and unintelligible jargon. Reprinted over sixty times and published in many languages it became the standard book of Quaker theory.

Thomas Aldam of Warmsworth, near Doncaster came to Fox's aid in 1652 when the preacher was battered with stones and clods of earth after he attended Warmsworth Church. Aldam was later chosen by Fox to be one of his first four disciples and afterwards was known as 'The First Friend'. The other three disciples were James Naylor of West Ardsley, Richard Farnsworth of Balby and William Dewsbury of Allerthorpe. Thomas Aldam's grandson John Aldam married Elizabeth Ghest, the aunt of John Eddison the bog-improver and Aldam cousins feature frequently in the early letters.

In 1658 Thomas Aldam travelled to all the gaols in England and wrote accounts of the sufferings of the imprisoned Friends. He took the list to Oliver Cromwell who refused to allow the Quaker prisoners to be released. In a fury, Aldam snatched his thick felt hat from his head (Quakers had to wear hats at all times, even indoors) and with tremendous strength tore it in front of him muttering: 'So shall thy government be rent from thee and thy house.'

Thomas Aldam is mentioned in many Quaker histories. His son, another Thomas, born in 1648, also suffered severe persecution and along with William Penn frequently visited the Rodes at Barlborough Hall. This Thomas Aldam's wife was Anne Stacye [38] whose family were among the tightly-knit group of Quakers living within ten miles of Gateford House who sailed to

---

37 Robert Barclay, *An Apology for the True Christian Divinity*, first published in 1678

38 Various spellings – Stacye, Stacy, Stacie, Stacey

Thomas Aldam
tears his Cap before Cromwell, saying: So shall thy Government be
torn from thee and thy House". A.D. 1658.

Thomas Aldam tearing his hat in front of Cromwell in 1658 by William Bell Scott
(copyright Religious Society of Friends in Britain)

Edith Eddison, (3rd from the left, middle row) St Thomas's Hospital 1906

New Jersey in three little ships in the spring of 1677, five years after the intrepid George Fox had explored the land with Indian guides.

Repeatedly imprisoned in York Castle for non-conformity, Thomas Aldam, embarrassed by his father's extreme behaviour (including the hat-tearing), refused to wear a hat for the rest of his life. He lived at Warmsworth and built the Friends Meeting House near to the White House where his father had lived.

At the beginning of the eighteenth century Quakers were mainly from middle class yeomen families. The movement did not appeal to the nobility or the gentry, though there were exceptions including the Rodes of Barlborough, the Aldams, Robert Barclay and William Penn. Various prohibitions excluded Quakers from the great English universities and professions with the exception of medicine. For this reason Quakers gravitated towards commerce and manufacturing and by the middle of the nineteenth century British Friends were relatively affluent. When the average yearly wage was £50, (roughly £2,500 today) the average annual income of English Friends was £182 (£9,100) for every man, woman and child. The average life span of a Quaker in the 1850's was over fifty-three years, which was more than double that of the general population.

Many members of this small community did well because they were conscientious and, faced with the necessity of making a living, worked hard, were

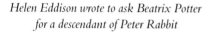

Helen Eddison wrote to ask Beatrix Potter for a descendant of Peter Rabbit

Elizabeth Fry 'the ultimate gay Friend' who wore purple boots with scarlet laces

focused, prudent and responsible. Education was the central character-build-er for Quakers but Britain's Anglican public schools would not accept them and they were debarred from taking degrees at the principal universities as this would have required affirmation of the Church of England's '39 Articles'. Thus many Quakers were educated outside the English mainstream in their own schools with free-thinking teachers.

At a young age they often plunged straight from school into practical ap-prenticeships in Quaker family businesses. Fourteen year-old Samuel Gurney, was apprenticed to his relatives the Fry's where he gained early commercial experience. Edwin Eddison left school at fifteen and although he battled with ill health, became a precocious lawyer at eighteen. His younger brother Booth Eddison also did well after good schooling and an early medical apprentice-ship. So those who began working early were often ahead of those who had gone to university. The roll call of the Quaker school, Grove House at Tot-tenham between 1828 to 1878 with an intake of thirty boys a year, include the names Barclay, Lloyd, Gurney, Foxe, Pease, Backhouse, Hanbury and Bevan, all of whom were to provide leaders in their fields.

Science was considered a safe subject for Quakers who were urged to study nature as a way to involve them with the inscrutable ways of the Creator. This led them through different courses to botany, farming, medicine and experimenting with minerals. They did not spend their fortunes on grand houses, carriages, clothes, amusements or fast women. Instead they spent their money on observatories, botanical gardens and in forming scientific societies. Samuel Galton, a Quaker despite being an arms manufacturer, was a founder member of the Lunar Society (1765–1813). He invited the group to meet at his house in Birmingham to try out some of his experiments and his butler was heard to ask afterwards 'where will the lunatics be meeting next'?

This emphasis on nature and science very much suited the intellectual Booth Eddison whose letters to his brother Edwin before he went to school brim with stories about his pigeons and life on the farm. He was the first of several generations of medical Eddisons and eventually became the head of the British Medical Association. Edwin's granddaughter Edith Eddison of Epperstone Manor also had a distinguished nursing career when she worked under Sir George Makins at St Thomas's Hospital in 1906 and later received the Royal Red Cross from Queen Alexandra as Matron of a Dublin hospital during the Troubles. Her sister Helen Eddison had slightly less ambitious surgical aspirations when her dull diaries soar at one point with the drama of her surgical operation on an ill-fated, crop-bound chicken. She applied and failed to train as a nursery nurse, so retired to live at home, killing tedium by gardening and making rabbit hutches. At the beginning of World War II she wrote to Beatrix Potter asking if she could buy a descendant of Peter Rabbit to breed from – to which the crusty author wrote back saying that Peter lived and died a bachelor and anyway he was a Belgian hare not a rabbit.

Industrial Revolution

The Quakers' lack of higher education seems to have intensified the Friends' sense of rejection by society but attitudes gradually mellowed and respect grew for their benign steadiness, their demonstrably happy family lives, their honesty and their financial success. People were impressed by their enlightened relationships with their workers, their efforts in prison reform and their early anti-slavery stance.

The forced exclusion of Quakers from the universities and professions partly explains why so many of them were in trade and industry but does not explain why they did so well. The golden years from 1815 to 1870 have been classified by historians as the Age of Reform when British industry and society were being transformed at breathtaking speed. In 1800, when many of the Quaker businesses began their growth, only one person in 500 was a Quaker. Sir Adrian Cadbury has calculated that the foundations of a large percentage of Britain's Industrial Revolution were laid by just 0.2 percent of the population. Successful Quaker firms include the Darby and Reynolds ironworks at Coalbrookdale; Huntsmans steel industry in Sheffield; Allen & Hanbury, (later Glaxo), Ransom's pharmaceuticals; Cadburys, Rowntrees and Frys chocolate manufacturers; Huntley & Palmers; Peak Frean and Carr's biscuits; Horniman's tea; Colman's mustard; Ransom's machinery; Albright & Wilson's chemicals; Bryant and May matches; Clarke shoes; Tompion the clockmaker; Lloyds, Barclays, Gurneys and countless other banks. Their success was helped along by their scrupulous plain dealing, industriousness and the loyal support of other Friends in business.

According to David McClelland's *The Achieving Society* [39] Protestants were six times more creative than the mainstream population. From McClelland's work it can also be calculated that the tiny group known as Quakers were technically and socially 70 times more creative than the mainstream population.

In the very early days of Quakerism, the largest single occupational group was connected with textiles. Later on in the century more were farmers and more joined the expanding group of wholesale traders. They rejected the haggling over retail prices and returned to the medieval practice of fixed prices which was fairer to both producer and buyer. The Quaker George Eddison, born in 1679 changed from the family milling and farming tradition to join the cloth trade which was at that time surging forward on a great wave of economic growth. He prospered and was able to retire to the more gentrified countryside of Nottinghamshire where his son John was to farm at Gateford with scientific brilliance.

Georgian Quakers, rather like the Jews (of whom at that time there were about 10,000 in Britain) segregated themselves by their distinctive humble manners, antiquated sombre dress and plain speech and above all by their rule of not marrying out of the Society. This caused a decline in Quaker numbers from about 38,000 in 1700 to about 20,000 in 1800 which made this small

---

39   David McClelland, *The Achieving Society*, D. Van Nostrand, 1961

society more select as its proportion of merchants and professional men rose, while its artisan numbers declined.

Quaker women dressed plainly without superfluous lace or decoration. In her portrait Ann Eddison's ruff was not exactly plain and her bonnet has elaborate pleating which was tiresome to iron. Quaker wives wore no wedding rings, considering them to be badges of a hireling ministry.

Quakers considered it frivolous to have their portraits painted, or even to own portraits. Luckily John and Ann Eddison dismissed this custom and defiantly hung their portraits downstairs. William, Henry and Ann, their first three surviving children, were painted in oils but there seems to be no trace of an oil painting of their third son, Edwin. Their mother Ann was painted and several copies were made, presumably one for each of the children. Benjamin Eddison of Raymoth Farm, her brother-in-law, also defied these rules and was painted by a good painter at Osmaston, and Edwin commissioned William Poole of Sheffield to paint him in 1832. This portrait hangs in our hall today.

The fact that the Eddisons were painted so much is puzzling. Thomas Clarkson (1760–1846) in *Portraiture of Quakerism* wrote:

> Neither, as a general rule, would a person in going through the houses of Friends find portraits either of themselves, or any of their families or ancestors, except in the latter case, they had been taken before they became Friends. The first Friends never had their portraits taken with their own knowledge and consent. Considering themselves as poor and helpless creatures, and as little better than dust and ashes, they had but a mean idea of their own images. They were of opinion, also, that pride and self-conceit would be likely to arise to men from the view and ostentatious parade of their own persons.

Clarkson goes on to say:

> They believed also if there were those whom they loved, that the best method of showing their regard to these would be, not by having their fleshly images before their eyes, but by preserving their best actions in their thoughts as worthy of imitation; and that their own memory, in the same manner, should be perpetuated rather in the loving hearts, and

kept alive in the edifying conversation of their descendants, than in the perishing tablets of canvas fixed upon the walls of their habitations. [40]

Walter Scott while having his portrait painted was surprised to hear that the artist C. R. Leslie had painted several Quakers and said scathingly 'They must have been what are called wet Quakers.' The artist assured him that they were not, but the acerbic Scott remarked that at least they were 'damp Quakers'.

Were the Eddisons damp Quakers? Their need to perpetuate their identity was strong. The elderly owner of the Quaker Meeting house at Blythe (now a private house), told us that she knew that Eddisons were buried there. Kicking aside the earth on a moss-covered rockery in the corner of her garden, a flat stone was partially revealed. Bending down to read the inscription, I was able to make out the name HENRY EDDISON (second son of John and Ann). This was surprising as Quakers did not even approve of memorial stones and suggests that the Eddisons were more than just a little damp.

The Quaker aversion to portraits was followed by another curious rule. Strict Quakers had a choice of just three pictures in their houses. You often saw one of these pictures, sometimes two, but never three. They were:

1. Penn's Treaty with the Indians – an engraving of Benjamin West's painting

2. A print of the plan of a slave ship

3. A plan of the building at Ackworth School, the Quaker School near Wakefield in Yorkshire.

Quakers had officially shunned portrait painting fearing that it might be over-flattering. But on the invention of the new technology of portrait photography in the mid-nineteenth century, Friends were innocently unaware of yet undiscovered techniques to improve images and believed photography to be unerringly truthful. The Eddisons avidly embraced this new form of portraiture judging by the large number of early carte-de-visit photographs found in old soap boxes in the Bedale attics.

40   Thomas Clarkson, *A Portrait of Quakerism*, 1806

A Quaker Meeting

At the time of Edwin's birth at the beginning of the nineteenth century, there had been a greater distinction between Strict Quakers and those who were not so strict. Strict Friends dressed plainly and those who flouted the rules were described as 'gay' Quakers. Elizabeth Gurney (1780–1845) of Earlham Hall, (later Elizabeth Fry the prison reformer) was the ultimate gay Friend wearing purple boots with scarlet laces, a scarlet cloak (made from a bale of cloth, imported from Belgium by her father, who had mistaken it for a drabber colour) and bright frocks, when it was more usual for Quakers to wear dresses of dun or dove-grey. Edwin's sister Mary, with some sort of fashion sense, enjoyed trimming her hats and making frivolous screens using feathers, plundered from her taxidermist brother's discarded plumage.

Music, singing and dancing were not encouraged as they stirred up lusty emotions. Novels were out. The theatre damaged the personality and painting was dangerous on account of the unbridling effect of colours. Furniture was meant to be plain and decorations on cradles were expected to contaminate babies. It sounds as if the Eddisons were on the whole non-strict. There is no

Earith Monthly Meeting c. 1837 by Samuel Lucas of Hitchin
(copyright Religious Society of Friends in Britain)

mention of music and dancing in their early letters even though, according to the Gateford inventory of 1852, they owned a Broadwood piano.

Edwin Eddison was educated at the highly respected Joseph Tatham's Quaker School in Leeds, where he later reluctantly lodged while learning law. There were benefits because he married into the Tatham family whose leather-bound family tree, going back to 1580, I found hidden under a pile of clothes in the Bedale attics.

The Tathams of Tatham in Lancashire were brave and defiant early Quakers. Marmaduke Tatham of Wray was sentenced to have his tongue torn out in 1660 and later on various Tathams emigrated to Pennsylvania which was a hotbed of Friends. An area of 45,000 square miles had been given to William Penn in 1681 by Charles II in order to extinguish a debt of £16,000 owed to the estate of his father Admiral Sir William Penn who had conquered Jamaica in 1655. Pepys remarked acidly in his diary, '*Penn's son had become a Quaker or some very melancholy thing*'.

In 1841 when the Tathams were well settled in America, the Oregon Trail opened up and covered wagon trains forged their way across the continent.

The Californian Gold Rush came a few years later in 1849 and by the 1860's the majority of Indian nations had been driven to the west of the Mississippi basin. President Ulysses S. Grant took the imaginative step in 1869 of calling on the Society of Friends to supervise many of the Indian Reservations and treaty areas.

Friends always behaved honourably to the Indians, even in the very earliest days of settlement, although their purchase of land from the Indians in Pennsylvania was questionable at a time when the natives still had no concept of privately owned land. But on the whole the Quakers' intentions were good. The need to survive in this new land was paramount and it was here that they acquired their skill at dealing with refugees.

In the bitter winter of the Irish Potato Famine in 1845–46 Friends were invaluable, organising soup kitchens and providing shoes and clothing for the destitute. Aghast at the devastation, they provided smallholders with seeds and set up model farms. The young John Fowler [41] who was taken to Ireland at that time by his father, a rich Quaker corn merchant from Melksham in Wiltshire, was horrified by what he saw and racked his brains for farming solutions which led to his invention of the first steam plough in 1858.

In 1860, towards the end of Edwin Eddison's life, it had become clear to Friends that their Society was in terminal decline. To many, their behaviour and dress regulations were offensive and the rule restricting marriage to those within the Society was intolerable. These irritations and other issues were put right in reforms and the Society just managed to survive. In 1858 the essayist, John Stephenson Rowntree wrote, 'the paralysing effect of an eagerness to be rich … the prevalence of the commercial prosperity to which the profession of Quakerism is specially favourable – were two of the reasons for the decline.' [42]

Rowntree found even more fundamental problems. Priest-less quiet worship was uninspiring; men and women needed to be led and inspired to God. They were too cut off from the world and the Quakers' disavowal of baptism and the Lord's Supper made it impossible for them to associate with other Christians; also the Society was too harsh in its discipline. But the main reason for the decline, in Rowntree's view, was the harsh choice between mar-

41   Edwin's son Robert Eddison was a partner in John Fowler and Co.
       Engineers, Leeds.
42   John Stephenson Rowntree, *The Friend*, 1858.

riage within the Society and the risk of disownment, a choice women could avoid by remaining spinsters and thus driving down the Quaker birthrate even further. In the first half of the nineteenth century, Rowntree reported, the Society disowned some 4,000 members under the marriage rule, a policy he rightly characterises as 'suicidal'. The inbreeding was inevitable as Quaker rules were strict, but the network was close and there were many advantages and supports between them all, particularly in the business and banking worlds. Generations of social isolation and persecutions meant that the clan feeling was usually strong.

Quakers considered their church was a community not a building and their Meeting Houses emphasized this. The younger Eddisons dreaded the long, sometimes five-hourly meetings when they had to sit still and listen to spasmodic outpourings of their elders. In these meetings an icy chill fell when elders disowned a member who fell short of its standards. Edwin's wife, Hannah Maria underwent the frosty experience when she was rejected in 1830 but the fact that Edwin's mother-in-law, Hannah Tatham was also disowned for marrying William Baker, a non-Quaker, may have softened the blow. The Quaker noose on the family gradually loosened but the Friends' influence over the years had been a positive and the Eddisons' dampness over the portraits rule was a blessing. Seeing them peer from their frames satisfies curiosity and gives a comforting sense of continuity.

8
The Booths

*When but a mere child the degradation and helpless misery of the poor
stockingers of my native town wandering gaunt and hunger-stricken
through the streets … kindled in my heart yearnings to help the poor.* [43]
General Booth, Salvation Army founder.

The dark eyes of Edwin's mother Ann Eddison (*née* Booth) beam from
her portrait in our dining room. On the bookcase nearby, the salt-glazed
loving-cup, with one handle missing, is inscribed with her grandmother's
name, *Elizabeth Booth, June the 10th 1734*: the date her famous son Abraham
was christened.

On a raw February day 1799, half-way through the reign of George III,
twenty-nine year old Ann Booth married the forty-three year-old Quaker
John Eddison of Gateford House: both thought to be rather old for marriage.
The Booths of Annesley Woodhouse were much involved with the profitable
frame-knitting industry and lived near where the first Luddite frame-smash-
ing incident took place, so it was no surprise to find mention of the Luddite
uprising in their letters.

The best known book of Reverend Abraham Booth, an early protester
against the slave trade, was *The Reign of Grace* [44] which has been in print more
or less continuously since it was published. The Salvation Army leader, William Booth, (no relation, but also from Nottinghamshire) was recommended
the book as a student but finding its language both florid and obtuse is said to
have hurled it against the wall after reading only thirty pages.

Abraham Booth's grandfather, another Abraham, born in 1675, farmed at
Blackwell in Derbyshire but his son Robert, born in 1700, later moved to
the village of Annesley Woodhouse in Nottinghamshire where he rented land

---

43   *Ashburton Guardian*, 22 August 1912.
44   Abraham Booth, *The Reign of Grace*, 1768. A remarkable *tour de force*,
      discusses how salvation is brought about, since Divine Grace cannot be
      refused or earned.

The link between the Booths and the Eddisons

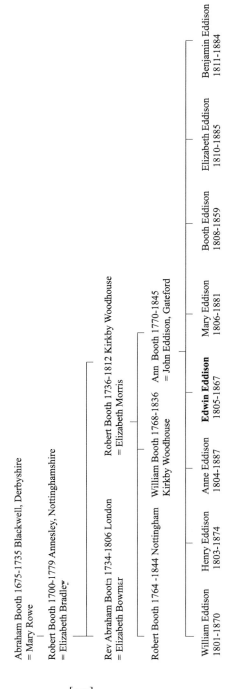

Abraham Booth 1675-1735 Blackwell, Derbyshire
= Mary Rowe

Robert Booth 1700-1779 Annesley, Nottinghamshire
= Elizabeth Bradley

Robert Booth 1736-1812 Kirkby Woodhouse

Rev Abraham Booth 1734-1806 London
= Elizabeth Bowmer

= Elizabeth Morris

William Booth 1768-1836   Ann Booth 1770-1845
Kirkby Woodhouse   = John Eddison, Gateford

Robert Booth 1764 -1844 Nottingham

William Eddison   Henry Eddison   Anne Eddison   Edwin Eddison   Mary Eddison   Booth Eddison   Elizabeth Eddison   Benjamin Eddison
1801-1870   1803-1874   1804-1887   1805-1867   1806-1881   1808-1859   1810-1885   1811-1884

*Elizabeth Booth's loving cup which
commemorates the birth of her son
Abraham in 1734*

*Selina Hastings, Countess of Huntingdon
whose bible studies at Donington Hall
were attended by the Booths*

from the Duke of Portland, owned several cottages and various plots of land. Robert's eldest son was the Reverend Abraham and his second son, another Robert (father of Ann Eddison), was born in 1736 – the year small-pox raged so virulently in Nottingham that burials exceeded births by 380.

The Booth family like many others in the eighteenth century were greatly influenced by the Christian Revival led by John Wesley and George Whitfield which spread across Britain like wildfire. One of the early converts to this movement was Selina Hastings, Countess of Huntingdon, whose fierce, but plain face can be seen in the National Portrait Gallery. The Booths attended her bible studies at Donnington Hall and were swept up in the fervour of new ideas.

The Reverend Abraham Booth started his working life in the hosiery business but his interest in books deterred him from becoming an apprentice. Aged twenty-three he married Elizabeth Bowmar, a farmer's daughter, who looks reassuringly homely in her portrait painted in middle age.[45] Abraham

---

45   The portrait is with Mrs Alison Denny, a descendant of Rev Abraham Booth.

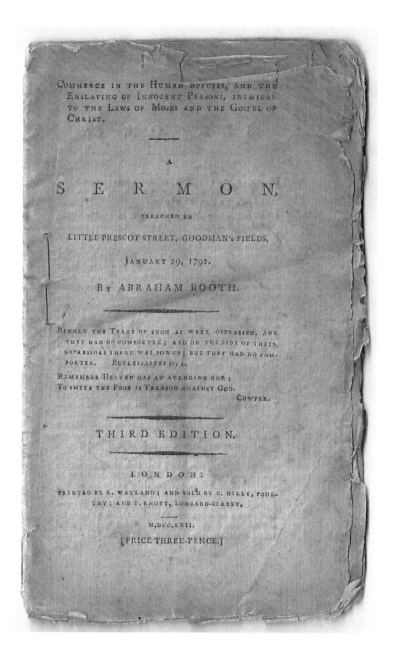

COMMERCE IN THE HUMAN SPECIES, AND THE
ENSLAVING OF INNOCENT PERSONS, INIMICAL
TO THE LAWS OF MOSES AND THE GOSPEL OF
CHRIST.

A

S E R M O N,

PREACHED IN

LITTLE PRESCOT STREET, GOODMAN's FIELDS,

JANUARY 29, 1792.

By ABRAHAM BOOTH.

BEHOLD THE TEARS OF SUCH AS WERE OPPRESSED, AND
THEY HAD NO COMFORTER; AND ON THE SIDE OF THEIR
OPPRESSORS THERE WAS POWER; BUT THEY HAD NO COM-
FORTER.   ECCLESIASTES iv, 1.

REMEMBER HEAVEN HAS AN AVENGING ROD;
TO SMITE THE POOR IS TREASON AGAINST GOD.
                                        COWPER.

THIRD EDITION.

L O N D O N:

PRINTED BY L. WAYLAND; AND SOLD BY C. DILLY, POUL-
TRY; AND T. KNOTT, LOMBARD-STREET.

M,DCC,XCII.

[PRICE THREE-PENCE.]

Abraham Booth declared that the European slave trade was theft

set up a school with his wife in Sutton-in-Ashfield and in 1768 published *The Reign of Grace.*

For thirty years Abraham was a pastor of Prescot Street Baptist Church in Goodman's Fields, London, writing many books and preaching important sermons, one of which was among the attic papers. It was a tattered document costing three-pence, dated 29 January 1792 [46] with twenty-five grubby pages crudely stitched together. It proclaimed that slavery is wrong and that the European slave trade cannot be justified as bondage, which the Old Testament described as a form of restitution for injuries done to society.

Abraham declared that the European slave trade was theft and that God the creator was the universal proprietor. No one had liberty or life except by the grant of God and God's moral and ethical laws did not justify the English buying negroes and selling them to other nations. In the Old Testament the Canaanite bondsmen were under the protection of divine law which prohibited cruelty. The Reverend Abraham would have urged people to see that the cruel storage of slaves in transport ships was brutal. He would have been appalled at the practice of throwing sick slaves overboard en-masse so that the insurance on them could be claimed.

In a letter from the Bedale attics dated 1797, Abraham Booth sympathises with his brother Robert about the death of his sixty-three year old wife Elizabeth from a stroke. It was the year the Bank of England had suspended cash

46   S.W. archive

payments with disastrous consequences for manufacturing districts. In another letter written in July 1800, Abraham describes how the high price of bread has caused three days of riots in Nottingham which the military were unable to quell. Three months later, when the price of bread had risen so high that people were starving to death, soup houses were opened and two saintly merchants bought huge amounts of corn to sell at low prices to the poor.

The Smallpox Scourge

In 1800 Robert Booth tells his daughter Ann Eddison that her uncle Abraham had been to Nottingham to have his face dressed as much flesh had been lost. He also writes that one of Abraham's children who had just recovered from small-pox has just died from the added complication of 'hoping cough' (sic). In a much used copy of John Wesley's *An Easy and Natural Method of Curing Most Diseases* [47] there is an optimistic cure for whooping cough: 'rub the feet thoroughly with hogs lard before the fire at going to bed, or to rub the back with old rum. It seldom fails or in desperate cases, change of air alone has cured.' One of his many useless small-pox remedies is: 'In violent cases, bleed in the foot; bathe the legs in warm water twice a day; and apply boiled turnips to the feet.'

The face of Lady Mary Wortley Montagu was ravaged by smallpox. Intrigued in 1717 by the Ottoman practice of inoculation known as variolation, she watched old Turkish ladies with nut-shells full of the 'best sort of small pox', going round injecting people at parties and describes the scene:

Lady Mary Wortley Montagu

47 This copy, dated 1774 belonged to the author's great-great-great-great-grandfather Joseph Tatham born in 1732, who started the Quaker School in Leeds. (S. W. archive).

The Cow Pock __ or __ the Wonderful Effects of the New Inoculation!__ vide. the Publications of ye Anti Vaccine Society.

*James Gilroy's cartoon of Jenner vaccinating patients who feared it would
make them sprout cow-like appendages*

The small-pox, so fatal, and so general amongst us, is here entirely
harmless, by the invention of engrafting, which is the term they give it.
There is a set of old women, who make it their business to perform the
operation, every autumn, in the month of September, when the great heat
is abated. People send to one another to know if any of their family has
a mind to have the small-pox; they make parties for this purpose, and the
old woman comes with a nut-shell full of the matter of the best sort of
small-pox, and asks what vein you please to have opened, and with a large
needle puts into the vein as much matter as can lie upon the head of her
needle.[48]

Thomas Dimsdale [49] the Quaker physician had long been interested in small-
pox inoculation and in 1767 he published *The Present Method of Inoculating for*

48   *Letters of Lady Mary Wortley Montagu, Vol 1* (Aix:Anthony Henricy 1796)
     pp 167–69
49   He was a Quaker but was later disowned for marrying out of the Society.

the Small-Pox which brought him overnight fame and the next year led to a summons from Russia to inoculate Catherine the Great and her son Paul. On a later visit he inoculated the Empress's grandchildren. Despite his apprehension,[50] shared by George III who feared a major diplomatic crisis if things were to go wrong, Dimsdale carried out the procedure successfully and was created a Baron by the Empress for his efforts. He was given £1,000 for his journey and the Empress presented him with £10,000, and £500 per annum for life as well as fabulous gifts which the family still own today. Edward

The Quaker Dr Thomas Dimsdale was created a Baron by Catherine the Great

Jenner (1749–1823) like any other doctor of the time, carried out variolation to protect his patients, but went on to make the discovery in 1796 that vaccination with cowpox was a much safer protection from the dreaded smallpox.

Consumption was another scourge of far too many Booths. John Wesley's book *Primative Physic,* 1774 has twenty-two hopeless cures, including:

Throw Frankincense on burning Coals, and receive the Smoke daily thro' a proper Tube into the lungs

Every morning cut up a little Turf of fresh Earth, and lying down, breathe into the Hole for a Quarter of an Hour, I have known a deep Consumption cured thus.

In the last Stage, Suck an healthy Woman daily. Tried by my Father.

---

50   The operation was kept secret and relays of horses were at the ready in case the inoculation should go wrong and Dimsdale needed to escape from Catherine's angry subjects.

Cottage knitting frame

The Stocking Business

Nottinghamshire was a key area for the stocking-frame industry and the Booth's involvement in stockings is mentioned in the early letters; even the Reverend Abraham owned stocking frames. In a letter he acknowledges receipt of £6 for Frame Rent from Taylor and Co. Hosiers in 1803 and thanks his brother Robert for not making any reduction on account of cleaning the frames or for repairs.

The hosiery industry originated in the sixteenth century in Calverton, a sheep farming area of Nottingham which was a few miles from where the Booths lived. In 1589 the Reverend William Lee tried to imitate the action of a pair of knitting needles on a machine. One account said that Lee, heir to an estate, was deeply in love with a young woman who was keener on her knitting than on his attentions which caused him to invent a machine that would make knitting by hand redundant. A more likely story is that William Lee was

Wensleydale knitters. Four figures knit and gossip round a pump,
the shepherd knits as he walks behind the sheep and the woman in the background knits
as she walks through the village. By George Walker, Engraved by Robert Havell

a poor curate, whose wife had to knit steadily to further their finances, so he was driven to invent a knitting machine to make family life tolerable.

The knitting machine could make six hundred stitches a minute as against the one hundred achieved on average by a good hand-knitter. A stockinger who owned his own frame could earn up to thirty shillings a week (roughly £75 today).

The typical knitter's home was a three-storey cottage with a living room on the ground floor, bedroom above and on the top floor, a workroom with a long mullioned window under the eaves to provide the most light. Knitting frames were expensive, so those who did not own them hired them from the hosiers. There were about 8,000 stocking frames in England at the time of Daniel Defoe (1660–1731), who noted when riding round the country that 'one would scarce think it possible so small an article of trade could employ such multitudes of people as it does.'[51]

51   Daniel Defoe, *A Tour through the Whole Island of Great Britain*, 1763

Before the invention of the frames, knitting stockings by hand had been mainly women's work and they would sit outside their cottages in good weather chatting away happily. At Bala, in North Wales, knitters of both sexes and all ages would gather on a mound called Tomen-y-Bala to do their knitting together. Thomas Pennant wrote that Bala had a vast trade in woollen stockings:

> From two to five hundred pounds worth are sold each day, according to the demand. Round the place women and children are in full employ, knitting along the roads; and mixed with them Herculean figures appear, assisting their omphales in this effeminate employ. During winter the females, through love of society, often assemble at one another's houses to knit; sit round a fire, and listen to some old tale, or to some ancient song, or the sound of a harp, and this is called Cymmorth Gwau, or, the knitting assembly.[52]

At Dent, in Yorkshire, the pace at which women produced knitted garments became legendary. Known as 'the terrible knitters of Dent' they maniacally knitted stockings as they drove their peat carts into the town, often with a wooden knitting stick attached to their belt to hold one needle while their right hand held the other, leaving the left hand to hold the reigns. Other jobs, such as milking the cow or churning butter could be done while using a knitting stick. Tourists would come and watch, which embarrassed the men who then left the knitting to the women.

At the beginning of the nineteenth century there were around 30,000 knitting-frames at work in England and 9,000 were in Nottinghamshire. The stocking frames were normally operated by men as they required considerable physical effort. A machine only produced a flat piece of material which was then taken off the frame and seamed up by women to form a fully fashioned stocking.

Profits were pitiful. Knitters paid a weekly rent for the frame and also had to pay a woman seamer and buy oil for the machine. They had to spend many hours a week travelling, collecting the raw materials and even more time delivering the goods. If a machine broke down the knitter was expected to be his own mechanic which further eroded the pittance he earned.

52   Thomas Pennant, *A Tour in Wales, 2 Vols.*, 1778–83

WHEREAS,

Several EVIL-MINDED PERSONS have assembled together in a
riotous Manner, and DESTROYED a NUMBER of

FRAMES,

In different Parts of the Country:

THIS IS

TO GIVE NOTICE,

That any Person who will give Information of any Person or Persons
thus wickedly

BREAKING THE FRAMES,

Shall, upon CONVICTION, receive

50 GUINEAS

REWARD.

And any Person who was actively engaged in RIOTING, who will
impeach his Accomplices, shall, upon CONVICTION, receive the
same Reward, and every Effort made to procure his Pardon.

☞ Information to be given to Messrs. COLDHAM and ENFIELD.

Nottingham, March 26, 1811.

*A poster printed at Nottingham in March 1811, offering a reward for
information leading to the conviction of machine-breakers*

Growing desperation caused knitters to rent extra frames so that they could
teach their children to operate them and this extra production by child labour
led to a further increase in the birth-rate. Government committees in 1778
heard that 'pauper children toiling for 4s.6d a week were enslaved to long
hours which destroyed the nerves and the bodily strength of grown men and
women'. Did the Reverend Abraham Booth have qualms about renting out
stocking frames? Could it have entered his head that this cottage industry was
slavery by another name when he delivered his sermons on the 'Exploitation
of Negroes'? He probably left the whole operation to his brother Robert.

The demand for stockings was reduced when the fashion for trousers began to replace the elegantly stockinged male leg and was further affected by
Napoleon's boycott of British trade. Soon there were too many workers try-

ing to earn a living from the depressed industry and, with the rising price of food, machine sabotage was inevitable.

In 1811 during the depression many hosiery workers in Nottingham were obliged to sweep the streets for paltry payment. They gathered in the Market Place determined to take vengeance on the hosiery manufacturers who had reduced stocking prices and sixty-three frames were broken in the village of Arnold which was worryingly near the Booths' village of Annesley Woodhouse.

Heavily disguised Luddites smashed two hundred more frames during the next three weeks; 'Luddite' was a term said to have come from the name of the young Leicestershire lad called Ludlam who, when asked to 'square his needles' by his father, took his hammer and beat them into a heap. A thousand frames were broken in Nottinghamshire alone and the next year breaking a stocking or lace frame was made a capital offence.

The rebellion spread and the leader of each assembled group – styled General Ludd, or Ned Ludd – stood guard while others smashed the frames wearing black handkerchiefs over their faces. Sometimes they destroyed all the furniture in the houses and burnt the stacks. They proceeded to Sutton-in-Ashfield, three miles from the Booth's village, where they destroyed about seventy frames but were later dispersed by the military who took several prisoners.

Luddites were not the first to break machines nor were textile workers the only ones to do so. Weavers in London rioted against engine looms in 1675 and in 1768 spinners at Blackburn rioted against Hargreaves' 'spinning jenny'. In 1776 a crowd of eight thousand attacked machinery in cotton towns and villages around Manchester and 'a most riotous and outrageous Mob' assembled at Birkacre, near Chorley, where Arkwright had just built a factory. Most of the carding machines were destroyed and the building was set alight.

The first Luddite martyr was a nineteen year-old rioter, Thomas Helliker, who was convicted for refusing to name his accomplices and hanged in 1803. The term Luddite did not come into use until 1811, so the episode may well have been known as the Hellikite Rebellion, which does not sound as menacing as Luddite. Searching through William Booth's diary for 1812 I found a mention of the Luddites in an entry on 26 January: 'Luds' broke 30 frames at Bagthorpe and Underwood; fetched a frame of Betty's from Betty Eyres for fear of 'Lud'.'

It is not known whether Booth frames were wrecked but Luddite gangs tended not to smash frames owned by masters who paid fair wages, or were making fully fashioned stockings at the proper price; as the saintly Abraham and other Booths were in this category they should have been left alone.

The winter of 1802 was particularly cold and poor Abraham, now sixty-nine and feeling his age, gloomily contemplates his death. He writes: 'My Asthma increases, and my cough is very troublesome, so that I have not been able to preach twice on one day for a long time, nor at all for three or four weeks.'

In the the summer of 1805 (the year of Edwin's birth), fearful of an invasion by the French and depressed that the Nottinghamshire wheat is mildewed, Abraham is looking forward to being gathered by the good Lord. He finally dies in January 1806 and in his will [53] he forbids eulogy at his funeral. But in a long elegiac poem written on his death two effulgent verses give a picture of old Abraham Booth:

Worn in his Masters work, and full of years
The venerable Booth in dust is laid;
Like th' autumnal shock of golden ears,
Triumphant to the garner home convey'd!

His was the hoary head with glory crowns
By wisdom marked with dignity and grace
His was the deep research; the judgement sound,
And his the soul sincere, and honest face.

In his will Abraham ordered his stocking frames to be sold along with all his publications and the copyright of his books. Among his bequests he leaves £100 to his son Isaac; to his son Robert all his clothes, his plate, his pocket watch, £300 5% Navy Annuities; and to his daughter Ann half the furniture, linen and china, £400 5% Navy Annuities. The daughters, Sarah and Rebecca were left £250 and the granddaughters, Elizabeth Parkin and Mary Wightman were each left £150 5% Navy Annuities. His sons, the executors of his will, were left £800 3% stock of the year 1726 together with the remaining furniture, linen and china. The Reverend Abraham Booth left a considerable sum.

Abraham's brother the farmer Robert Booth who died in 1812, had four unmarried sons and four daughters, one being Ann Eddison of Gateford. His

53   Ernest A. Payne, *Abraham Booth and some of his Descendants.*

son Robert, a guardian of Ann's eight children and a churchwarden of St Mary's Church, Nottingham, was the shrewd business man who built the first hosiery warehouse in Nottingham. He was prosperous and, surprisingly for someone involved with trade, was described a gentleman. In his will he left a number of stocking frames rented out to cottagers and real estate in the area of Kirkby Woodhouse. He died unmarried in 1844 at his house in Plumptree Street, Nottingham and was buried in the vault in front of Kirkby Woodhouse chapel, surrounded by smart iron palisades. Robert was pernickety. Just before he died he wrote the exact arrangements for his funeral in a little brown note-book [54] found in the Bedale attics. Terrified of being buried alive he writes: 'John Dreary to make a deal shell and a well made oak coffin furnished with plain brass handles, to be brought on Friday evening, and not to be closed till 8 o'clock on Wednesday morning'.

Then there is a long list of attending and absent friends who would receive silk funeral gloves and the unpleasant funeral biscuits with the exact order of the mourners in the procession and a seating list for the carriages. Mrs Betty Coulson, his brother William's housekeeper, 'an old friend' is seventh in the procession.

Brother William Booth, also styled a gentleman and also unmarried, had died earlier in 1836 of consumption, the scourge of the Booths. He had farmed, collected taxes, owned stocking frames and in his will he left consid-erable sums to his nephews and nieces. Mrs Betty Coulson, who also owned stocking frames, was left an annuity of £603 (£30,150 in today's value [55]) and the use of his house till her death. She must have been a good friend although her precise position in William's household is unclear. She is mentioned in a long letter from a Booth descendent, James Granger, writing in 1909 to Dr John E. Eddison. He describes how on a freezing day in January 1841 when he was fourteen, he was asked by his grandfather to take some money to Mrs Coulson. Concerned that he might lose his way, his grandfather drew a map of the landmarks on the road from Nottingham to Kirkby Woodhouse and made the boy promise to return the same day. Young James was worried about the large amount of money he had in his bag which was £60 (roughly £3,000). Snow was on the ground and the poor boy found the twelve miles heavy going. When he arrived Mrs Coulson was ill in bed and refused to see

---

54 S. W. archive.
55 For simplicity all 19th century values are multiplied by a factor of fifty.

him until it was dark, so he was compelled to stay the night. The next morning he set off for the hard walk home, relieved not to have the money in his
bag because a rough-looking man walked closely beside him for several miles
but, to his relief, eventually took a turning off the road.

In his letter James Granger stressed that although Mrs Coulson was unmarried, it was normal in the seventeenth and eighteenth centuries for unmarried
ladies in her position to be dignified by being termed Mistress or Mrs, and, he
insisted: 'no doubt she would be looked up to in Kirkby Woodhouse during
Uncle William's time and after, as higher than most there.'

9
A Murder in Australia

*We desire to be delivered from any suspicion of a wish to check the 'march
of improvement'; but the 'march of quackery' seems to be running just now
very strongly side by side with it.*

The Times, 29 January 1828

After the mad king George III died in the summer of 1820, there would only
have been slight interest at Gateford in the crowning of the Prince Regent as
the antics of the royal family were shocking to respectable Quakers. Benjamin
Haydon, the painter, with a good seat in Westminster Hall captures the bum-
bling chaos of George IV's coronation:

> The sun began to light up the old gothic windows, the peers to stroll
> in, and the company to crowd in, of all descriptions, elegant young men
> tripping along in silken grace with elegant girls trembling in feathers and
> diamonds, old peers and old peeresses, some in one dress and some in
> another … all happy, eager, smiling, and anticipating. Some took seats they
> had not any right to occupy, and were obliged to leave them after sturdy
> disputes. Others lost their tickets. The Hall occasionally echoed with
> the hollow roar of voices at the great door, till at last the galleries were
> filled.[56]

Haydon reaches a crescendo describing the entrance of King George IV
whom he calls 'the fat Adonis of fifty':

> The appearance of a Monarch has something of the air of a rising sun;
> there are indications that announce his approach, a streak of light, the
> tipping of a cloud, the singing of a lark, the brilliance of the sky, till the
> edges get brighter and brighter, and he rises majestically into the heavens.
> So was the King's advance. A whisper of mystery turns all eyes to the

---

56   *The Autobiography of Benjamin Haydon 1786–1846*, published 1853.

throne! Suddenly two or three run: others fall back: some talk, direct, hurry, stand still, or disappear. Then three or four of high rank appear from behind the Throne; an interval is left: the crowds scarce breathe! Something rustles, and a being buried in satin, feathers and diamonds rolls gracefully into his seat. The room rises with a sort of feathered, silken thunder! Plumes wave, eyes sparkle, glasses are out, mouths smile, and one man becomes the prime object of attraction to thousands! The way in which the King bowed was really monarchic! As he looked towards the peeresses and foreign ambassadors, he looked like some gorgeous bird of the east.

But there is no mention of poor Queen Caroline who was fighting frantically to gain entry to the Hall. She had horrified the Prince with her coarse behaviour and was said to have smelt unwashed. At a ball Lady Bessborough

1812, OR REGENCY À LA MODE.
(*Drawn and etched by W. Heath.*)

Caricature of the Prince Regent as 'the fat Adonis of fifty'

found her a short, very fat, elderly woman with an extremely red face. An anonymous rhyme current at the time ran: 'Most Gracious Queen we thee implore/To go away and sin no more/But if this effort be too great/To go away at any rate!'

Three months after this event eighteen year-old Henry Eddison writes to his younger brother Edwin advising him to ask his mother for money for law books. There were 122 circulating libraries in London in 1800 and 268 in the provinces but Edwin needed specific ones for his law studies. Books were expensive: novels cost 7s 6d, history books a guinea and for those who could not afford good books, novels were reduced to little 'chapbooks' printed crudely on the cheapest grade of rag paper with worn type and illustrations from battered old blocks. Because they were so flimsy they rarely survived. Paper was expensive and people used chap book sheets for wrapping and there are even contemporary references to its use as 'bum fodder.' In one of the Bedale trunks there was a thin wrinkled page of a chap book with a ballad titled *The King God Bless Him* with a verse that would have cheered young Henry Eddison:

THE KING
GOD BLESS HIM.

Pitts, Printer, wholesale Toy and Marble Warehouse,
6, Gt. St. Andrew Street, Seven Dials.

A goblet of Burgundy, fill, fill for me
Give those who prefer it Champagne,
But whatever the Wine, it a Bumper must be,
If we ne'er drink a Bumper again;———
A goblet of Burgundy, fill, fill, for me, &c.

Henry was kind and was concerned about Edwin's problems. He explained to him that their mother was always ready to lend money when it was necessary, stressing that '*she had a very slight idea of what was necessary*'. He advises Edwin to go to the Philosophical Lectures in Leeds which he says are fun, though Henry's idea of fun was more rakish. He also made sure that Edwin had enough quills for writing and sent freshly plucked ones from the Gateford geese. London alone used 20 million goose quills a year at that time and so fierce was the demand that many were pulled from living birds, an agonising and sometimes fatal process. Travellers occasionally found denuded geese lying at the side of the road where quill robbers had left them shocked to death. It was said that the best feathers were plucked from live birds or from dead ones still warm.

Henry is profoundly depressed and writes to sister Ann of his fear of never enjoying good health. 'I can assure you that my enjoyments in life were never less than at present. Time I never valued less; for no sooner has the day dawned than I am almost ready to wish its total annihilation.' His ennui has reached a serious low. But his advice to his younger brother shows signs of paying off and Edwin thanks his mother profusely for the five guineas, although this is not nearly enough to cover his costs for the next two years which Mr Payne had advised might be as much as £14. His mother is cautious because Edwin is on trial because of his health and she insensitively tells him that she thought he might not live beyond the age of twenty-one.

Edwin assures her that he is much better apart from some headaches which he blames on his lodgings. He is reluctantly living with the Tathams at his old school which is cheap but he longs for a room of his own. The Tathams are feeling the pinch and, as there is no fuel for a fire in his room, Edwin tells his mother that he has heard of a Quaker family who live further out in the country away from the smoke and filth of Leeds, and who are willing to take in lodgers.

Further costs for his mending, washing, tailor and shoemaker are mentioned in the letters. He needs a suit of clothes and asks for more money for books, explaining that Mr Payne wants him to start his clerkship as soon as possible otherwise he is wasting time. He huffily writes to his mother: 'I am not particularly uncomfortable, but you are not ignorant that to acquire a sound knowledge of the law requires the Lucubrations [57] for 20 years for a

57   To study by candlelight.

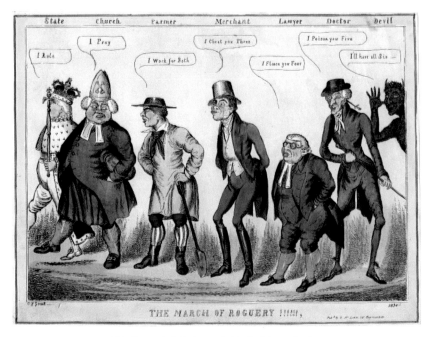

Edwin needed clothes suitable for his profession.
The March of the Roguery by C. J. Grant

judge, but even a common solicitor … must undergo a great deal of arduous study.'

There is more indignation and he returns an embarrassing suit of old clothes:

> they are more worn and shabby than any you could find of my fellow Articled Clerks here … I am in the Articled Clerks Society and as they are almost all the Sons of Wealthy Gentlemen, Doctors, Surgeons and Attorneys, it is quite necessary to attend to appearances – or I should be taken very little notice of. I have not room to speak of its advantages but if you don't think it right for me to remain a member you must speak.

The summer is boiling hot. Edwin now needs some nankeen trousers.[58] Optimistic about his health and to encourage his mother, he says that they should

58 Buff coloured cotton cloth first made in Nanking, China.

Edwin at 20 was only 5 foot 4½ inches tall

last two or three summers as he thinks he has stopped growing (he is seventeen). Four years later we know from his lists of family measurements that he was only 5 feet 4½ inches tall.

Edwin has some embarrassing health questions and begs his mother not to show his letters to anyone and tells her his large bills for shoes are justified on health grounds. Dr John Arthington Payne (the brother of his boss), an expert in neuralgia, has told Edwin to take a daily walk on Woodhouse Moor, but on hearing the distance he walks daily to the office, decides it is not such a good idea after all. The doctor questions him thoroughly about the pain and like all the other doctors stresses the importance of keeping his bowels open.

Edwin now writes too graphically about his spots wanting his mother's advice. 'They contain a sort of serum and sometimes if irritated they produce pus and are very pungent'. He also wants to know about 'opening medicines she thought the most tolerable.'

Leeds in 1858

She might have found some recipes for purges in John Wesley's *Primitive Physick, or an Easy and Natural Method of Curing Most Diseases*[59] published in 1774. Wesley, like many of the clergy at the time had a direct and practical interest in the health of his parishioners and alongside his message of salvation advocated a frugal diet, regular exercise, early rising and personal hygiene, coining the adage 'Cleanliness is next to Godliness'. Like William Buchan, some of his remedies were dangerous but others simply worked because people believed they would. As Buchan put it: 'How the mind affects the body, will in all probability ever remain a secret'.[60]

Edwin's next testy letter to his mother is again about money problems but he starts gently, saying he is sorry that she is having trouble with the servants, suggesting that she pays them more as Mrs Tatham gives £8 a year to her lowest maid. Defending his request for 'Nankeen Trowsers' (which are disapproved of by everyone at Gateford) Edwin sniffily writes that he did not expect his mother to ask people for their opinion. Brother William has suggested that 'drab single milled Kerseymere'[61] would be smarter; Edwin sends back

59 The copy from Joseph Tatham's library, dated 1775 in S.W.'s archive.
60 *Buchan's Family Physician*, published 1769.
61 Twilled cloth of very fine cashmere wool.

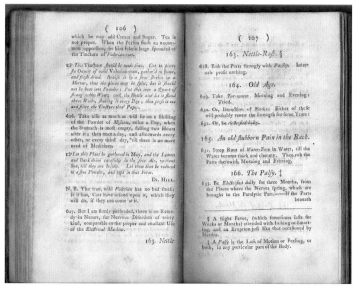

Pages from Joseph Tatham's copy of John Wesley's Primitive Physick *1775*

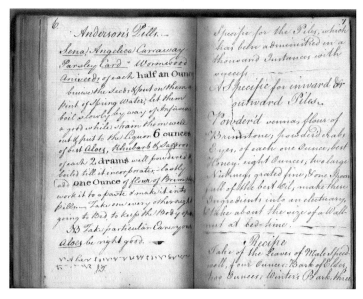

Joseph Tatham added useful recipes at the back of Primitive Physick

some white stockings which are too short and includes more bills. Still in pain, he describes his day as an articled clerk:

I do tolerably well for from 9 o'clock in the morning to 8 in the evening I am only absent from the office about 2 hours and nearly one is spent in walking backwards and forwards as I walk above ½ mile 6 times over. It is a very disagreeable part of the town now, for we are surrounded by factory chimnies and in the midst of smoke. It is in winter very dirty and in summer a very dusty road. I suffer more than I like from the pain in my side.

Leeds is becoming horrible. Among the visitors with memories of pre-industrial times were Mrs. Siddons and Mrs. Jordan, two actresses not afraid to speak their minds. Mrs. Siddons describes Leeds as 'the most disagreeable town in His Majesty's dominions God bless him' and Mrs. Jordan found that sleep was impossible: the beds being 'so bad and so dirty'.[62] A German princeling, Hermann von Puckler visiting Leeds for the first time, notes that 'in twilight a transparent cloud of smoke was diffused over the whole space which it occupied, on and between several hills; a hundred red fires shot upwards into the sky and as many towering chimneys poured forth columns of black smoke'.[63]

Perhaps this is why the Tatham's school had dwindled to seven pupils. Even so, Edwin urges his mother to send Ben, his bright farming-mad thirteen year-old brother to the school. Ben eventually goes there but it is not a success as Mr Tatham, the only teacher, was often absent and the boys had too many holidays. Ben precociously remarks that he would prefer to do more work and begs to be sent to a better school.

The two guardian uncles put pressure on Edwin to come home more often, which is hard as he is far from well. Begging Henry not to tell their mother, he says sadly that he thinks he will never get better. But now it is Edwin's turn to worry about Henry, who has given up his apprenticeship and has drifted back to Gateford. Young Edwin suggests to his mother that his elder brother should rise earlier, study six hours a day and go round the sheep before breakfast and after tea and then go to bed at 9pm.

62   Mrs A. Kennard, *Mrs Siddons*, 1887
63   Hermann von Puckler-Muskau, *Touring England, Ireland and France in 1826, 1827, 1828*, published 1833

In November 1823 Edwin visits his father's seventy year-old cousin George Eddison, a corn merchant living at Holbeck Lodge, Leeds which was also known as Steam Hall, as it was the first house in the world with central heating generated by steam, having been built in 1802 by Matthew Murray[64].

Edwin's interest in family history was sparked off by the elderly George Eddison on this visit. He told Edwin many stories about the family and that his great-grandfather, another George Eddison, born in about 1679, had died at Gateford House and that he had a brother Thomas[65] who does not appear on the later family trees.

'I shall want more money to discharge my tailors and shoemakers bills' Edwin now writes to his mother. It was hard on shoe leather trudging six miles a day. He also needs six new shirts, two black silk handkerchiefs, four nightcaps, four nightshirts and some white neck cloths, as black silk had become unfashionable. Alas the white ones went brown quickly in 'this dirty smoky place.' The depths of the collars he insisted, were to be exactly four and a quarter inches, the neck size, fifteen and a half inches. 'I wish them to be of good quality because I think nothing is lost by that and it prevents people from suspecting me of avarice … as I am not one of those who live to dress but I would dress to keep my life – I also want some more white worsted stockings.' He ends crossly: 'I must remind you that in packing my box you enclosed some tarts for Benjamin without wrapping them up in paper and the syrup smeared some of my books, and I mean this as a hint that I do not wish you to do so again.'

Money was frequently mentioned in the letters and the two uncles were not always in agreement about how much of the eight children's inheritance should be advanced to them. Edwin was a stout defender of what was correct and his legal knowledge was useful. In a letter to his mother in October 1824 he presumes that she has been informed that there is some argument about their father's will as to whether each of the children can be allowed more than

---

64   Matthew Murray 1765–1826, pioneer engineer, steam engine and machine
      tool manufacturer, who designed the first commercially viable steam
      locomotive, the twin cylinder Salamanca in 1812.

65   This information led me to the side-alley of research into the idea
      that Thomas was the great-grandfather of the American inventor
      Thomas Alva Edison.

£500 before Ben's coming of age in 1832. Edwin has had much advice about this from his boss Mr Payne.

There were serious money worries in December 1825 when a banking crisis hit the country. Edwin's letters give a taste of the panic, describing crowds flocking into Leeds, coaches racing up, and from London loaded with gold and Bank of England notes telling of exhausted cashiers working long hours, doling out money and reviving themselves with little swigs of wine. He urges her…

> … to send £10 in Bank of Englands if you can. You will have heard of the stopping payment by the Wakefield Bank, Wentworth Chalford and Rishworths. In consequence of this Bank having stopped, four Post Chaises each with 4 horses were sent express from London and arrived here on Friday night with Gold and Bank of England paper, and the bank William Brown and Co, our bankers, received 15000 £ in Gold. All the five banks received large supplies of gold and Bank of England paper … the town is filled with Country people as though it were a Market day. Even Beckitt Blaydon and Co's notes were refused on Saturday night though I imagine they are worth at least two millions … It is expected here that all the banks in England will be run upon … to give you an idea of the money that has paid here in gold and Bank of England papers, two Masters and court of clerks were engaged at the Union Bank from 9 o'clock on Saturday morning till 6 at night paying out … without taking anything but wine.. and they were all in a complete sweat … The respectable tradesmen are now sticking papers in their windows to say they will take any of the Leeds notes.

Edwin becomes ill again and needs a break. A letter in wobbly inebriated handwriting arrives from Henry giving brotherly advice and the name of a fashionable boarding house, warning that he must dress for dinner and always drink wine rather than beer. A ball is held there once a week which he says would do Edwin good but he advises against any expensive female pleasure parties in Whitby or Filey. Henry writes: 'Mother desires you to stay as long as you can be spared and she will bear a Handsome part of the expenses. I should not think of staying but less than a fortnight were I in your place.'

It is not clear if the advice was taken. Edwin was wary of Henry's choice of smart places and the perils of drink and he was increasingly worried that his elder brother was drifting through life. In years ahead Henry wanted to broaden his horizons by joining others on trips abroad, but for some reason these trips never materialized. Perhaps he had ambitions to go as far as Australia.

A travel-battered red diary dated 24 July 1830 was at the bottom of the Bedale trunk. It had a bottle stain on its leather cover and tucked inside I found Henry Eddison's black edged funeral card. The owner of the journal had scribbled his initials in indelible pencil on the first page, but only the letter 'W' could be made out – the next letter, covered with a watery stain, might just have been an 'R' or a 'P'. Inside was a gripping account of a sea voyage on the merchant ship *Resource* which left England for Australia on 4 July 1830.[66] The writer appeared to have travelled with a carefree spirit with his gun and dogs on board but from time to time he was irritated by crowds of passengers, over-eager females, maids falling pregnant and flocks of albatrosses overhead. There was a drama when the '*beast of a captain*' who was ill for most of the voyage, stabbed the boatswain twice. In spite of being severely wounded the boatswain went to a ball on a Man of War and then nearly died but recovered to survive the six month voyage. The diary had descriptions of a landing in Rio and the voyage ends in Van Diemens Land, now Tasmania, and from there the writer travels on to New South Wales. The diary ends abruptly in April 1831. It was impossible to make out who this person was, why the diary was in the Eddison trunk and why Henry's funeral card been put in the diary when he died many years later.

Only surnames were listed for passengers on the *Resource* but reading that the writer had bought land at Duns Plains, New South Wales, I wrote to Helen Jeuken the archivist at the Bathurst District Historical Society whose initial response was unhelpful saying that the initials W P and W R were not enough to go on and that she needed more information. So I wrote again copying out the last days of the journal which described the roads, the scenery and his companions when the writer first inspected his estate. The last entries told of an evening he spent with some 'desperate jolly fellows' after receiving an invitation to a ball and supper at Government House.

These extracts revived the archivist's interest as by chance she had come across a magazine article written in 1940 describing a terrible story. She enclosed the article which tells of the travels of a retired sea captain, William

---

66   From the *Norwich Mercury* 27 February 1830: 'Fine Teak ship, 500 tons, first rate passenger vessel, superior accommodation, and carries an experienced surgeon. Henry Shuttleworth, Commodore.'

Australian bush rangers c. 1830

Van Diemen's Land (Tasmania)

Payne[67], a rich man who had bought land at Dunn's Plains in early 1831 and had declared himself blissfully happy with the beautiful new property. One evening just as the sun was going down, four months after the deeds were signed, he went out wild fowling and did not return. The next morning his

---

67 His father William Payne Esq of Frickley Hall was described by Arthur Young, the agricultural writer as 'a gentleman well known for his skill in agriculture.' Frickley Hall later came into the possession of William Aldam.

body was found by his servant. He had been brutally murdered by a gang of marauding bush rangers with blackened faces.

This was indeed shocking. I had spent many days deciphering the pencilled account with the help of my brother, wondering why the journal had been kept. Searching the family tree I discovered that the murdered man was the brother of Richard Ecroyd Payne, Edwin's boss. On his retirement from sea-faring life, William Payne, finding farming unprofitable and wanting to in-crease his capital, had bought a considerable amount of land in Australia.

The archivist sent maps of his 3,280 acre estate with a sizeable house and a beautiful garden. William Payne was a bachelor and it is not known who inherited the property after his murder. His obituary in the Sydney Monitor states:

> Mr Payne who arrived in this Colony at the commencement of the present year, was bred an English gentleman farmer, practically and theoretical; the library at Frickley being stored with all the standard works on Agriculture, and the periodicals of the day. It was Mr Payne's intention to shew an example of English farming in many points not practised here, if it were possible, as he said, to avoid falling into that state of apathy and carelessness, which struck him with surprise as pertaining to the settlers generally. A few years ago he travelled through France and Switzerland, from which he obtained much valuable information. His loss to the Colony is therefore to be deplored, especially on account of the manner of it, as it may tend to prevent Emigrants of the same useful and superior class, from adventuring to New South Wales.

There was a long account of the bush rangers' trial in the Sydney Herald on 28 November 1831 which described the men coming to rob the house after the murder. A kitchen boy asked them how his master had behaved and was told by one of them that 'the b... is in hell now, he had a beard like a ghost and we have made a ghost of him.' The boy explained to the court that his master had never shaved from the time he left Sydney and he was then able to identify William Payne's clothes; a striped shirt, a black waistcoat, a green shooting coat and a green forage cap. The three members of the gang were found guilty and were hanged; their bodies cut down and delivered to the surgeons for dissection.

Two months after Payne's murder there was a Quaker exodus from England to New South Wales. James Backhouse the botanist [68] (a fellow pupil with the Payne brothers at Tatham's school) set off with George Washington Walker for a six year journey to research the condition of the penal settlements and the welfare of Aborigines and the free settlers. Ironically they were too late to visit their unfortunate school-fellow William Payne. Could the unsettled Henry Eddison have been planning to join them?

The Quaker James Backhouse researched the condition of the penal settlements and the welfare of the Aborigines.

Twenty year-old Edwin has now been learning the law for four years with Richard Ecroyd Payne and it had been suggested that he was about to be made a partner. To safeguard himself, Edwin considers moving elsewhere and does some research into the different population returns in neighbouring towns. He decides that he wouldn't accept a partnership of less than a third with annual profits of £1200 a year, this would give him £400 per year.

Needing more money he asks the uncles to advance him £750 as he knows that his forthcoming year in London for further studies will be expensive. However Mr Payne does not want to lose him and agrees to a partnership with no premium where Edwin would have a quarter of the profits and after seven years, half the profits. He expects the profits to be around £1500, bringing his income to a handsome £750 a year in seven years' time.

68   James Backhouse 1794–1869, Quaker missionary, traveller and botanist, studied flora in Australia 1832–1838 and developed one of the best known plant nurseries in England. He was a nephew of Jonathan Backhouse who, along with Edward Pease and Francis Mewburn, built the world's first passenger railway in 1825.

At the end of January there is a sombre letter to his mother. Edwin is not very well. The surgeon now calls the disease a Masked Fever: a fever that did not show itself but lay lurking in the system. Edwin tries to give a better description of how he feels, saying that he had fainted and vomited in the office, then had taken some warm water, chamomile tea and gruel and walked to his lodgings half a mile away where he had more broth and went to bed in acute pain which had kept him awake for three nights. He is now desperate for a cure.

Edwin has great confidence in Mr Thackrah of Leeds who had gained the prize for his treatise on the blood, offered by the great Sir Astley Cooper (whose grisly lectures in London were to cause Edwin to sink to his knees a few years later). Mr Thackrah purged him then made him sweat profusely and expected him to become delirious. He felt surprisingly better in the morning.

But more clothes are needed and he asks his parsimonious mother for four pairs of white worsted socks as soon as she can find time to knit them. (No wonder her portrait [69] shows her with a ball of wool and knitting at hand). Edwin also needs twelve more shirts before he goes to London. Ann Eddison would have baulked at the expense and her heart sinks when he says: 'I only write to tell you what I dare say you don't want to know. That I want some more money to pay my half year's bills. I think £5 will do. I have written to Uncle about my money concerns as I shall be of age in ten days time.'

Elder brother Henry goes back to Sheffield in a melancholy mood. He writes about the misery of mingling with individuals with whom he has absolutely nothing in common and longs to be with his circle of dear friends at Gateford. He wishes the dull reality of his life would dissolve and he could indulge in the '*fairy candles of imagination*' [alcoholic hazes?].

A few months later brother Booth Eddison is furious about their mother's tight purse strings and writes to Edwin:

I think I may very well compare Mother and her Purse to a well built, firm and durable Pump and Well, in days full of good and lasting waters, pipes strong … and permanent, … though the handle is heavy and always requires lifting. Now this pump I must also say has a very commendable quality that though the handle is heavy you may always if you will be at the trouble of lifting it, and pump as much as will do you good.

69   This portrait is with S.W.

Edwin, soon to be free from these problems, sits down at his desk and scribbles lists of clothes that he will need for an exciting time ahead. He is to go to London to complete his studies.

10

A Year in London

*I felt a completion of happiness … I just sat and hugged myself in my own
mind. Here I am in London…*

James Boswell's Journal, 10 April 1772

A frozen twenty-one year-old Edwin steps down from the coach at the Peacock Inn, Islington in December 1826, blows on his fingers and looks around
for a Hackney to take him to his lodgings at 6 Gower Place, near Euston
Square. The first stage of his journey from Worksop to Leicester had been tedious enough but the last stage from Leicester to London had taken a numb-
ing thirteen hours.

A street urchin holding his nose against the stinking Thames (Punch, 18 June 1859)

Having served five years clerkship in Leeds, Edwin is soon to sign the contract for a partnership with Mr Payne but, before this, he has to spend a year on further studies in London with the legal firm of John Morris. It is his first visit to London and he is bursting with excitement

London at that time was a disgusting place. The streets were caked with excrement, buckets of ordure were thrown out of windows and the sewage system caused vile stenches to blast through the town. Filth piled up in court-yards and nearly every house had a cesspit below causing nauseating smells to waft through even the best of houses, which was why drawing-rooms were often on an upper floor. Cesspits overflowed into open sewer trenches along the streets before flowing into the Thames but the air was often worse indoors when the windows of many houses were sealed at sunset for fear of the night air laden with coal smoke and sulphurous fogs. It was said that entire families were asphyxiated during the nights.

Edwin was lucky not to arrive in the summer when the stench was at its worse. Behind Kings Cross Station, a short distance from his lodgings, a mountain of the city's waste was stinking of boiling bones and rotting rubbish. Unsurprisingly, there was a major cholera epidemic four years after Edwin arrived. Matters did not improve for decades and when he came back to London several years later to meet the young Queen Victoria he was again sickened by the same foetid atmosphere.

This deplorable situation was allowed to continue until the 'Great Stink' of 1858, when the smell of the Thames became so unbearable that the House of Commons hung up curtains soaked in chloride of lime and Members even considered relocating upstream to Hampton Court. At this point a new sewer network for London, one of the century's great engineering projects, was sanctioned.

It is interesting to see 'pattens' on Edwin's shopping list before going to London. These were wooden soles mounted on iron rings to lift his shoes above the squelching filth. Fortunately his lodgings in Gower Street, (costing five shillings a week), were close to his office, which was not far from the site of the newly founded secular University College London – often called the 'Godless Institution of Gower Street'.

This was not a healthy place for Edwin with the constant fear of epidemics of cholera, typhoid, diphtheria and smallpox. Coal fires which heated homes for much of the year caused nagging headaches, clothes were seldom washed, the underclothes of the poor were worn till they rotted and baths were rare for most people.

From details in the biographies of Disraeli and Gladstone (roughly the same age as Edwin) it is interesting to see that both men of enormous vitality had many health problems. Disraeli battled with exhaustion, asthma, a throat condition, bleeding gums, Bright's disease, bronchial asthma, bronchitis, catarrh, depression, gout, indigestion, influenza, nephritis, tinnitus and uraemia and a dose of venereal disease. The tougher Gladstone was addicted to long walks and tree felling but his medical details included erysipelas, strain and exhaustion, bronchitis, gastric attacks (to the exasperation of fellow diners he chewed each mouthful of food thirty-two times), lumbago, gumboil, pneumonia, insomnia, tonsillitis, laryngeal catarrh, influenza, cataract and finally cancer of the cheek which killed him.

At first Edwin was pretty healthy. His excitement is palpable in his long letters home and within ten days of his arrival he is visiting his London relations and dining with his cousin, the medical student Wilson Overend [70] who was much the same age. Wilson was to have successful medical career and his portrait by G. F. Watts now hangs in the Cutler's Hall in Sheffield. Wilson's uncle, John Overend, born in 1769, was the original partner in the vast Overend and Gurney Bank which crashed in 1866. Edwin may have been attracted to Hannah Overend because he took her to see the Chancellor and twelve Judges of England, a sight he knew few ladies had seen.

Wilson Overend, surgeon to Sheffield Infirmary. Painting by G. F. Watts, Cutlers Hall, Sheffield

One evening after dinner, Wilson Overend and Edwin went to a lecture by the great Sir Astley Cooper, celebrated for his work on hernias, ligaments and neuralgia of the testicles. Wilson was used to the foetid atmosphere of the theatre but Edwin fainted after three quarters of an hour. He writes airily that this was not unusual and that he recovered after ten minutes and stood manfully for the rest of the evening.

---

70   Wilson's father, Hall Overend, a well known physician, had founded the first medical school in Sheffield.

As a teacher of surgery Sir Astley was considered the best. A pupil of the famous John Hunter, he was made a baronet for removing a sebaceous cyst from the scalp of King George IV and was surgeon to both William IV and Queen Victoria. He was known for saying; 'If you are too fond of new remedies, first you will not cure your patients, secondly, you will have no patients to cure'. One of his pupils was the poet John Keats who worked hard on the corpses procured by the body snatchers and was far from squeamish. He may have been inspired on the dissecting benches for his poem about Isabella, who dug up her murdered lover's head in the forest and kept it planted in a pot of basil. Keats once caused a man's death, having been lost in thought after opening his temporal artery. He was so appalled by this mistake that he decided to abandon medicine and to devote himself to poetry.

It is astonishing that so many survived the operations at that time as hospitals were awash with dirt, infection and stench. Surgeons cut and sawed away in germ-soaked coats and top hats; theatres were packed with unwashed students and scenes of pandemonium were aggravated by the screams of patients strapped down on operating tables. Surgeons needed to work flat out as fifteen minutes was the maximum time that patients could survive the pain and shock to their nervous system.

Many surgeons had limited knowledge of anatomy and Keats had the job of dresser to one of the worst: a William Lucas, known as Butcher Lucas, who carved his way through vital organs, leaving his assistants to sew up the wounds.

Keats admired Sir Astley for his sweetness of manner, his courtesy to patients and the way he insisted that his students spent as much time as they could in dissection; although this involved the surgeon in the illicit trade of body-snatching, with charges scaled to the state of the corpses. Stealing clothed bodies was a felony carrying the death sentence: to snatch a naked corpse was a mere misdemeanour. The only bodies legally available for research were those of executed criminals, whose sentence included anatomizing (the fate of the Australian murderers of Edwin's relation, William Payne). The same fate awaited the deranged Liverpool broker who assassinated the Prime Minister Spencer Perceval in the lobby of the House of Commons in 1812.

Edwin made the most of his time in London, calling on John Moon who had married his cousin Ann Aldam. They invited him to dine and he expected an unpleasant visit but was mistaken. The Moons lived in tradesman-like style in a small house in Millbank about a mile from their shop in St Martin's Lane.

The surgeon Sir Astley Cooper who was known for saying; 'if you are too fond of new remedies, first you will not cure your patients, secondly, you will have no patients to cure'

John Keats worked hard on the corpses

Charles Lamb was instantly cured of 'Quakerism' after seeing a man 'under all agitations'

The house was awash with noisy babies, one of whom, George Washington Moon, was to become a well known poet and writer.

He also visited Booth relations on his mother's side, including a Mrs Robinson at 44 Piccadilly and took 'pot-luck' with Mr and Mrs Wayland [71] where he met Nancy Booth who lived in Mansel Street with her niece, Lettice Wayland. He visited the Stephensons [72] too, who lived in Bow Lane in Clapham. George Stephenson was a successful silk merchant whose eldest son, Leader Stephenson, owned a large silk mill in Taunton. Edwin describes a cosy evening with them starting with tea at 7pm, then their daughter, Jane plays the piano, her brother, Joseph the flute and other sisters sing. Edwin describes their house as:

> *furnished in what I suppose would be considered a good plain London Merchants style, and I expected to see them live much more expensively than they appear to do from their carriage, servants etc. We had gravy soup, a plain joint of Boiled Beef, an apple pudding and cheese to dinner with a glass of Champagne to it, but I don't suppose they regularly drink Champagne for dinner. We had steel forks.'*

The Stephensons' Champagne does not sound particularly appetising with the gravy soup and boiled beef. The normal drink at dinner was small-beer or sparkling ale which, being alcoholic, was much safer than well water. An alternative was fortified marsala which was first exported from Sicily by John Woodhouse in 1773: the trade being carried on by the Yorkshireman, Benjamin Ingham who with his nephew, Joseph Whitaker made a fortune in the nineteenth century.

Georgian breakfasts usually consisted of tea, weak coffee, bread rolls, meats, eggs, and possibly plumb (sic) cake if you were still hungry. This kept people going through the long day until the main meal, dinner at 2pm, later to be moved to 4pm.

Ordinary dinners had two courses: the first, soup served in tureens, one set at either end of the table and removed when people began the main course. This might include roast joints, boiled rabbit smothered with onions, French beans, pease and apple puddings, leg of lamb, whole fishes, meat pies and veg-

---

71   Rev Abraham Booth's daughter Mary married Daniel Wayland.
72   Alice Booth, b. 1764, the daughter of Rev. Abraham Booth, had married George Stephenson.

etables. These might appear together on the table and people chose what they wanted. Louis Simond, an American touring England in 1811 complained that the vegetables, thought to be the best in the world, appeared without sauce and were frequently cold. The main fish on the table would probably have been surprisingly inexpensive salmon and oysters or eel.

Alongside the meat and fish were savoury dishes made with sweetbreads, tongue, little mushrooms and small meat patties. To sink the faint-hearted, ornamental jellies, floating islands, blancmanges, and other wobbly dishes were also spread around.

An inelegant ritual of mouth cleaning sometimes took place at the end of a meal with the help of glasses of coloured water placed before each diner as Louis Simond described with disgust:

All (women as well as men) stoop over it, sucking up some of the water, and returning it, perhaps more than once, and with a spitting and washing sort of noise, quite charming – the operation frequently assisted by a finger elegantly thrust into the mouth! This done, and the hands dipped also, the napkins, and sometimes the table-cloth, are used to wipe hand and mouth.

More discreet individuals would clean their teeth in private. Brushes and tooth powder were expensive. Wordsworth used stripped and frayed dogwood twigs and others used sage leaves and parsley.

After the victory at Waterloo, travel to the Continent became easier and hostesses began to copy the French custom of serving dinner *a la russe* with food served directly to the diners whilst it was hot, but more staff were needed.

Queen Victoria's preference for eating late in the evening annoyed fashion-able people but nevertheless this caused dinner to be converted to an evening meal from 1840 onwards. Luncheon, or nuncheon (from *noneschenche* noon drink) was a new idea which provided snacks for bored ladies to break up long mornings with a biscuit, a piece of cheese and a glass of sherry. But for most people dinner in the late afternoon was the first meal since breakfast.

Gout was caused by too much indulgence. George III's strategy to avoid overeating was to select one dish and stick to just that. There were many diet fads and one of the nastiest was Byron's, which was potatoes boiled in vinegar. But serious overeating caused obesity and tourists were eager to see the leg-endarily fat British waddling about the streets. Louis Simond wanted to see *Jacques Roast-Beef*, the well known caricature of the rotund Briton.

In 1827 Edwin was enjoying life in London. With so much to see he had never been happier than when exploring the city and, like Charles Lamb, he loved covering great distances in London by night and by day. Lamb's describes his enjoyment in a letter to Wordsworth in 1817:

> The lighted shops of the Strand and Fleet Street, the innumerable trades, tradesmen, and customers, coaches, waggons, playhouses; all the bustle and wickedness round about Covent Garden; the very women of the Town; the watchmen, drunken scenes, rattles; life awake, if you awake, at all hours of the night; the impossibility of being dull in Fleet Street; the crowds, the very dirt and mud, the sun shining upon houses and pavements, the print-shops, the old book-stalls, parsons cheapening books, coffee-houses, steams of soups from kitchens, the pantomimes - London itself a pantomime and a masquerade – all these things work themselves into my mind, and feed me, without a power of satiating me. The wonder of these sights impels me into night-walks about her crowded streets, and I often shed tears in the motley Strand from fullness of joy at so much life.[73]

Lamb, impressed by William Penn's books and entranced by early Quakers, wondered whether he should become a Friend, but after attending a meeting and seeing a man 'under all agitations and workings of a fanatic who believed himself under the influence of some inevitable presence' was instantly cured of Quakerism. As he wrote in his *Essay of Elia A Quaker Meeting*: '… it was some years ago, I witnessed a sample of the Foxian orgasm. It was a man of giant stature … I saw him shake all over with the spirit – he seemed not to speak but to be spoken from.'[74]

Edwin often walked through Covent Garden where there were gambling dens, brothels, a large number of Turkish baths and traders in every kind of commodity with stalls selling anything from crockery to live hedgehogs which were sold as pets to eat the armies of beetles from householders' damp basements. He was keen to visit more of his relations and, wearing his pattens stepped through the filthy streets, sometimes in danger from robbers as this was before Sir Robert Peel started the Metropolitan Police. The choking fog

73 Penelope Hughes-Hallett, *The Immortal Dinner*, Viking 2000.
74 Charles Lamb, *The Complete Works and Letters of Charles Lamb*, Modern Library, 1935

'The London Particular', turned morning into night for days on end, making London so dark that the shops had to be lit up; and in the streets vehicles constantly bumped into each other and horses had to be led by men carrying torches. However, none of this seems to have deterred Edwin's excursions to the various Law Courts and joining the crowds to see the Lord Mayor's Show. He visited The British Museum, The London Institution, Westminster Abbey and watched George IV going to Parliament. There were visits to Covent Garden, the Haymarket Theatre, the English Opera House and in the Spring he invited Henry and his sisters to come and stay. In a letter home Edwin admits to being greedy and asks to be sent ham, honey and a bottle of the Gateford orange wine if his mother can be trusted to pack them properly.

In January 1827 Edwin is admitted as an Attorney of the Court of Kings Bench and is just about to be admitted as a Solicitor in Chancery when Henry comes to stay laden with parcels. Their mother has sent a box of food ahead which has been delayed by ten days and arrives broken with one of the pheasants spread-eagled under the ham. A Miss Vessey has sent a pork pie, Miss Downing some mince pies and Uncle Benjamin Eddison, three hares. Edwin, with some irritation, tells his mother how much each parcel had cost him: 4s 5d, 4s 3d and 7s 8d, but admits that the honey and jams were excellent.

Henry of course enjoys London far too much but Edwin loves having him to stay. Slipping into the Nottinghamshire vernacular he writes to sister Elizabeth and his mother: 'we have got the malt and hops, brewed some beer and drank thereof and we think it very good, and we should like it no worse at all if we had had a small "pace of the chase" that come from the dairy at Gateford.'

With little spare money to eat out, he relies on cold meats and meat pies in his rooms and his landlady brings bowls of hot potatoes from the kitchen. Henry, the food connoisseur, notes with pride that the Gateford mutton is held in high respect.

Much more keen on his appearance than the economical Edwin, Henry writes that he has just bought some lambswool stockings which are marked and drawn at the heels. He scorns his mother's laboriously knitted worsted ones. The portrait of Henry painted around this time shows the influence of Beau Brummell – his hair is brushed fashionably forward and he looks handsome in his high collar and tailored jacket with slightly padded shoulders.

The sisters, Ann and Mary were thrilled to visit Edwin in London that year. Their guide book to the Tower of London was carefully stored among the papers in the Bedale trunk. Hand-stitched and with a blue sugar-paper cover, it

The Eddison sisters' guide book to the Tower of London

gives the admission fee as two shillings, the warder's fee one shilling and entrance to the Crown Jewels Room another two shillings. It describes the Menagerie Royal, a private zoo belonging to English monarchs from King John to King William IV which was opened to the public in the 18th century. From the early 13th century it occupied quarters beside the Tower's western entrance with some 300 animals in cages and dens high above the river. The first elephant seen in England, given to Henry III in 1255 by Louis IX of France, was housed in a wooden shed. Unfortunately it was fed prime cuts of beef and good red wine which killed it. A lioness called Elizabeth fell ill and died in 1603. That year on 24 March her royal namesake followed and later the same century the death of another beast presaged the death of Charles II. In the eighteenth century Smollett recorded that a lion roaring at a female visitor was proof that she was no longer a virgin. Perhaps the two Eddison sisters were jumpy walking past the cage.

In the Crown Jewels Room the treasures were protected from the public by large squares of plate glass illuminated by the light of six gas lamps with the power of forty-eight candles. Ann and Mary as Quakers would have only been slightly impressed by the New Imperial Crown revolving under a bell of plate glass. Under the reign of the unpopular George IV the monarchy had become an irrelevance so the stern reminder at the end of the guidebook that the King's powers are limited is particularly interesting.

Edwin has another try at getting money out of his mother for his brother Booth who has a passion for natural history. He needs two ounces of broken-eyed needles (costing sixpence) to stick through insects, along with an expensive book, *Stokes Botanical Maleria Medica*. Edwin chides his mother for not putting the expected ten shillings in her last letter.

Then on a more friendly note Edwin writes that he has sent her three pomegranates, a pint of Brazil nuts and a coconut and adds:

> *I have sent you a ½lb canister of Fry's chocolate Powder which I like very well and find it also very cheap. A canister cost me 2s and will serve me to breakfast for a month. I merely put a teaspoonful into the coffee pot and pour boiling water upon it and it makes 3 or 4 teacups quite as strong as I like it. Though chocolate drinkers would think it very poor stuff I suppose.*

Some say the Quaker Frys had introduced this cheap beverage hoping it would stop the poor drinking alcohol. Joseph Fry of Bristol (1730–1789), a third generation Quaker, was an apothecary who studied diet and encouraged the use of chocolate as a drink; he became involved in its manufacture and then was involved with a soap boiling firm, which was later bought by the Lever Brothers. His son Joseph Storrs Fry took over the business on the death of his father and was the first to introduce factory methods for making chocolate. He was also the first to use a Watts steam engine to grind the beans.

After pacifying his mother with pomegranates and chocolate, Edwin is still rather angry because she has:

> given Henry his London 20 £ because he is so poor. I think I am fully entitled to it on that ground, for I am the poorest child you have, by several hundred pounds. I have no money to spare for what is not absolutely necessary. Indeed I mean to spend half your twenty (if it come) in Law books, for I can do nothing without them. You will believe this when I tell you … that the law library of the late Lord Gifford … sold for nearly a thousand pounds … I intend to spend at least 500 £ in a library.

He ends his letter:

> I have no intention of marrying till I am 26 or 27, … and I shall have a third of the business by that time which may perhaps be 600 £ a year I shall then begin to think about it, if I live, and intend to marry at all.

When his year in London comes to an end Edwin returns to Leeds to become a partner with Mr Payne. During his time away he was being kept abreast with news of the exciting development of the steam railways. The family's Quaker connections were heavily involved with the birth of this epoch-making invention.

11
Founding the Railways

You enterprised a railroad … you blasted its rocks away … and now, every fool in Buxton can be at Bakewell in half-an-hour, and every fool in Bakewell at Buxton.

John Ruskin, *Praeterita*

'Given to E. D. Eddison by Emily Mewburn in 1890' – a scribbled note on the back of my pencil drawing of George Fox, the founder of the Quaker movement, made me wonder who Emily was. The name Mewburn appeared frequently in the letters and research led me to a remarkable point in British history: Emily's father, Francis Mewburn (known as the Railways' Solicitor) was very much involved in the birth of the Stockton and Darlington railway. Emily had given the pencil drawing to her friend, Libby Eddison who was Edwin's niece.

The world's first steam railway journey took place in 1804 when Richard Trevithick's and Andrew Vivian's unnamed locomotive hauled a train from the Pen-y-darren ironworks to Abercynon in South Wales. Trevithick then visited the Newcastle area later that year as several colliery owners were interested in his invention.

In the summer of 1818, Darlington and Stockton, both towns in the Tees valley, became involved in a race. The mayor of Stockton had undertaken to ask Parliament for the necessary powers to build a canal that linked the River Gauntless at Evenwood with the River Tees at Stockton. Stockton's canal did not pass anywhere near Darlington and the town was in danger of becoming an industrial backwater if Stockton soaked up all the investment available from London. If Darlington failed to build its own transport system, the town would have to rely on horse carriers.

Two Darlington Quakers, Edward Pease, a former wool merchant with major coal-mining interests in the North East and Jonathan Backhouse, a banker, joined forces with their non-Quaker lawyer, Francis Mewburn to promote the idea of building a railway line running from the collieries around Bishop Auckland to Darlington together with a canal to run from Darlington to Stockton.

Francis Mewburn, known as
'The Railways' Solicitor'

Jonathan Backhouse rushed off to
proposition rich London Quakers

George Stephenson described
himself as 'only the engine-wright
at Killingworth'

The Quaker Edward Pease proposed
a railway between Darlington
and Stockton

Pease proposed a railway all the way between the two towns. This was considered the best option, although local people thought it a ridiculous idea, while the Duke of Cleveland, who later made good profits from the railway, objected, saying that the line would interfere with his fox-coverts.

Time was of the essence. The Stockton canal promoters were already in London lobbying MPs, seeking investment and enjoying the support of local landowners, Lord Stewart and Lord Castlereagh. However the Darlington railway promoters had the advantage of Backhouse's financial connections and were in the stronger position.

Somehow Backhouse had to raise £125,000, the enormous cost of the line. He put in £20,000 himself; the Peases put in £6,000; others put in a further £11,000 and Leonard Raisbeck put in the one Stockton contribution of £1,000. Backhouse then collected the remaining £80,000 from Quaker bankers across the country.

When George III died in 1820 the election delayed the project, so the Bill only began its passage through Parliament in 1821. At the Committee stage, sitting in his hotel room in London, Mewburn nearly had a fit. Reading the Parliamentary small print, he was shocked at a small section that caught his legally trained eye. It appeared that 80% of the capital supporting the scheme had to be raised first before it could progress beyond the Committee stage. Later in his hotel room Mewburn carefully checked the figures and found that they were £7,000 short. With only three days to raise the capital, Backhouse rushed off to proposition rich London Quakers while Mewburn raced round finance houses desperately trying to raise the capital. They failed. But at the very last moment Edward Pease himself produced the necessary £7,000.

It was said that Pease had no hesitation in signing the cheque for this final amount, which further strengthened his, and the Quakers', hold on the Stockton and Darlington railway. Taking charge of the project, which was nicknamed 'The Quaker Line', he was called 'Father of the Railways'. The Bill received the Royal Assent from George IV on 19 April 1821 and the Act of Parliament, sixty-seven pages long, was mostly written by Francis Mewburn. It laid out how the line would be used in minute detail but there was no mention of coal exports, or the use of steam engines: just that the wagons would be hauled by 'men or horses or otherwise'. Nor was there any mention of 'passengers', yet the Stockton and Darlington Railway's great claim to fame was that it was the world's first passenger railway.

At the end of 1821 two strangers from Killingworth called at the house of Edward Pease in Darlington. They were Nicholas Wood and George Stephenson who had heard of the passing of the Stockton and Darlington Act and were eager to be involved. Pease was impressed with Stephenson, finding him honest, sensible and modest. He spoke with a strong Northumbrian dialect and described himself as 'only the engine-wright at Killingworth'. He told Pease that 'a horse on an iron road would draw ten tons for one ton on a common road' and added that the *Blucher* locomotive that he had built at Killingworth was 'worth fifty horses'.

Pease had the foresight to recognise this unknown genius and accepted Stephenson's invitation to visit the Killingworth Colliery. When he saw the *Blucher* at work he realised George Stephenson's claims were correct and promptly offered him the post as the chief engineer of the Stockton & Darlington Company. It was now necessary for Pease to apply for a further Act of Parliament to add a clause giving permission for the Company 'to make and erect locomotives or moveable engines'.

In 1823 Edward Pease joined with Michael Longridge, George Stephenson and his son Robert Stephenson to form a company to make the locomotives and their first, *Locomotion*, was finished in September 1825. Very surprisingly there was great criticism in the press at the idea of passenger travel. The editor of the Tyne Mercury wrote hotly, 'What person, would ever think of *paying any thing* to be conveyed from Hexham to Newcastle in something like a coal-wagon, upon a dreary wagon-way and to be dragged for the greater part of the distance by a *roaring steam-engine*!'

Edward Pease's nineteen year-old son Joseph Pease was given the task of drawing up the prospectus for the new company. He, like his father, had been well educated at Joseph Tatham's Quaker school in Leeds and was in the same year as Edwin's brother William Eddison[75]. Success was to follow Joseph Pease through life: he married Emma Gurney from Norwich and was the first Quaker M.P. For religious reasons he refused to take off his top hat when he entered the House of Commons as can be seen in the 1833 group portrait by Sir George Hayter[76]. His daughter, Elizabeth Lucy Pease married the engineer John Fowler of Leeds who invented the steam plough[77] and who was in

---

75 Through the great network of Quaker intermarriages, the Peases and the Backhouses were both connected to the Eddisons.

76 National Portrait Gallery.

77 Two stationary steam engines, one at each end of the field, which pulled the plough share back and forth.

*George Stephenson driving the world's first passenger train at the opening of
the Stockton – Darlington Railway 27 September 1825*

partnership with Robert William Eddison, Edwin's eldest son. A fine statue of
Joseph Pease was later erected in Darlington.

Edwin and his family may well have been at the grand opening of the
Stockton & Darlington rail road on 27 September 1825 but Edward Pease
missed the celebrations as his son Isaac had died the night before. Large
crowds watched George Stephenson proudly manipulating the controls of *Locomotion* as it chugged forward pulling six wagons filled with sacks of coal and
flour, a covered coach bulging with the directors and proprietors, followed by
twenty-one coal wagons fitted up for passengers and lastly six more wagons
loaded with coals. A man with a flag walked ahead but had to jump out of the
way when Stephenson demonstrated the speed of the engine, accelerating to
fifteen miles an hour. Later Stephenson paid tribute to Pease, saying he was 'a
man that could see a hundred years ahead'.

At the grand opening, Francis Mewburn, the railway solicitor toasted the
success of the enterprise and boldly predicted to those present that soon Darlington people would be able to leave Darlington on any morning to attend
an opera in London in the evening and be home again by breakfast time.

In the Eddison trunk from the Bedale attics there was a much folded scrap
of paper dated 28 August 1839. Someone had written in pencil:

*Mr Stephenson told me that he left school at 8 years old and has been working
ever since. He pulled turnips at 2d per day – porridge and bread and cheese that
2d provided the milk for the family, six children. He was a collier afterwards and
saved a hundred pounds by mending clocks and watches after his work that he gave
to his parents and saved another. He then invented a safety lamp, similar to Sir H.
Davy's, as safe but not equal to his and for that he received 1000 guineas.*

He and his son have expended about 30,000,000 £,[78] in Rail roads etc etc. His son took the prize for mathematics at Edin. College and was sent to Columbia at 20 a chemist – civil engineer and something else for a mining company. He staid there four years.

He thinks the earth was once a ball of fire, surrounded by dense vapour, as the earth cooled, the crust cracked and formed hill and valley, the vapour became water and then the lights shone through the thin air. The light produced by striking iron and flints and is produced by the current of air producing a vacuum when the electricity being the lightest part of the air rushed in and meeting with oxygen or hydrogen, takes fire, the sparks are pieces of iron heated by that fire.

The function of the engines on the rails produces electricity which circulates round the carriages which he thinks is very beneficial to human life.

He has lowered the price of coals at Leicester 50% and will do the same for Oxford, by competition I suppose. He says the Bradford railroad will do.

When the Liverpool–Manchester line (the world's first twin-track passenger railway) was nearing completion in 1829 a competition was held for locomotives; Stephenson's new engine the *Rocket*, which he built with his son, Robert, won with a speed of 36 miles per hour. The grand opening of this line was held on 15 September 1830 when tragically the first death on the railways occurred. The Tory MP, William Huskisson had been invited and as he crossed from his carriage to speak to the Duke of Wellington in another carriage, he failed to hear warning shouts and was knocked down by the *Rocket* which ran over one of his legs. George Stephenson immediately used the *Northumbrian* to take him for treatment, steaming at the unprecedented speed of thirty-six miles and hour but the man died later that day. Lady Wilton, who was in the same carriage as the Duke of Wellington (who haughtily dismissed the new steam railway as a project which would encourage the lower classes to move about needlessly), described the scene to Fanny Kemble, saying that 'the train passed over his leg, squashing and mangling it in the most horrible way'.

As usual, one Quaker success led to another. Quaker engineers went on to develop a device to fix rails to sleepers, Thomas Edmondson invented the railway ticket and the machine which stamped it. Another Quaker, the cartographer George Bradshaw, compiled the 'Bradshaw's Guide', the indispensable

---

78   I have not been able to find out if this remarkable sum is believable.

Inaugural journey, Liverpool–Manchester Railway, 15 September 1830

listings of timetables, fares and connecting stations, which became the essential guide to all rail journeys.

'Railway Time' was the name given to the standardised time arrangement first applied in November 1840 by the Great Western Railway in England, when a number of different local times were synchronised and a single standard time applied which was later to be taken up by all the other railway companies in Great Britain. The original Bradshaw's Guide was before 1840, but the later editions adapted to the new 'Standard Time.'

The historian Sir Llewellyn Woodward wrote that that the railways were the greatest physical achievement of the human race within a comparatively short time. For Victorians the railways widened their horizons. People used to dogged, dangerous journeys now took to train excursions with ease. Holiday resorts opened up and the public in general welcomed the ubiquitous metal tracks that snaked around the countryside; but most of all the railways were the cause of the rapid expansion of industry around the world.

Money poured into the banks.

12

Eddison Bigamy

A potent quack, long versed in human ills,
Who first insults the victim whom he kills.

George Crabbe 1754–1832, *His Mother's Wedding Ring*

The very poor harvest in the summer of 1828 produced a wave of disturbances with machine smashings and turmoil which seemed on the point of ripening into national revolution. However Edwin is preoccupied with other things and is sprouting his lists again. He measures each member of his family against a door frame and then urges them onto the scales to be weighed.

	Weights st. lb	ft. in
William Eddison	10.. 11	5.. 6
Henry	11.. 1	5.. 9¾
Ann	8.. 3	5.. 4
Edwin	9 .. 4	5.. 4 ⅜
Mary	8.. 3	5.. 2⅞
Booth	8 ..10	5.. 4⅜
Elizabeth	6.. 8	5.. 0 ¾
Benjamin	7..10	5.. 2 ¾
My Mother	7.. 5	5.. 1

Twenty-three year-old Edwin, now a partner with the lawyer Richard Ecroyd Payne, is earning good money and grandly sets up house in 10 Albion Street, Leeds as he has a position to keep up and marriage is on his mind. His eye is on a girl he has known for a long time and he needs to impress her with a well furnished house and the inheritance owing to him is now very necessary. Another list was among the papers: eighteen foolscap pages noting all his

First page of Edwin's house inventory 1828

house contents. The total setting-up costs were: £315.9s. (roughly £16,000), the most expensive section being upholstery at £131.16s. (£7,000).

This impressive list is far too detailed to itemise here. He bought many things from a family friend, the Quaker philanthropist, Thomas Firth of Toothill Hall whose father Robert Firth had died a few months earlier. The furniture was mainly mahogany, but some bedroom items: a faux bamboo chest of drawers, a crib 3ft by 6ft and a wash stand were all painted in drab (a dull light brown). There were a number of looking-glasses and plenty of deal furniture for the servants' rooms.

One can imagine the lovely plain Georgian interiors: wooden floors, muslin curtains flapping in the breeze, elegant chairs and delicate china. There was an Imperial Venetian carpet that he bought for the drawing room at £6.6s.6d; wallpaper at 9/6d a piece, and 40 yards of black reeded moulding. From his boss, Mr Payne he bought a set of mahogany dining room chairs and glorious crimson moreen [79] curtains which he then dyed to a duller colour.

The extensive linen list includes several double damask tablecloths and copious napkins, Irish linen sheets, gingham, a fine quilt, brown Holland blind cloth and Witney blankets, double and single. Then he adds a little note: 'N.B. *For a more accurate list of linen see the one made out by my sister Ann in a Book.*'

The ironmongery bought from Thomas Firth included 3 sets of fire irons, a warming pan, brass water cans, telescope metal candlesticks, a tin gravy strainer, many snuffers, a green fender, a japanned slop pail, a foot bath, a treacle can, a tinned wire fireguard, iron saucepans, a brass kettle and stand, sugar nippers, a meat saw, a long Dutch oven, a meat screen, a bath brick [80] and more.

Among the glass, china and earthenware are tart cups and jelly moulds. There is a 180 piece blue and white dinner service with the British Flower design which had been introduced that year by Spode (a bargain for £5 5s), some of which was in the basement cellars at Bedale.

For the kitchen there is an elegant dresser that would have fitted well in the Georgian interiors in books illustrated by Randolph Caldecott [81]; a deal

---

79 Stout corded fabric, woollen or cotton, often watered.

80 Patented in 1823, bath bricks were the predecessor of the scouring pad used for cleaning and polishing. They were made in the town of Bridgwater from the fine alumina and silica particles that were washed down the River Parrett.

81 Randolph Caldecott 1846–1886 illustrator of childrens' books such as *John Gilpin, The three Jovial Huntsmen, Elegy on a Mad dog, The Queen of Hearts* etc.

table, a church pew, a step ladder and an oak round table. For the scullery maid there was a washing tray, an oval tub, and a washing-up tub. He had all his silver engraved and spent 14 guineas (roughly £700) on wine and spirits from Thomas Firth including 2 gallons of rum, 2 gallons of brandy, 2 gallons of gin, 24 bottles of rich pale sherry 13 years old for 4s 6d, and 24 bottles of old red port for 4s 2d.

His parsimonious mother Ann would have passed out at the £40 (£2,000) spent on office furniture. Every little item is accounted for. Even two new window screws are listed at 2 shillings the pair.

Clothes are one useful way of judging a person's character and Edwin's next list helps to form a better impression of him.

> *2 hats, 2 top coats, 1 cloak, 5 coats, 5 waistcoats, 9 pairs trowsers, 2 pairs of*
> *Wellington Boots, 9 pairs of shoes, 3 pairs slippers, 2 pairs pumps, 1 shoe horn,*
> *3 pairs gaiters, 4 clothes brushes, 4 hair brushes, 3 nail brushes, 1 toothbrush,*
> *2 shaving brushes, 1 hat brush, 3 razors, 2 razor strops, 17 Day shirts, 6 Night*
> *shirts, 5 Night caps, 25 pairs white cotton stockings, 6 pairs blue stockings, 7 pairs*
> *white worsted stockings, 2 pairs of cotton drawers, 11 coloured silk pocket*
> *handkerchiefs, 1 travelling cotton neckerchief, 21 Cravats, 2 Black silk neckerchiefs,*
> *4 Lawn handkerchiefs, 9 Coloured cotton handkerchiefs, 3 Flannel waistcoats,*
> *2 Dressing gowns, 9 pairs of gloves, 3 pairs of Black silk stockings, 3 Speckled*
> *stockings, 1 Straw coloured stockings, 2 Umbrellas, 1 Comfortable* [82] *, 48 Collars*

The speckled and the straw coloured stockings sound carefully chosen and he would have worn the black silk stockings with pumps in the evening. The large number of cravats [83] necessary in the dirty atmosphere of the city, had been elevated into a cult by Beau Brummell who suggested that they should be starched to the consistency of fine writing paper. Those who wore massive cravats were called 'incroyables'; the high collars, forcing heads to point snootily skywards, tended to make men look absurd.

The nine pairs of '*trowsers*' on Edwin's list would have been worn skin-tight to the knees and extended to the mid calf or below. Longer ones were anchored in place by straps that buckled under the instep, an idea possibly

---

82 A long narrow woollen scarf.

83 Cravats developed from Croatian mercenaries who wore scarves in battle and were honoured by Louis XIV in France during the seventeenth century.

introduced by Brummell: a device which delighted smart cavalry regiments and, according to George Orwell in 1947, 'gave you a feeling like nothing else on earth'. These trousers made male legs so alluring in ladies' eyes that Pope Pius VII condemned them as sinful and the garments were taboo in Rome until 1827.

On this list Edwin only had two pairs of underpants compared with the seventeen day shirts and forty-four pairs of stockings. Drawers (they were drawn on) had only just been invented; before that men had nothing but their much longer shirts to tuck into their trousers. Men's drawers, similar to shorts with buttoned flaps and a drawstring, were invented in 1806. Women wore crotchless drawers which came to below the knee, two separate legs joined at the waist: thus a pair. Only some of the clothes could be cleaned in those days, so the stench of the unwashed bodies and unclean clothing would have been insufferable to our noses and a good deal of itching and scratching went on due to bed bugs, fleas and lice: an activity ignored in historical dramas today. Clothes were of unsurpassed elegance at that time. The five coats and two top coats on Edwin's list would have been cut in a figure-hugging style devised by Brummell whose clothes influenced European male fashion for the next hundred years. His style was based on perfect fit, faultless construction and exquisite attention to detail.

'Skin tight trousers gave you a feeling like nothing else on earth'. Caricature of Beau Brummell by R. Dighton 1805

Edwin in his new abode still needs the family money owing to him so he works out exactly how much is due to the eight children from their father's estate. John Eddison's 1812 will stated that £500 was to go to each child on coming of age but Edwin feels the children should be advanced double the amount as the value of money has changed since then.

The young lawyer revels in his first home. The walls, woodwork, stairs are being whitewashed and the newly dyed curtains are being hung. The furniture looks wonderful and gallons of drink await his guests. Then shocking news arrives from Gateford. Edwin's sporting cousin, Benjamin Eddison, son of his guardian Uncle Benjamin of Raymoth Gilead

Farm has bigamously married a Mrs Farrer. Edwin is practically apoplectic. He dashes off an indignant letter to his mother in June 1828:

the conduct of Benjamin's wife is such as to exclude her for life from all respectable society if we are to believe the old proverb that a woman can only lose her character for once and that is for ever – that my Aunt's conduct is such as to disgust everyone who has any delicate feeling left and any sense of propriety to uphold … If my Aunt or Uncle seem disposed to impose upon you, speak out as in duty and Christian rectitude and tell them that a whore and adulteress is a person with whom you do no wish to associate.

He writes again in August still fuming:

George Woolam in speaking of my cousin Benjamin and Mrs Farrer, said that Farrar's mother had lately been over to Worksop and during her stay was very near to his house. He observed how fond my Aunt Eddison was of Mrs Farrer and how anxious to introduce her. I asked him whether he considered that any person of respectability in Worksop would visit her and he said, ' no, certainly not!' and he said he believed Mr Farrer was living. Of Farrer's being alive, I feel to have no doubt. At any rate I have not a shadow of doubt about his being alive at the time of Benjamin's Marriage to Mrs Farrer.

This is serious and such a scandal could put off a potential bride. Bigamy was punishable by seven years transportation and, even after sentence, Mr Farrer could bring an action against Benjamin for damages. Bristling at the immorality, Edwin's language as he continues the letter, is flowery with rage:

Let her think and do as she likes. Let her drive her chosen harlot before your window and let them go to on that broad way and to that destination whether all beggars on horseback go. I may seem severe and unchristian in my last remark. But punishment is not with me save in this that I look on the conduct as odious and therefore they may rest assured they are not at peace with all judgement … I do not intend ever to call at Benjamin's house with any view of paying a civility.

No more is heard about the story. Mrs Farrer is not on the family tree, nor any wife for Benjamin, whose death is not recorded. Was he transported or did he leave the country in disgrace? This is unlikely, as he is mentioned again in 1831 and is known to have had a son, ironically, called Edwin. A search revealed an

Edwin Eddison Farrer had been born 10 March 1823, so Benjamin must have got Mrs Farrer pregnant and the child was named quite blatantly. The illegitimate Edwin wrote The History of Worksop under the name Edwin Eddison, which was well received when it was published in 1854 (this was the book I found on the internet which by a very strange coincidence had belonged to my great-grandfather Francis Eddison of Syward Lodge, Dorchester.) Edwin was thirty-one and had dropped his mother's name by then, driven, perhaps, by shame.

Five months later on, Edwin, recovered from this disgrace, is full of warmth and appreciation for his guardian, the solid, reliable Uncle Benjamin Eddison. He writes on 26 November 1828:

> *Dear Uncle,*
>
> *… I am informed that there is an artist in Worksop or the neighbourhood, who has been taking the likenesses of several individuals and is said to be rather clever. If you will not think it unreasonable to trespass on your time and patience I shall feel it an obligation if you will sit to him at my cost. You are aware that you are the last of your generation of all the descendants of my Great Grandfather and therefore there is no other person left if you refuse. I know you have an aversion to it but you must remember you are my Uncle Eddison and though from the daily trouble you have had from me and the rest of us for nearly seventeen years I think you awfully entitled to exemption from any duty except what is really needful, yet you must remember that it may remain long after you and me to show to our posterity if any there should be, the face of the worthy Uncle of 8 fatherless children. If it do really seriously annoy you to sit I must be content for you to use your discretions, but if there be any other artist – whom you know for instance, the man who took you at Osberton – I shall be very glad to have one from his pencil – though as that at Osberton is a family painting, likely to stay as long as the house stands, I would rather have you done by another Painter. But any way or by any man rather than not at all. I am not yet very wealthy, but nevertheless I can, with pleasure raise a few pounds for my Uncle's portrait – whoever you may get, I shall not grumble at his fee.*
>
> *With love to my Aunt and Cousins, Your Affectionate Nephew Edwin Eddison*

This information about a portrait of Benjamin was useful as I had bought a small blackened painting of a man with soft grey hair at the auction of the contents of my grandparents' house in 2002. After the picture was cleaned, the name J. C. Bentley, January 1829 was just discernible on the back. Edwin's letter also mentions a painting done of Benjamin at Osberton a nearby estate to Gateford, and the seat of the Foljambe family. Perhaps he sat for Queen Victoria's painter, John Partridge who was painting the Foljambes at the time and perhaps this better painting has been lost.

Edwin now sounds happy and reasonably healthy at his work in Leeds. His next letters to his mother are chiefly about investments, mortgages and financial advice. The family scandal had abated and foolishly he now tempts fate saying that his health is 'the best for twelve months'. Wretchedly the pain strikes with a vengeance in June 1829 and

Edwin commissioned J. C. Bentley's portrait of his uncle Benjamin Eddison

this time he treats himself with fomentation, fearing rightly, that leeches did him more harm than good.

Dear Mother,
I am a good deal better than I was last week though my side is not yet quite well. My servant also is better and I have not the least occasion at present for anybody to nurse me. I find fomentation to mend me as soon as any thing or indeed sooner than any thing that I have yet tried; or if I have bran I put it in a flannel bag with very little water and it will keep hot several hours sometimes. I find relief this way quite as soon as from leeches and I think it is preferable on many accounts. It is less trouble and less weakening and I think it is better to avoid bleeding as much as possible though I have no doubt when the pain is very bad I could not get more certain relief than by using it. With love to all Edwin E.

Things get worse and on the advice of his surgeon, Mr Thackrah he goes home to Gateford to rest for ten days. Again he is advised to use leeches to suck his blood and, as they are difficult to buy in Worksop, he brings some squirming creatures along with him on the coach in a jar.

Alarming occurrence. Chorus of Unprotected Females: 'Conductor! Stop!
Omnibus-man! Here's a gentleman had an accident and broke a jar of leeches and
they're all over the omnibus!' John Leech, Punch, 1850

Buchan in his book *Family Physician*[84], was adamant that 'no operation of
surgery was so frequently necessary as bleeding.' He says: 'But though practised by Midwives, Gardeners, Blacksmiths etc we have reason to believe that
very few know when it is necessary. Even physicians themselves have been so
much the dupes of fashion in this article, as to render it the subject of satire
and ridicule.' He goes on to explain that bleeding was necessary at the beginning of all inflammatory fevers: after falls, blows, bruises or any violent hurts
received externally or internally. He says that 'it is likewise necessary for persons who have had the misfortune to be strangled, drowned, suffocated with
foul air or whenever the vital motions have been suddenly stopped. Not so
good for swoonings or hysteric affections… the bleeding to be performed as

---

84   This book, also known as *Domestic Medicine* was published in 1769 and went
      through countless editions. It was republished in 2012 as *Can Onions cure Ear-
      ache?* (Bodleian Library) with a forward by Professor Robert Winston, who
      points out that although some of his remedies were dangerous, others worked
      simply because people believed they would.

As an all purpose treatment, cupping was an alternative torture to leeches.
Print by Thomas Rowlandson

near the part affected as possible, preferably with a lancet, but where a vein
cannot be found, recourse must be had to leeches or cupping.'

In the early 19th century the use of leeches had become a mania and they
were prescribed for every human ill throughout Europe; for obesity, colds,
asthma, vomiting, consumption, dysentery and even for nymphomania. This
frenzied use peaked between 1820 and 1845, the time when Edwin most
needed medical help. It was not a painful ordeal. He would have felt a slight
prick, then nothing as the anaesthetic in the leech's saliva was pumped into
the bite from ducts between its teeth. The leech expanded to roughly seven
times its normal size, like a plump cigar and after twenty minutes it released
its hold and dropped into a container to be killed, if it was lucky, with alcohol.

In the mid 1800s some six million leeches were used each year in Paris
hospitals alone and, in order to supply the hospitals young women waded into
lakes and ponds to lure the leeches onto their bare legs; even horses were used
for this purpose. In Germany by the end of the century, leeches had become
extinct through over-collection.

Wordsworth wrote about a dispirited leech collector in his 1802 poem
Resolution and Independence: 'Once I could meet with them on every side / But

Women waiting for leeches to attach themselves to their legs
by George Walker, engraved by Robert Havell

they have dwindled long by slow decay / Yet still, I persevere and find them where I may.'

In 1824 Byron denounced his doctors as 'a damned set of butchers' when they insisted on a treatment that included attaching 20 leeches to his brow as a cure for fever. He died a few days later.

The ghoulish use of leeches by 19th century physicians gradually lessened with Pasteur's discovery of germs. However, they were used on James Joyce in 1922 in an effort to halt his advancing blindness and in 1953 Stalin, dying from cerebral bleeding, was leeched by the terrified physicians charged with keeping him alive by any means possible.

Edwin's health takes a long and unnecessary battering under this medical caprice which worries his anxious partner Mr Payne. He goes back to work, still doubled up with pain but finds he cannot go on. He writes to his mother describing a further application of leeches and deploring the foul air of Leeds:

> *The pain is much less and the swelling is gone down. I had 16 leeches on Saturday evening and I had 23 on yesterday. I have not been dressed yet and do not mean to leave my bed until I am quite free from pain. I can nurse myself very well here but the air at Gateford has an advantage in purity over the Leeds air which I feel more now I am an invalid than I should at any other time.*

Then the pain becomes unbearable and he thinks he is really going to die. Two days later he braces himself for more treatment. He is appalled when the doctor tells him that he does not think he will recover. He writes to his mother:

At about 5 o'clock on Monday evening the pain quite ceased and I began to feel sorry that I had sent for Thackrah. I sat up at my writing till ten o'clock and then went to bed and had a large Blister on which is to be perpetual for about 10 days whether the pain continues or not. The Blister kept me awake most of Monday night and rose very well and yesterday night at about seven I had it dressed. Soon after the dressing I had a slight pain in the left groin which gradually increased both in vigour and extent till it reached up to the kidneys and in a short time became so severe that I felt in doubt some time whether it would prove fatal. However Mr Thackrah and his assistant Mr Scholefield both came and by the application of Laudanum and Camphor it was reduced in about 3 hours. In the evening I was in a hot bath for ½ hour, and I felt much better for it though a good deal reduced. Mr Thackrah had a long conference with Mr Payne yesterday … He told Mr Payne he thought I should never completely recover … I must be very temperate in diet, go to bed early and not attend too closely to business and as I valued my existence, I must refrain from vibrant exercise. I feel much better this morning. William Overend slept with me last night and I have not suffered for want of nursing. Miss Tatham has been exceedingly kind. I do not see any necessity for either Ann or Mary to come as unless the pain should return. Thackrah says I should not want leeches again.

Your affectionate son Edwin.

Samuel Pepys, like Edwin was plagued with bad health and he too, looking back from middle age, wrote that he could not remember any period of his life without pain. His condition was so bad that he often passed blood or, as he put it, made 'bloody water upon any extraordinary motion'. For Pepys it was the pain of a kidney stone which forced him to submit to an operation in which he was held down by several assistants, then a stone as big as a Real Tennis ball (smaller than a lawn tennis ball) was removed. But, like Edwin, his pain-racked childhood may have given him the physical stoicism which seems to have provided them both with the determination to make something of their lives.

13
Romance and Riots

I chose my wife as she did her wedding-gown, not for a fine glossy surface,
but such qualities as would wear well.

Oliver Goldsmith, *The Vicar of Wakefield*

Romance is in the air at Gateford. A dithering Mary asks her brother Edwin for advice about her engagement and he replies guardedly, using (unusually for him) the formal Quaker 'thees' and 'thous' saying:

I have no wish to catechise thee, but I have an earnest wish for thy happiness. All that I have to advise thee is that if thou like John Ryalls better than any other man thou knows ... unless thou believes that his conduct health, character and property are much as to give thee a reasonable prospect of matrimonial happiness for life, thou ought not to marry him ... remember thy own conscience is the only safe guide. Think seriously and decide seriously.

In a small albumen print Mary's fiance John Ryalls looks a fine dignified man. He was a churchwarden and one of Lord Scarborough's tenant farmers living in the village of Eakring. But marriage with Mary Eddison was not to be as she took Edwin's stern letter to heart. In the end John Ryalls married Elizabeth Mason, the daughter of a bewhiskered clergyman. However the Ryalls name came into the family later on when their daughter, Sarah Ryalls married Edwin's fifth son, Francis Eddison.

The ending of her engagement to John Ryalls gave Mary a nervous collapse. In an honest letter she poured out the details to her new admirer, John Dougill, but this did not put him off. Her little red diary notes the course of this new courtship along with the last days of old Uncle Benjamin Eddison at Raymoth Gilead Farm.

Romance was infectious. While Mary sorted herself out, Edwin was positioning himself for marriage; he had already noticed the attractive Hannah Maria Baker, granddaughter of Joseph Tatham, who started the Quaker school in Leeds in 1756. Hannah Maria's mother, Hannah Baker (*née* Tatham) peers beguilingly from a green-framed miniature; her brown eyes are alert and her

*Miniature of Hannah Tatham before
her marriage to William Baker*

*Hannah Baker, Edwin's mother-in-law
who inherited the Adel estate.
A watercolour by Sir John Gilbert RA*

Sarah Ryalls

*Edwin's son Francis married
Sarah Ryalls in 1872*

hair is caught upwards by black velvet ribbons [85]. In 1805 Hannah had married William Baker, a London merchant described as a gentleman, whose family had owned land at Acle in Norfolk since the seventeenth century. A beautiful exercise book found in the Bedale trunk titled *Letters to William Baker at South Town School 1791* [86] had been written by Thomas Wright, his teacher, in copperplate writing embellished with flourishes so perfect that the book looks as if it had been printed.

There had been some disgrace when Hannah Tatham was expelled from the Society of Friends after her wedding to William Baker who was not a Quaker. Newly married, she had had to cope with two major tragedies: her first-born son died at the age of eight months (Hannah Maria was born two years later), then her husband William Baker died after only four years of marriage. So to be near her sixty-eight, year-old mother, the unhappy widow travelled the long distance from London to Leeds in 1809 with the infant Hannah Maria screaming from a hammock swinging inside the coach.

Hannah Baker had a strong character and concentrated her energy on supervising the education of her daughter Hannah Maria. I found a bundle of Hannah's letters in tiny envelopes, written when she was in her eighties to her ninety year-old cousin, Elizabeth Clay of Rastrick House near Huddersfield. The letters are bursting with family matters: among them worries about her granddaughter and namesake, Hannah Eddison, Edwin's only daughter who married the Reverend Charles Middleton, a man loathed by her brothers.

Now living frugally in Leeds with her mother, Hannah Baker is not yet aware of a sizeable inheritance coming to her under the will of her brother, George North Tatham, a rich flax spinner and woollen magnate of Leeds who owned the Adel estate. Hannah was co-heir to this estate, most of which had been bought from William Carruthers in 1850 for £29,700, but George North Tatham died just three months after the purchase. He left £12,000 to his nephews in Philadelphia and the estate went jointly to his sisters, Hannah Baker and Eliza Tatham and his niece Mary Ann Tatham: the latter was later bought out by the other two, and when Eliza Tatham died in 1860 Hannah Baker acquired the entire Adel estate.

Sadly, Edwin did not keep his love letters. Perhaps they were just too personal. He had no prospective father-in-law to ask for the hand of Hannah

Maria and his only reference to the coming celebration is in a letter asking his sisters, Mary and Ann to be bridesmaids. He must have left the Society of Friends at some point before the marriage as there is a note in the Minutes of the Brighouse Quaker's Monthly Meeting:

Hannah Maria Eddison a Member of our Religious Society having contrary to our testimonies been united in marriage by a priest to a person not in membership with us, we hereby disown her as a member of our Society, yet we desire her present and eternal welfare.

Edwin, disliking anything that smacks of Catholicism or episcopal authority, writes tersely: 'This is a very indefinite term (priest). We were married by the Clerk in Orders at the parish Church of Leeds.'

The wedding was on a cool November day in 1830 after which they settled down in the freshly painted house in Albion Street, Leeds. Hannah Baker lived nearby and had great respect for her legally-minded son-in-law and writes to him in 1839 about a business idea concerning her nephews:

My Dear Edwin,
Sudden thoughts are sometimes best, therefore on the spur of the moment I may inform thee that it has just come into my head to query whether we could not avail ourselves upon of these lead machines to save the 800£ now in George Baker's hands from final wreck? [87]
First I would suggest that his stock etc should be converted into money, then that one of these machines should be set up at Newcastle, or some such improving town, on a plan, something like the one in London, that thou a should furnish the capital required, which perhaps, and not exceeding 2000£ at first, that George and his brother Benjamin [88] *should work the concern with a certain salary for services, allowing Hanson and Co as in London 2½ and 10% on the respective profits on each kind of pipe and that the remaining profits be divided into three parts thee to take one, me one and G & B one (I do not mean that my name should appear) this I think may be done without placing the whole amount of capital in greater jeopardy than it is at the present time, if thou likes the idea, I think Hanson and Co should be spoken to without much loss of time, as I fancy most large towns*

---

87   Her husband's brother George Baker born *c.* 1777.
88   Sons of her brother James Tatham.

Hannah Maria Baker who married
Edwin Eddison

Hugo Eddison ill, 1832. A drawing by
George North Tatham

will shortly set up these machines, because, the carriage of the Article is such that
it will not admit of its being sent to any very great distance. I have not mentioned
this idea to anyone as yet, if thou thinks it is not practicable here let it drop. In
a few days or a week, I expect we shall hear Benjamin's report of the London
establishment, so for the present I will leave the subject,
I remain thy aff mother, H. Baker.

There are no letters from Edwin on this matter so he may not have encouraged his mother-in-law. However the lead-pipe business that Hannah Baker's
Tatham nephews started in Philadelphia in 1840 grew steadily and became
the largest in America with factories and shot towers[89] in Philadelphia and
New York.

Benjamin Tatham was soon able to buy a grand house in 4th Avenue, New
York and being a conscientious Quaker helped to improve the wretched conditions of Negroes and Indians. A veil was drawn over Quaker ethics of owning shot towers to make ammunition for the American Civil war but Hannah
was delighted at their success and was further thrilled when Henry Billington

---

89   Towers in which molten lead was dropped from a height to become shot
      for bullets.

Tatham's daughter Anna Paulina married Edwin's eldest son Robert William Eddison in 1862.

The newly married Edwin admires the female touches being added to his bachelor abode; the nursery is equipped with fresh curtains and painted furniture and the couple await visits from the family. Hannah Maria's gossipy letters are a welcome relief to Edwin's precise missives. She describes a visit by her sweaty cousin, Tom Tatham, who had just got engaged to his cousin Maria Tatham. 'He arrived yesterday, piping hot I dare say for his is of a most perspiring nature'. She also says that the portrait of Edwin's Uncle Benjamin has not yet arrived, but hopes it will soon be dry enough.

This has to be the portrait of Benjamin Eddison of Raymoth Gilead Farm which had been lying unloved in the Bedale attics until it was rescued by my mother [90]. The subtle colouring of Benjamin's face is impressive and the crisply painted clothes are rather like those in Raeburn's portrait of William Glendonwyn at the Fitzwilliam Museum, Cambridge.

There is mention of this portrait in a letter from Edwin's youngest brother, Benjamin. He describes old Uncle Benjamin sitting for a painter in Sheffield called Poole in 1831 who finished the picture after six sittings.

The artist of Benjamin Eddison's portrait was identified with the help of Professor Duncan Robinson [91] He thought it had been done by a good regional painter who may not have painted anyone particularly well known and suggested that Poole, mentioned in the letter, was the likely artist.

Not much is known about William Poole of Sheffield except that he was President of the Sheffield School of Art. His subjects included William Wentworth-Fitzwilliam, 4th Earl Fitzwilliam, a portrait in a similar style to Benjamin's. A local reference librarian in Sheffield Central Library found a book that had a brief mention of Poole which says that although 'he had a large number of commissions, he lacked ambition which spurs men on to great endeavours; being content to pass his later years chiefly in the enjoyment of literary pursuits and those that knew him enjoyed his ready wit and power

90   With the author.
91   Duncan Robinson, CBE, FRSA, DL, Master of Magdalene College,
      Cambridge, previously Director of the Fitzwilliam Museum, Cambridge,
      a leading authority on British Art from the eighteenth century onwards.

Uncle Benjamin Eddison (1858–1832) Co-guardian of Ann Eddison's eight fatherless children. Portrait by W. Poole of Sheffield

of quotation…competent judges thought that some of his work equalled that done by Raeburn'.[92]

Ten months after the wedding, Hannah Maria feeling 'vastly queer and un-comfortable' asks her sister-in-law, Elizabeth Eddison about a monthly nurse.

92   *Hallamshire Worthies*, 1926.

During her last month of pregnancy there are disturbances in the area. Angry crowds mass in the streets of Nottingham and when Elizabeth arrives fresh from Gateford she is full of the latest news of the disruptions.

After the death of King George IV and the dissolution of Parliament in 1830, electoral reform was on many people's minds. The Tories had won a majority but their Prime Minister, the Duke of Wellington, opposed reform and had to resign. Charles Grey, a Whig succeeded him and proceeded with the parliamentary reforms. The Reform Bill, or the Representation of the People Act 1832, was then brought forward. The Second Reading was approved by only one vote which made further progress of the Bill difficult; however the motion was carried by nine votes and then it was decided to take the decision to the people.

Public violence broke out in Derby on the evening the Lords rejected the Reform Bill and a mob attacked the jail. Lord Grey's Government committed to reform, extended voting power to middle-class men, small landowners, tenant farmers and shopkeepers. The rioters were protesting against opponents of the Bill. Nottingham had elected pro-reform MPs and supporters claimed to have gathered 12,000 names for a petition supporting the Bill. In the countryside the riots were brutally suppressed; there were about twenty executions and hundreds of men were sentenced to imprisonment or transportation to Australia.

To understand the Eddisons' anxiety, it is interesting to read alongside their letters an account of the anger of the Nottingham people written by Francis White [93] which makes the riots immediate. White tells of crowds gathering in the streets of Nottingham on the morning of 9 October 1831, eagerly awaiting the rumble of coaches bringing news of further disturbances. People begin to smash the windows of those who had signed the Anti Reform petition; then the mayor reads the Riot Act and hurriedly calls in the only remaining troop of the 15th Hussars. Shops are broken into and market stall-holders stay away. On the edge of the forest a windmill is attacked, the sails cut and the damaged machinery lies in the flour. A gang of tough youths armed with dismantled iron railings proceed to the Carolean Colwick Hall where the owner, Jack Musters, is a leading anti-reformer. He is away fishing at the time and his family hide trembling in the shrubberies whilst raging youths attack the house. This was all much too near the homes of the Eddisons and Booths.

93   *Nottinghamshire, History Gazetteer and Directory*, 1864.

The Duke of Newcastle is opposed to reform and his property, Nottingham Castle, is pillaged. According to Francis White, tapestries are torn down and sold to bystanders for 3/- a yard and a fine equestrian statue is destroyed. Two boys are crushed and scorched to death when they try to steal lead, glass and marble and their bodies are found fused together. The mob set fire to a large silk mill at Beeston and go on to attack Wollaton Hall, a magnificent Smythson house owned by Lord Middleton.

The nervous militia eventually get the upper hand and, with the mob bellowing at their heels, they march unruly prisoners through the town holding their swords high and firing wild warning shots down the high street, unfortunately shooting a helpless old pensioner doing his best by acting as a special constable. In the evening the soldiers gallop along the pavements and charge the crowds near the market place, striking unsuspecting rioters with the flat of their swords. The disturbances last three days and the damage in Nottingham is serious. Mansfield, only ten miles from Gateford also suffers much damage.

Five days after the riots, young Ann Eddison, with news of the riots ringing in her ears, writes a letter to her sister Mary describing the drama of the 15th Hussars, quartered at Worksop, two miles from Gateford, being ordered to quell the mob. She writes: 'We are sorry to hear my Cousins had their windows broken and also much surprised for they are quiet about Politics and Mrs Booth very kind to the poor.'

She is further agitated by a calamity that happened in the middle of the disturbance

> Mrs Machin had Russell and Dethick [doctors] *sent for in a great battle on Wednesday. And had a painful operation performed. The child's life was obliged to be taken ... She was three months off her expected time. The corpse was deposited in Shireoaks chapel and I am glad to say Mrs Machin is doing better than they could expect. Mr Machin says he must keep her in bed a fortnight.*

Hannah Maria goes into labour three weeks after the riots and a rather feeble little boy is born. Mary Eddison, in charge of the nurses, is appalled when people think the red-faced baby looks like her. She insists that he looks exactly like florid old Uncle Benjamin Eddison. But something is not right.

Three days after the birth Edwin has not been allowed to see his son. Writing to his wife from his office he pours out his views on the naming of the boy, indicating that he expects a production line of children.

My dear H. M. E.,

I have no great objection to any of these names but I much prefer Hugo … from my great veneration for the name of Hugo Grotias (or rather for the man more than his name) [94] *and partly because it is not a common name in the family …*

I give thee the accompanying names to look over but I shall want some very very strong arguments to drive me off my predilection, and if I do give up it must only be on condition that the next boy be called Hugo. Thou remembers it was a bargain that I should give names to all the boys and thou to all the girls … Thy affectionate Husband, Edwin Eddison.

He ends on a wry note:

PS Mary says you are not ready to admit one and will not be for some time so by way of amusement as I am busy and cannot wait any longer, I have been writing this on my office stool whereon I intend some day to make young Hugo try to earn his living if it please Providence to spare him so long.

So Hugo it was – for his brief life. The sickly baby struggled on for five months until his death. Among the letters in the trunk and carefully wrapped in tissue paper, there were several pencil drawings of the pop-eyed baby: drawings imbued with love and anxiety. There is no account of the actual cause of his death; several Eddison first-borns died young but a serious outbreak of cholera had hit unhygienic Leeds in 1831 and, according to a contemporary report, seventy-five cartloads of sewage were removed from a cul-de-sac known as Boot and Shoe Yard in Kirkgate where many had perished.

Hannah Maria and Edwin are of course devastated by the baby's death. At the funeral an epitaph is chosen from *A Child in a Country Churchyard* by his great-uncle the Reverend Abraham Booth:

Ere sin could blight or sorrow fade,
Death came with friendly care,
The opening had to heaven conveyed
And bade it blossom there.

94   Hugh Grotias 1583–1645, philosopher, lawyer and political theorist.

Writing to his mother seven years later after the death of another son, Alfred, from measles, Edwin remembers the earlier agony saying, 'I was stripped to the very dust that I was made of.' In the end, six sons and one neurotic daughter survived out of the nine children. Leeds was now an unsuitable place to bring up a family so after the birth of the third child they move to the countryside: to Ashfield House, Headingley Hill, near Adel, away from the smoke and grime of the town.

Mary Eddison having been busy with Edwin's marriage and the birth of Hugo, now has her own important decision to make when John Dougill, her new suitor, appears on the scene. Her small red diary of 1832 glows with her social life but there are difficulties ahead on the tiny pages when she describes the dying days of florid old Uncle Benjamin Eddison of Raymoth Gilead Farm.

14
Mary Eddison's Little Red Diary

Whitest thoughts in whitest dress
Candid meanings best express
Mind of quiet Quakeress.
    Charles Lamb, *The Album of Lucy Barton*

In her photographs Edwin's younger sister Mary Eddison has a cheerful face and wears unexciting Quaker clothes. She was a bright spirit and this attracted her two suitors. After turning down John Ryalls she had a nervous breakdown but before very long she was being courted by another admirer, the Quaker John Dougill. The Dougills lived at Darley, a wild spot in Nidderdale, near Knaresborough, where the family was said to have lived since 1496 and where, during the reign of Queen Anne they had built Dougill Hall and Dougill Farm.

A brown paper packet in the Bedale tin trunk contained the 1767 Gretna Green marriage certificate of Gracie Spence and John Dougill. Gracie was not a Quaker and the marriage upset the family. Joseph Dougill, the child of the elopement, was Mary's father-in-law who had some odd habits. There was a page from his book in the trunk which was covered with endless calculations about letters and words from the Bible. He obsessively recorded that the word 'and' occurs 46,227 times; that the 21st verse of the 7th chapter of Ezra contains the alphabet and that the first record of a man being buried in a coffin was in the 26th verse of the 50th Chapter of Genesis. Perhaps he had nothing better to do.

More genealogical clues emerged when my cousin Simon arrived one day with five bursting suitcases of linen that he had originally intended to take to Oxfam. I spent a fortnight washing countless sheets, pillows, bolster cases and large damask tablecloths. Simon had seen a little blue label attached to a greyish sheet which had cross-stitched initials in the corners: W B 1832, A E, E D E. The blue label said that the sheet had belonged to William Booth, born in 1768 and that it had been handed on to his unmarried niece Ann Eddison

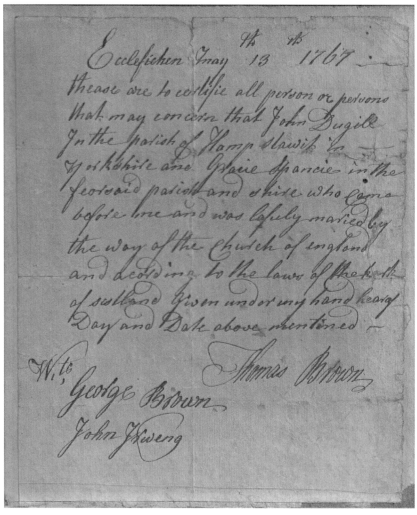

John and Gracie Dougill's 1767 Gretna Green marriage certificate

Mary Eddison married John Dougill

(Edwin's sister) who passed it on to her niece Elizabeth Dougill Eddison.[95] The sheet must have been treasured as the initials are exquisitely stitched. Elizabeth Dougill Eddison, who died childless, passed it onto her great niece Constance Moseley[96].

It must have been Constance who had saved a threadbare damask table-cloth found in one of Simon's suitcases. It is very frail with initials in each corner; the oldest punched out with small holes, the others in cross-stitch. In the weave of the damask, the figure of a king sitting on a prancing horse with little tubby ships behind can be discerned. There was some lettering – *Friedrich August Koningpollen, Danzig*, which probably represents the King of Saxony and Poland, born 1696, or maybe his father, Fredrick Augustus the Strong, born in 1670, who was known to break horseshoes with his bare hands and to throw foxes with a finger. The tablecloth belonged to the Dougill family

95 Daughter of Anne Eddison of Shireoaks. She passed on the Booth loving-cup
    and the portrait of Benjamin to my grandfather, Francis Eddison at Bedale.
96 Mary's daughter Elizabeth Dougill who married her first cousin, Edwin's son
    John Eddison.

Jane, Joseph and Grace Dougill

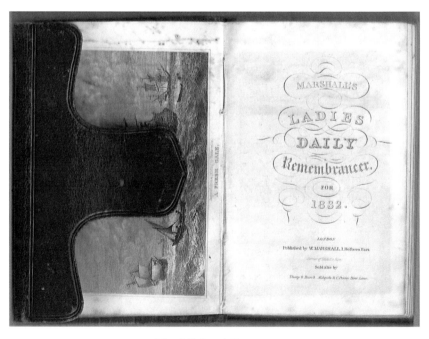

Mary's little red diary 1832

and the initials in the corners were: EMV EHV WEB JMD which indicates that the owners were:

Edward Veepon of Airton 1702–1756. A Quaker, the author's great-great-great-great-great grandfather who married in 1735. (Was it a wedding present?)

Elizabeth Veepon 1746–1810, his daughter who in 1771 married:

William Bilton 1743–1815 of Darley, and their daughter:

Jane Dougill (*née* Bilton) 1776–1848 who married the eccentric:

Joseph Dougill 1768–1822. Their son John Dougill married Mary Eddison.

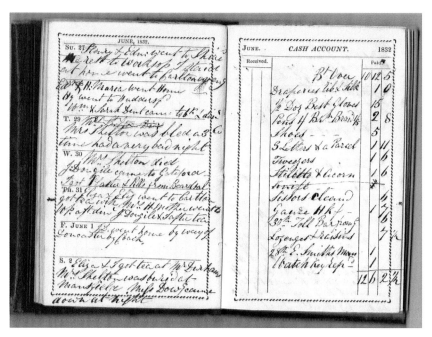

Pages from the little red diary telling of illnesses

Mary Eddison's romance moves forward in the summer of 1831 when John Dougill suddenly proposes. This may have taken her by surprise. She turns him down with chilling formality and bossily reprimands him for not dating the letter:

> *Sir, Feeling conscious of the high compliment conferred upon me … I can no longer delay answering you … It is my firm resolution for a considerable period to remain disengaged for various reasons known only to myself… I am obliged by your consideration about my cough. It is now so much better that I beg you will not trouble yourself to send anything for it. As a man of business you surprise me much by sending a dateless letter …*

Three months later he must have become closer as she daringly calls him 'My Dear Friend' and tells him that she is bored with helping her sister-in-law, Hannah Maria with the new house and says 'alterations and preparations of houses have no charms for me.'

The next month her letter begins with surprising intimacy 'Dear John.' Brother Henry is against the marriage but there is determination as she writes, 'but I think it is much better for me to have a little opposition'. While helping Hannah Maria with the sickly baby Hugo, she is longing for John to visit Leeds and tells him 'we have not a spare bed to offer a friend at present, but Edwin wishes me to say the half of his will be at thy service'. This is not an invitation to share the marital bed: in those days it was usual for married couples to have separate bedrooms.

Cholera raged in 1832. There were 796 cases in Nottingham and a Quaker, Mr Samuel Fox gave land for burials away from the churchyards. Mary Eddison's tiny diary for that year *Marshall's Ladies Daily Remembrancer* was one of the very few amongst the papers. It is a beautiful object, red calf with blue marbled end papers, closing leather flaps and a inside pocket for extra notes. It opens with a delicate engraving of ships titled, '*A Fresh Gale*' with two more engravings of fashionable ladies in ornate hats, flouncy dresses with wasp waists. One of the dresses is festooned with feathers – much too enticing for a good Quaker girl. In minute print there are 141 pages of short stories, poetry, songs, hackney and stage coach fares, stamp rates, tables of wages and a list of London bankers.

This diary gives a real feeling of the time. Amongst her monthly expenses Mary records the costs of tooth cleaning, tongue scrapers, stay-laces, a stiletto acorn knife, bronze slippers, gauze hose, green paper for feather screens, lute-

Fashionable ladies

strings, black gloves, a black dress, a black apron and even black pins (for Uncle Benjamin's funeral), hair wire, a carpet bag, an anti-slavery tract, 10 yards of black galloon [97] and 1 dozen love apples [98].

It is an important year for Mary and Gateford is full of fun. That year the young Princess Victoria toured the Midlands in order to see some of the country over which she would one day be Queen. After visiting a coal-mining town near Birmingham, the Princess comments in her journal that everything was black: the grass, the people, the houses and even the poor little ragged children.

Henry Ryalls, the brother of Mary's earlier suitor, is on the scene at Gateford, hunting, coursing and shooting with her brothers. The Aldams, Tathams, Overends, Radleys, Heppenstalls, Machins, (Henry Machin was High Sheriff

---

97 A lace-like tape with gold or silver thread for trimming.

98 Tomatoes.

There was constant hospitality at Gateford House

that year), Vesseys, Girdlers and John Dougill pay frequent visits. Parties of friends make visits to Welbeck Stud, to Wallingwells, the seat of Sir Thomas Woolaston White and to watch the fireworks at Worksop. Mary busies herself making feather-work screens, lining her winter shawls and helping Aunt Eddison's servants to make pork pies and to bottle the orange wine from three year old casks at Raymoth Farm. There are many dinner and tea parties and there is a record of meal times in one of the letters: 'We have altered our dinner hour to half past 2 o'clock I am happy to say, for 4 o'clock dinners do not suit me a bit'.

Cousin Wilson Overend, the same age as Edwin, often calls in to deal with his cousins' ailments. He is now surgeon at Sheffield Infirmary and later became a Justice of Peace and Deputy Lieutenant of two counties. He visits old Uncle Benjamin Eddison at Raymoth who has serious tummy trouble and who has sheepishly admitted to raiding the kitchen at two o'clock in the morning to eat a veal pie which may have been none too fresh. He is now extremely ill.

Benjamin's wife is not in good health either and she asks Mary to look after her seventy-six year-old husband. It is tiring work but Mary manages to snatch walks in the park and dinners at Gateford across the fields with her fiancé, but Benjamin dies after twenty-two days of harrowing sickness during which Mary nursed him night and day. Struggling to haul him out of bed when he needs the commode, she is alarmed by his shivering spasms and in the 1832 diary she describes it all vividly:

17th April   Mother came in the p.m. Uncle was obliged to have old things under to save the bed. Ann and I were with him the night. Very restless.

21st April   Uncle had four hours sleep. I sat up. He twice got to the chair.

24th April   Uncle gets weaker evacuations come from him sadly.

25th April   Shivers and fits in the p.m. And we thought Uncle would die. Made sad work in easy chair.

26th April   Uncle was most tiresome and would have William all day. Kept getting up continually to chair.

27th April   William assisted me most of the day. Uncle would be up and down all day. Could not turn him, soon as he was laid on one side of the bed, he wished to be on the other. He rambled all night

28th April   About 6 o'clock Uncle began to lay still and at 10 his Breathing altered and he complained, and wished us to pray that he might die, and at ½ past 2 he quietly breathed his last.

In the middle of this ordeal a letter arrives for Mary announcing the death of her little nephew, Hugo. This is almost too much to bear, particularly as she had helped to look after the sickly baby from birth. Exhausted after her uncle's death, Mary trails home over the fields in the early morning for breakfast at Gateford, worrying about the black clothes she needs to borrow for the funeral. The family assemble, including grey-faced Edwin and Hannah Maria, both in deep shock as it is just eight days since their baby's death. Understandably Hannah Maria is too ill to attend the funeral and the others are all cross and tired. Elizabeth scolds Henry and their Mother goes to bed before dinner. Three days after the funeral they are all run-down and ill.

Uncle Benjamin's sister-in-law, Mrs Shelton, after 'a usual good dinner' now becomes seriously ill. Beardsall, the Worksop surgeon, bleeds her three times but five days later she is dead. Mary, ill again, is given pills and a horrible blister plaster is attached by the assiduous Beardsall.[99]

Mary's fiancé, John Dougill comes back to Gateford and soon normal life resumes with gatherings of cousins and friends; visits to the dentist and more trips to neighbouring houses, Osberton, Clumber, Worksop Manor, Chatsworth and Haddon Hall. They hear of the cholera epidemic in Sheffield but this does not put them off dining on oysters at Upperthorpe with their cousins the Aldams.

Trouble lies ahead for twenty-six year-old Mary. Her mother opposes her marriage to John Dougill, insisting that it is too soon after her last engagement and she refuses to give her consent alluding to the fact that Mary upset everybody three years earlier when, at the very last moment, she called off her marriage with John Ryalls. Memories of her hysterics are raw.

Young women's neurotics were often due to stultifying boredom. They tended not to have such a good education as their brothers and, as Quakers did not encourage the arts, their days often passed with time-filling tedium helping out every now and again with home duties, in contrast to their mothers who were fully in charge of countless household activities. The widowed Ann Eddison had the satisfaction of running the farm, looking after the investments, keeping meticulous accounts and being in charge of the smooth running of Gateford. Her daughters obediently bided their time but Mary was the only one to marry.

John Dougill writes persistently several times a month and Mary coldly records the cost of his letters. Letter-writing was expensive because of the high price of the best quality rag paper and the charges were worked out by the sheet, the weight and, most importantly, the distance travelled; the recipient had to pay when the letter was delivered. Parcels were extremely expensive to send.

Booth supports Mary, knowing how difficult their mother could be and sends her a letter saying he will present her marriage at the Monthly Meeting. So nothing can stop them and the wedding is arranged. But tension is still in

99 Blisters, produced by a chemical on the plaster, were painfully punctured with scissors and another plaster would be applied to the raw patch. It was not noticed that a disordered stomach would have carried on regardless; on the other hand the stomach could have sorted itself out by the end of a long blistering ordeal.

the air and Mary, exasperated by her fiancé's inefficiency over plans for the honeymoon, writes: 'Do as thou thinks best about writing to London about lodgings. There's not a doubt but we can find quarters when we get there if thou can't write to make them understand the apartments thou wishes for.'

They were married on a beautiful Spring day in 1833 with the lanes wreathed in cow parsley. The wedding was a subdued Quaker affair with much silence, a short exchange of promises and the signing of the certificate by all those present, followed by a family lunch at Gateford attended by the Aldams. But only two of her brothers were there.

There are two photographs of Mary after her marriage. One in a tiny envelope with her daughter's inscription, 'photograph of my mother, one of the best taken' in which she has an innocently wide and friendly smile. Her dark coloured dress conceals any suggestion of a good figure and her hands are protectively clutched at her waist. In a later photograph she is about fifty, still with her innocent smile and the same hairstyle, but there are dark rings under her eyes. There is only one photograph of John Dougill. He too has a friendly smile, but has serious eyes and is wearing a very tall top hat.

The next reference to the married couple is in June 1841. John Dougill tells his mother-in-law of the speedy delivery of their first child eight years after the marriage.

John writes: 'Thou will be rather surprised to hear that my Mary presented me with a Daughter ¼ before 12pm and so far mother and baby are doing very nicely. Mary was only middling yesterday and went to bed about 10pm At 11pm. I got up and got the doctor here and then went for the nurse, but all was over before I returned.'

Jane's birth was dramatically quick but she died within a year, like so many first-borns in those days. Over the next six years Mary gave birth to three more daughters: Elizabeth, who at the age of forty married Edwin's son, her first cousin, Dr John Edwin Eddison; Ann, who died unmarried aged thirty-nine and Mary Hannah, also a spinster, who died aged twenty-nine. So no grandchildren for the kind, motherly Mary, but her beautiful red diary lives on.

15
Queen Victoria

Great events make me quiet and calm;
it is only trifles that irritate my nerves.
Queen Victoria

King William IV died propped up in his leather chair in the early hours of the 26 June 1837. Benjamin Haydon the painter declares in his journal: 'thus died as thoroughbred an Englishman as ever existed' and, disapproving of the monarch, he writes:

> the people the King liked had all a spice of vice in their nature … one could judge of the King's nature by the companions he seemed to like … the account of his death is peculiarly touching. There must be something terrifically awful in the moment … his lips grew livid and he dropped his head on the page's shoulder, and saying "This is death!" died. [100]

Harriet Martineau [101], who was amongst the six bystanders who witnessed the presentation of the young Queen Victoria to the people outside St James's Palace, describes the occasion in her memoirs:

> There stood the young creature in the simplest mourning with her sleek bands of brown hair as plain as her dress. The tears ran fast down her cheeks as Lord Melbourne stood by her and she was presented to my mother and aunt.

---

100 Benjamin Haydon, *The Autobiography and Memoirs of Benjamin Robert Haydon 1786–1846*, published 1853.
101 Harriet Martineau (1802–1876) English writer, philosopher and controversial journalist. She was a political economist, abolitionist and life-long feminist.

Harriet had a good seat at the coronation 'with a pillar to lean against and a nice corner for my shawl and bag of sandwiches'. Observing the peeresses she writes:

> Old hags, with their dyed or
> false hair drawn to the necks
> and arms bare and glittering
> with diamonds ... the younger
> were as lovely as the aged were
> haggard. The first gleams of the
> sun slanted into the Abbey ...
> I had never before seen the full
> effect of diamonds. As the light
> travelled, each peeress shone like
> a rainbow.

Harriet Martineau had a good seat at Queen Victoria's coronation

Describing Victoria, she says 'her small dark crown looked pretty and her mantle of cloth of gold very regal. She herself looked so small as to appear puny.' Then observing poor Lord Rolle's homage to the Queen, she writes:

> the large, infirm old man slipped, and rolled over and over down the steps,
> lying at the bottom, coiled up in his robes. He tried again and again ...
> the Queen leaned forward and held out her hand. A foreigner in London
> gravely reported that the Lords Rolle held their title on the condition of
> performing the feat at every coronation.[102]

Two years after this event, on 26 June 1839, Ann Eddison receives a letter at Gateford from Edwin with an ominous black seal. The letter describes the death from measles of the new baby, the two month old Alfred:

> *He breathed much worse about midnight and grew gradually worse until 10*
> *minutes past 2 this morning when he expired in the easiest way you can suppose*

---

102 Harriet Martineau, *Harriet Martineau's Autobiography, Vol.1.*, Published 1855

it possible for life to depart. His patience under his suffering seems to me quite extraordinary. The ease with which he took his food and medicine the exceedingly mild manner in which he shewed dissatisfaction at any thing unpleasant to him and an appearance of what I might perhaps describe as angelic resignation – often fetched a tear and sigh with mingled feelings of grief and admiration.

The anguished Edwin and Hannah woke the three older children and took them to the baby's bedroom for their last farewell:

Robert William seemed quite aware of what he was sent for and without bidding said "goodbye Alley" and kissed his cold lips. Hannah seems at present very full of sorrow, she has just been saying "Papa I am so sorry I don't know what to do". Frederic showed no emotion of grief, but we could not get him to raise his voice above a whisper. He kissed his mouth and hand and at our suggestion said goodbye.

The baby had caught measles from the children of their grandmother's servants with whom they often played against their mother's orders and Edwin had angrily scolded them for their disobedience. But he is now in misery. Pouring out his emotions to his mother he tells her that he feels just as strongly now as when poor Hugo died seven years earlier and says that death rarely knocks at the door for one. His words are bleak:

I have just been to see him in the coldness of death and am strongly reminded that it is indeed an awful thing to die. At half past 12 I felt a wish for dawn of day to come and relieve him. On the first gleam of morning light I pulled up the blind but only to see the paleness and stillness of death shown in its full reality. He breathed but a few time more and his spirit returned to God who gave it.

Hannah Maria, grief-stricken and suffering from backache, tries hard to carry on. Edwin, who had been appointed the first Town Clerk of Leeds, distracts himself with Council matters; there is hunger in the town and violence is expected from the Chartists and Socialists who are threatening to break up an imminent meeting. The Civil Force has been alerted.

After Edwin has been Town Clerk for a while an invitation arrives from Buckingham Palace inviting him to meet the young Queen Victoria. He loves being fitted out in court dress: velvet coat, black silk breeches, lace collar and cuffs, white silk stockings and gleaming buckles on his shoes and breeches. He has also been asked to read an address to Prince Albert and the old Duchess of Kent. Sitting in his hotel after the event and perhaps suppressing Quaker sensibilities, he writes proudly to his mother:

Dear Mother

I merely write to tell you that I have today had the honour of kissing the hand of her Majesty Queen Victoria. – I thought of you many times whilst I was thrusting in St James's Palace amongst Earls, Viscounts, and Barons, Generals, Admirals, Mayors, Aldermen, Squires, Members of Parliament etc etc. I could hardly help laughing at the thought of just meeting you by accident in my grand court dress with crop lappets – with steel buttons, lace to my shirt and cuffs, knee breeches, white silk stockings etc etc and bending my stiff neck before her Majesty with Dukes and Lords stepping a little back to make room for my person in black silk and velvet. But I assure you though I was pleased and felt honoured with the smile from her Majesty, who has a beautiful hand and seems remarkably well and I think very good looking too. I was not a whit more happy than I used to be in a dirty smock frock building a Rabbit-cote.

Tomorrow I am to read the address to Prince Albert and the Duchess of Kent. I expect to leave here next Wednesday mg. I heard today from Henry and they are all well. Ann had been there.

My love to you all, your aff son, Edwin Eddison [103]

Royal hands had the same intoxicating effect on others. The writer William Cobbett's daughter writes in 1820, 'Papa has been to Court and kissed the Queen's hand, and a very pretty little hand he says it is'.

One morning Henry arrives at the door of Gateford House 'by coach, as you would expect' writes his exasperated mother. Seventy-three year old Ann Eddison is a weak old woman, now under five foot tall, her mouth sunken over toothless gums and her dark eyes reflecting worries over Henry's wild life and Edwin's bouts of pain. Writing a short letter in a shaking hand she begs Edwin to persuade Henry to stop seeing his dissipated friends as she fears his early death.

Edwin is not feeling too brilliant. He has a fever and the pain is again hammering in his side. The doctor prescribes the usual leeches and a gentle laxative: caster oil, magnesia with rhubarb. He is to avoid eating sweets or

103 Undated letter.

acidic foods but the good news is that he is allowed sherry. A holiday is recommended, so leaving young Hannah and Robert at home with nurses, Edwin and Hannah Maria set off by first-class rail to Hastings, rather than by the tooth-rattling coach. Their lodgings have a sitting room, three good sized bedrooms, a maid to wait on them and meals provided, all for two guineas a week. Hannah Maria, wheezing with asthma, amuses herself by writing long chatty letters to her medical brother-in-law, Booth Eddison whom she admires. He knows her well; after all he was a witness at the birth of her children.

Three photographs of Edwin and a watercolour painted in 1861 by Sir John Gilbert R A [104] show a man shorter than average for the day. At twenty-three he was 5 foot 4¾ inches (half an inch taller than Booth) and weighed 9 stone 4 pounds. Short sighted, due to too much lucubration [105] in his youth, his kindly eyes can just be made out behind steel spectacles; there is tolerance in his expression and his face does not seem lined by his years of pain. His hair is thick, possibly fair, and he has an Abraham Lincoln, Quaker beard, exposing a strong dimpled chin.

There is a letter amongst the papers about the family portraits. Edwin writes to sister Elizabeth on 4 September 1837, saying that three paintings have just arrived at their house in Leeds; he is not sure if the one of his mother is the original or a copy but he waxes lyrical about the good likeness of Uncle Robert Booth's portrait:

The best I ever saw. My mother's is not equal but is very good. That of my Uncle William is a likeness but not good. The expression is hard, painful and deathlike and less of that mildness and intelligence which my Uncle William's countenance expressed than I should have liked. However I am glad that I have got them. My Uncle Robert's is without exception the most correct portraiture of life that I ever saw, one might suppose the very hairs of his head had been numbered. I now wish very much that I had a likeness of my father.

Edwin is now floored by another bout of ill health and the family take off for a holiday to Seaton Carew, near Hartlepool stopping at the Golden Fleece in Thirsk en-route. On their arrival Edwin writes to sister Ann, describing with

104 With Christopher Eddison.
105 A term used for studying late into the night by candle or lamplight.

Uncle Robert Booth (1764–1844), Ann Eddison's brother
'The most correct portraiture of life that I ever saw, one might suppose the
very hairs of his head had been numbered'

delight the colours of the sea and the fluttering sails at sunset but he is soon
fractious and snappy with ten year-old Robert William who is behaving badly.

While they are away Edwin's old mother begins to fail. She is suffering
from pleurisy and has forebodings about the future of Gateford. Then one
cold February evening in 1845 surrounded by her family and with the embers

flickering in her bedroom fireplace, Ann Eddison, the matriarch of Gateford House dies aged seventy-five.

Edwin is deeply upset. He had been close to his mother and during his childhood she had been the only person he could confide in. Although he often resented her tight hand on the family purse, she had a steadying influence and under her authority life at Gateford had run relatively smoothly. Now all is about to change.

Details of Ann's funeral, carefully preserved among the family papers give readers the feeling that they are among the mourners sharing in the rituals and the misery. Quakers did not normally go into mourning; their clothes would have been subdued enough not to make much difference but the Eddisons were not strict Quakers and it appears that they may have wanted to make something more of their mother's funeral.

There is a receipt from John Skelton of Worksop for '5 dozen funeral biscuits and 1 dozen ginger biscuits,' presumably for those who found the former unpleasant. Stemming from an old Viking tradition, funeral biscuits were

The receipt for the funeral biscuits
which smelt of ammonia

often given to guests or sent to absent friends along with funeral gloves. The biscuits were small rich finger-shaped sponge cakes smelling of ammonia or were sometimes round shortbread biscuits containing caraway seeds, often stamped with a heart motif, wrapped in white tissue paper and sealed with black sealing wax.

Quakers of course disapproved of the usual plume bearers and the hired mutes who walked with suitably woeful expressions in funeral processions, wearing black cloaks, sashes, top hats with drooping black hat-bands. It is not certain whether mutes were at Ann's funeral but the receipts from the trunk give the impression of a certain amount of finery:

The clocks would have been stopped at the hour of Ann's death, crepe draped on the front door, the windows, the mirrors and a twenty-four hour vigil would have been kept on the corpse because people feared being buried alive. Candles would have been lit around the room and vases filled with flowers for decoration and to suppress the smell. The future of the house had become uncertain but a decision was eventually made that until the whole estate was divided equally among the children, the farming was to be carried on by Henry, although there were worries about Henry's ability to cope. The letters cease for a while. Then in the autumn of 1858 Edwin has another brush with royalty when Leeds is swept up with fervour over the visit of Queen Victoria with Prince Albert and the Princesses Alice and Helena who were coming to open the opulent new Town Hall.

Leeds had flourished in the Industrial Revolution causing men to pour in to find work, which lead to poverty and overcrowding. Dickens called Leeds 'the beastliest place, one of the nastiest I know' even though the drainage system had been overhauled after the outbreak of cholera in 1831 [106]. Poor working conditions, bad housing and the intense pollution of the air had all contributed to a high death rate which was constantly rising and new cemeteries became targets for highly organised groups of body snatchers [107]. But industry boomed and in 1851 the competition for the new town hall was won by an unknown architect, Cuthbert Brodrick. Edwin as Town Clerk was keenly involved; he watched the building rise and was determined that the royal opening would be an outstanding success.

The Town Hall, built in a Parisian Neoclassical style touched with a dollop of English Baroque, became a model for municipal buildings throughout the Empire. The entrance vestibule was 70ft high with a domed ceiling supported by arches and separated from the large hall by a glass screen. The floor tiles were from a firm in Stoke on Trent whose workmen were simultaneously fixing tiles of the same design in the Senate House in Washington. In the centre of the vestibule there was a colossal white marble statue of Queen Victoria

---

106 Edwin's faithful doctor Charles Thackrah campaigned for a proper
     sewage system, causing the waste to be channelled into the river Aire near
     Temple Newsam.
107 Newly interred bodies had to be guarded for five weeks; the corpses being
     buried twelve feet down with iron staves at intervals immediately above
     the coffin.

by Matthew Noble which was presented to the Corporation by the Mayor, Peter Fairbairn.[108] The Great Hall was huge and was to be one of the noblest public rooms in the country. An engraving in the London Illustrated News shows a soaring cathedral-like interior festooned with vertiginous Victorian ornamentation. Designs were coloured by John Crace at the cost of £1,600, but he did not manage to finish his work in time, so some of the rooms were 'merely distempered with plain tints'. The woodwork in the dining room was painted to look like knotted oak and in the drawing room imitation walnut was 'admirably executed'. The organ was immense: the largest three-keyboard organ in Europe with 6,500 decorated pipes.

Leeds was all agog and elaborate preparations were made for the huge numbers expected to turn up. All available accommodation near the station was booked and great stands were erected. At the approach of the Royal train, the Royal Artillery fired guns to warn the restless crowds; umbrellas were sent for at the first drop of rain but as soon as the Royal Party appeared, the rain stopped. Excitement intensified and cheers bellowed forth as the train steamed into the station. The tiny Queen was helped onto the platform by a cluster of notables who all rushed forward at once, including the Earl of Derby, Sir Harry Smith and Peter Fairbairn the Mayor, whose long silvery beard and rich costume 'resembled a Doge of Venice'. As the Royal party were eased into their carriages the cheering renewed. *The London Illustrated News* graphically described the event, recording how 'the beaming Queen turned to the Prince Consort and said a few words and then happily waved her pretty hand to the crowds'.

The procession of carriages headed towards Woodsley House, the home of the ecstatic doge-like Mayor and the crowds waved hats and echoed 'Hurrahs' to each boom of the 21 guns. The Mayor shot ahead in his carriage to be at his mansion to welcome the royal party. Seven minutes passed before the military escort arrived with two hundred mounted soldiers and the Queen's party swept by and in a moment was out of sight.

The greatest scene along the whole route was at Woodhouse Moor where there was said to be a staggering choir of 29,000 children. On the banks of the reservoir stood a further crowd of 70,000 people while a bandsman conducted the singing and men held up huge boards on which were printed in large

108 After studying engineering in Manchester, London, Paris, Glasgow, he had opened a machinery manufacturing business in Leeds.

The royal party meeting the Mayor of Leeds 1858

letters PREPARE TO SING! SILENCE! and DISMISS! PREPARE
TO CHEER! was not needed when the royal party arrived as it was impossible to keep the children quiet. *The Illustrated London News*, 18 September
1858, described the noise:

> Nearly 30,000 little trebles set a-going are not so easily stopped: and
> some time elapsed before the shouts ceased, and the thundering bass
> accompaniment of the populace outside, mostly the parents of the
> children – went rumbling away in a hoarse roar in the distance.

The conductor then waved his hand and 'slowly swelling upwards like a vast organ of human voices', came 'God Save the Queen'. Her Majesty held up her hand and the carriage halted in the centre of the moor till the singing stopped. The lucky crowd had a prime view.

The Mayor, Peter Fairbairn, who was born of poor honest parents and who had had very little education, made lavish improvements to his house for the royal party who were staying with him overnight. He was soon to be knighted. Edwin organised a great feast for the masses at the Town Hall of plum pudding and ale and wrote a jolly poem to be sung to the tune of 'Hunt the Hare'

Some future story of Leeds in her glory
Will tell of the time when Sir Peter was Mayor
How with beard like Mahomet he outshone the comet
And made all the wondering universe stare.
Nor shall Adel's renown be without its due crown
But fame shall record the magnificent tale
Of Queen's visit Festival science and best of all
Eddison's feast of plum pudding and ale.

16

Climbing Boys and Sad Sale at Gateford

When my mother died I was very young,
And my father sold me while yet my tongue
Could scarcely cry 'weep, weep, weep, weep.'
So your chimneys I sweep and in soot I sleep.
William Blake, *Songs of Innocence*

Thumbing through dull-looking legal documents among the family papers, some blue tissue-thin copies of business letters headed 'Climbing Boys' caught my attention. How was Edwin involved in the murky world of child chimney sweeps? The letters I discovered were addressed to a Peter Hall who had been a climbing boy from the age of six and was now an agent for the Climbing Boys' Society.

Chimney sweeping by very young children in the eighteenth century was taken for granted and, although by 1819 it had been proved that all but a few difficult chimneys could be better swept by machinery, people were resistant to change and many insisted that the practice of using children to sweep chimneys was still the best method. The Chimney Sweepers Act of 1840 prohibited child apprentices under the age of sixteen and forbade the climbing of flues by anyone under twenty-one. But by 1860 the number of children bought and sold as sweeps was increasing. There were terrible accidents. Children had to harden their flesh by rubbing their elbows and knees with salt which took years to become effective and they hardly ever had baths so their skin was blackened and often covered with suppurating sores. Soot causing cancer of the private parts was one of the many afflictions, and the

The Poor Little Sweep!

Edwin was involved in helping climbing boys

terror of unknown dangers was always present. Children could get wedged, suffocated by fumes and sadly were often burnt.

An Act of Parliament in 1864 tightened controls significantly. Lord Shaftesbury established the maximum penalty for a master sweep found employing children under sixteen at £10 and the minimum penalty at £5. But the abuse went on and children as young as four were still being trained, six being 'a nice trainable age'. Masters would take a child into a house to carry the brushes, then once the door was shut, they would furtively force them up the chimney. Magistrates were slow to convict as offences were often committed in their own houses and unless the boy died in the chimney the offence could be difficult to substantiate.

Sensational evidence was given by Peter Hall who had been in the business for forty years when he followed two boys to Wimpole Hall in Cambridgeshire and spoke with the servants of the house. He then took out a summons on Lord Hardwicke's housekeeper who had allowed the boys in. But the local magistrate said that he would sooner fine himself than his friend, the owner of the house, and Peter Hall was then stigmatised by Lord Hardwicke as a public informer.

Edwin was involved in helping climbing boys because Peter Hall had brought a case before York Magistrates over a master sweep's fine of a 'trifling amount' and Lord Shaftesbury asked Edwin to appeal against this. Writing to the clerk of the magistrates to find out more about the case, Edwin warned that the Act required a minimum fine of £5, an amount far greater than they had imposed. He wrote to Peter Hall saying that he had dealt with similar cases of these 'poor little fellows' and also that Lord Shaftesbury must appreciate that magistrates were unwilling to convict. He stressed that it was important not to relax the present law.

Edwin, extremely busy with his work, now had to consider what was to be done about his indolent elder brother, Henry. Immediately after his mother's death in 1845, Henry had been appointed one of the three Commissioners of the Enclosures of Nottinghamshire but was not coping with his personal life (drink being mainly the problem) and found it impossible to manage affairs at Gateford. His sister, Mary came from Finthorpe House, near Huddersfield to help from time to time and assisted her brother William to compile the inventory of the contents of the house for probate. His unmarried sisters, Ann and Elizabeth arrived from Toothill Hall to help, but the house was so full of stress that they soon left for Scarborough with headaches.

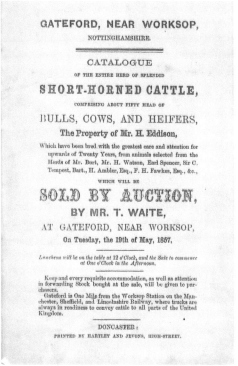

GATEFORD, NEAR WORKSOP,
NOTTINGHAMSHIRE.

CATALOGUE
OF THE ENTIRE HERD OF SPLENDID
SHORT-HORNED CATTLE,
COMPRISING ABOUT FIFTY HEAD OF
BULLS, COWS, AND HEIFERS,
The Property of Mr. H. Eddison,
Which have been bred with the greatest care and attention for upwards of Twenty Years, from animals selected from the Herds of Mr. Burt, Mr. H. Watson, Earl Spencer, Sir C. Tempest, Bart., H. Ambler, Esq., F. H. Fawkes, Esq., &c.,
WHICH WILL BE
SOLD BY AUCTION,
BY MR. T. WAITE,
AT GATEFORD, NEAR WORKSOP,
On Tuesday, the 19th of May, 1857,
Luncheon will be on the table at 12 o'Clock, and the Sale to commence at One o'Clock in the Afternoon.

Keep and every requisite accommodation, as well as attention in forwarding Stock bought at the sale, will be given to purchasers.
Gateford is One Mile from the Worksop Station on the Manchester, Sheffield, and Lincolnshire Railway, where trucks are always in readiness to convey cattle to all parts of the United Kingdom.

DONCASTER:
PRINTED BY HARTLEY AND JEVONS, HIGH-STREET.

Henry Eddison was reluctant to change his habits

There was further sadness in the spring of 1857 when '*The Entire Herd of Splendid Short-Horned Cattle, Bulls, Cows, and Heifers*' had to be sold. The sale catalogue shows impressive pedigrees, some eight generations long, with descriptive names for the cows such as Sprightly, Useful, Cactus and Ringlet.

Henry muddles along and quite enjoys being looked after by his sister Mary Dougill and her nineteen year old daughter Libby. He complains of cramp and asks pretty young Libby to rub him with something hot, then he asks her to wash his face and neck, but she baulks at having to shave the naughty old man. There is great worry about what to do with him. The Machins have indicated that they need the house.

Henry must have felt useless and offers to go with his dying brother Booth and his family who are travelling to Madeira. Unwilling to be burdened, Booth says no, and warns his brother to change his habits; knowing that the pains in Henry's arms are due to liver disease, he advises him to have warm

Mary and Libbie Dougill outside Finthorpe House, Almondbury,
drawing by Sarah Pashley

baths, regular exercise, proper food and early hours – a regime Henry was very unlikely to follow.

Edwin's children are now at school. Robert William and Francis are packed off to Benjamin Abbot's Academy, a school in Hitchin for rich Quakers. Abbot the founder was a friend of Faraday [109] and science was an important subject on the curriculum. Uncle Benjamin Tatham who lived in Hitchin was a friend of the local Ransom [110] and Lucas families and it is likely that he would have known other Quakers in the area, the Sharples, Tukes, and Seebohms.

Edwin's boys enjoy the school and write happily home for skates and plants for the school garden. They are soon joined by Booth Eddison's sons, Arthur and Alfred. Meanwhile the Dougill cousins Libby and Polly are at Polam Hall, Darlington, an expensive school costing 50 guineas a year (said to be five times more than other Quaker schools.) [111]

109 Michael Faraday FRS 1791–1867, English scientist who contributed to the fields of electromagnetism and electrochemistry.

110 William Ransom 1826–1913, founder of the UK's oldest independent pharmaceutical company.

111 The previous owner of Polam Hall was a distant relation, Jonathan Backhouse 1779–1842, whose father, a banker, married Hannah Gurney.

John Fowler of Leeds.
Inventor of the steam plough

The steam engine moves the plough backwards
and forwards across the field

Dan Woodall with Fowler traction engine

Francis Eddison's Steam Works in Dorchester c. 1885

On leaving school, Edwin's eldest son Robert enters his father's legal firm which he hates, so after a trip to America, he joins the agricultural engineering firm of John Fowler & Co. in Leeds and becomes a partner. John Fowler (1826–1864), born into a rich Quaker family from Melksham in Wiltshire, was destined to become a corn merchant like his father, but in 1845 his life was transformed by a harrowing visit to Ireland with fellow Quakers to help those devastated by the potato famine. He wanted to ease the dreadful situation and, realising that the current method of ploughing was too slow, he invented the steam-driven ploughing engine [112]. Much of his early equipment was made in Bristol in partnership with fellow Quaker, Albert Fry of the chocolate making family.

112 After years of experimenting he won the RASE trials held in Chester in 1858 with a portable engine manufactured by Robert Stephenson. The anchor carriage on the opposite headland allowed the engine to draw the ploughing implement backwards and forward across the field

John Fowler married Elizabeth Lucy Pease, daughter of the railway pioneer, Joseph Pease and Emma Gurney. He suffered a nervous breakdown and died of tetanus after a hunting accident in 1864. After his death, John Fowler & Co. was run by his brother, Robert Fowler in partnership with Robert Eddison. The firm was a world leader of steam powered land cultivation and later began production of locomotives, exporting to countries including Mexico and India. Fowler & Co. was the parent firm of Eddison Plant Ltd, established by another of Edwin's sons, Francis Eddison, who began his Steam Ploughing Works in Dorchester with John Fowler engines in 1870. He later moved to Fordington, a village near Dorchester which was extremely close to Thomas Hardy's house at Max Gate. The Eddison Steam Works are alluded to in Hardy's book' *The Mayor of Casterbridge* and the early morning works whistle was said to frequently exasperate the writer.

When Thomas Hardy died in 1928 he had two funerals: one in Westminster Abbey and another in the churchyard of his forebears where his heart was buried in a casket. Norman Stephens, Hardy's gardener, describing the time of Hardy's death writes: 'The hearse for the removal of the heart-casket arrived at about 7.55am … at 8.00am the solemn stillness was broken by the shrill call of Eddison's steam roller factory siren – a memorable noise at such a solemn moment…'.

17
Death of Edwin's Brother Booth and the Adoption of Bicycles

To array a man's will against his sickness is the supreme art of medicine.
Henry Ward Beecher

For a doctor, strangely in denial about the exact nature of his illness, Booth Eddison decides to sail with his wife and children to Madeira in January 1859. He hopes to be soothed by the benign climate, but just before the ship Eclipse sails from Portsmouth an irritating letter arrives from his brother, Henry who is longing to join them. Exasperated at this complication, Booth dashes off a letter from his cabin gently discouraging the idea as he is too preoccupied with his own troubles. He knows his fun-loving brother is not well which worries him, so he fills his letter with medical advice knowing very well that the alcoholic Henry will ignore it.

Booth Eddison FRCS

As he sets off for Portsmouth Booth notices an ominous swelling below his left ankle, which spreads to his feet, legs, hands and thighs as the voyage progresses. He is filled with dread and when the family arrive in Funchal all he can do is lie in a hammock soaking up the warm air which is blissful after the chill of Nottingham. At breakfast he rejoices in the cool morning breeze, exclaiming 'Oh! How delightful! This balmy air feels more like life to me.' The eminent Dr Lund, a specialist in tubercular diseases lives in Funchal which is helpful as Booth knows that tuberculosis is the chief part of his troubles.

Dr Lund calls immediately and diagnoses congestion of the kidneys which Booth had never suspected. Taking Eliza aside, Lund whispers to ask her to

The family tree of Booth Eddison

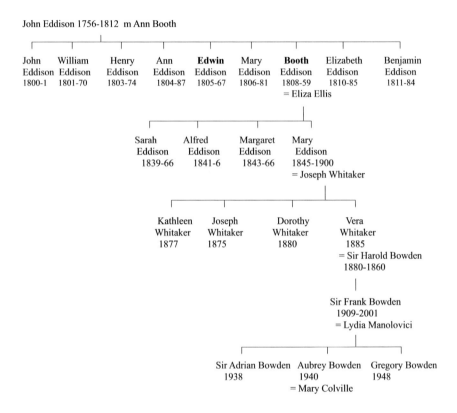

John Eddison 1756-1812 m Ann Booth

| John Eddison 1800-1 | William Eddison 1801-70 | Henry Eddison 1803-74 | Ann Eddison 1804-87 | **Edwin** Eddison 1805-67 | Mary Eddison 1806-81 | **Booth** Eddison 1808-59 = Eliza Ellis | Elizabeth Eddison 1810-85 | Benjamin Eddison 1811-84 |

Sarah Eddison 1839-66   Alfred Eddison 1841-6   Margaret Eddison 1843-66   Mary Eddison 1845-1900 = Joseph Whitaker

Kathleen Whitaker 1877   Joseph Whitaker 1875   Dorothy Whitaker 1880   Vera Whitaker 1885 = Sir Harold Bowden 1880-1860

Sir Frank Bowden 1909-2001 = Lydia Manolovici

Sir Adrian Bowden 1938   Aubrey Bowden 1940 = Mary Colville   Gregory Bowden 1948

save a little of his urine which he needs to examine. When he has gone Booth, who had been listening intently, hastily boils up some himself and is shocked to find an immense quantity of albumen. He knows things are far more serious than the pulmonary disease and realises that it could be the dreaded dropsy, or Brights Disease of the kidneys, a disease only discovered by Richard Bright in 1827, which certainly means a premature death. He knows that there is no cure and that his friends Watson and Gurney died of the same illness. Resigned to this wretchedness he writes long letters full of mournful farewells from his bed where he is enjoying the 'zephyrs and fragrant breezes.' Back at Gateford they are all shocked to hear he is sinking fast and that his recovery is doubtful.

Booth, the seventh child, was born at Gateford in the spring of 1808. He was bright and was reading well at the age of five. At ten he wrote to Edwin about his pigeons and Venter the dog mentioning brother William stuffing little birds:

I now take the opportunity of writing to thee. There are thirteen pigeons and I hope they will begin to breed soon but it is too cold for them yet. Cousin John Aldam has given Ben and me a knife each. William came home last Wednesday and he shot 26 little birds and a crow, he took 6 of them back with him to stuff. [113] *Venter is very well I think I have no more to say, a man that lived at the sand hill has been stealing coal from Ramoth and he is put in prison…*
I am thy aff bro Booth Eddison

A letter written in 1819 when he was eleven gives a vivid picture of life at Gateford. He tells of the jollities of Gateford Feast, the broiling of sparrows, and William stuffing again. Did they really eat sparrows?

Dear Brother,
When I wrote to thee last the Pigeons were breeding very fast but they have stopped and there is none but what can fly about … I have not killed any of the wood pigeons yet, they begin to look so pretty … I dare say Brother William will like a pair of them to stuff. We caught Betty Wards' cat on the wall plate in our kitchen one morning, we put Venter up and he soon fetched her down but as soon as she got out of the kitchen she was out of our sight and I have not seen her more than once or twice since then. I have almost got through my Latin Grammer I expect thou learns Latin too. I dare say thou has thought a great deal about Gateford feast. Ben and I went with the coursers they did not kill one hare and only one rabbit. There was a dancing at Gateford feast in Mr Smiths Kiln at night. Our Bill and I caught eleven sparrows on Friday night we intend to have a broil some night I wish thou could partake of them along with us … Cousin Benjamin hired a man at Retford Fair I believe he is a very queer one for they tell me that he stammers very much and that he is a drunkard. I do not think that we shall like him so well as we have liked George… from Thy Aff Brother Booth Eddison

113 He would have used a clumsy fowling piece because the shotgun, although invented in 1820, was not commonly used until 1840.

At the age of twelve Booth went to Tatham's boarding school in smoky Leeds where the numbers had dwindled alarmingly and standards had dropped. He is then sent to Isaac Brown's Academy the excellent Quaker School in Hitchin where Joseph Lister [114] had been sent to board at the tender age of five. Future pupils of the school were Myles Birket Foster RA, Joseph Pollard, botanist, the polymath William Ransom and the Barclays. Booth's passion for botany was fired at this school and at the age of seventeen, in his 1825 copy of *The Compendium Florae Britanicae* [115] he has translated the complete text from Latin on the 205 facing pages in his beautiful handwriting. His great interest in botany was closely linked with the herbal remedies of the day and in a box of old family books in the Bedale attics was his copy of the *Miscellaneous Tracts Relating to Natural History, Husbandry, and Physick, with the Calendar of Flora* [116] which contained a carefully pressed stem of Silver Hair Grass and meticulous text corrections. There was also a handsome leather-bound volume recording his library of books, many of which later lay scattered amongst the junk in the attics.

The distance to the school in Hitchin from home was about 100 miles; twelve dusty, bumping, rattling hours of discomfort by stagecoach, covering about 40 miles a day with twelve horse changes along the way. Luckily Gateford was only six miles from the Great North Road where Booth caught the coach but the journey was fraught with dangers. Highwaymen lurked along the route and top heavy coaches occasionally toppled over. Ann would have been unlikely to allow the boy to sit on top with the luggage. Inside it was warmer, but the seats were narrow and rank with the human stench of bodies.

I visited the 18th century building, now The Lord Lister Hotel, which once housed the school and the low ceilinged rooms and long corridors of bedrooms were redolent of studious Quaker boys. Nearby was Benjamin Abbot's Academy where the next generation of Eddisons were educated.

When Booth was fourteen, the guardian uncles talked of him going into the wool trade but Edwin, Benjamin and Mr Tatham objected. They knew the

---

114 Joseph Lister OM, FRC, PC, pioneer of antiseptic surgery.

115 S. W. archive.

116 Benjamin Stillingfleet, 1702–1771, *The Compendium Florae Britanicae*. Unable to afford black silk stockings, Stillingfleet wore everyday blue worsted ones while attending a literary society founded primarily for women. This was said to be the derivation of Blue Stocking, a name applied to a learned woman.

boy had a good brain and Edwin suggested that he should stay on at school until he was sixteen, thinking that he was still too small and too young for an apprenticeship. We know from Edwin's chart that Booth at twenty was quite short: 5ft 4½ ins tall, weighing 8 stone 10lbs. However he leaves school at fourteen and in 1822 begins his illustrious medical career. After a five-year apprenticeship at the General Hospital in Nottingham, he goes to St George's and Westminster Hospitals in London and then from 1827–1829 he is a student at St Bartholomews under the great Dr Abernethy and he also studies under Richard Owen, the founder of the hospital's medical school and the expert in palaeontology who introduced us to dinosaurs. It was Owen who convinced the Government of the need for a Natural History Museum.

Booth also studied at the London Ophthalmic Infirmary. He passed the exams of the College of Surgeons of Edinburgh; the Society of Apothecaries in London and spent five years as Resident Surgeon to the General Hospital, Nottingham, after which he studied at the Lying-in Hospital in Dublin and the medical schools of Paris. Then he started a practice in Leeds, which must have delighted Edwin and Hannah Maria, but remained there only for a few months having had an offer of partnership from Mr John Higginbottom of Nottingham. This partnership continued till he had his own practice in Nottingham in 1842. He sought to become honorary surgeon to Nottingham hospital but was defeated by Mr Henry Attenburrow, whose father had previously filled the same office for fifty-four years. In 1850, Booth was more successful.

His qualifications are recorded in The Medical Directory 1859:

Licentiate of the Royal College of Surgeons in Edinburgh, 1823 (aged 15)

Licentiate of the Royal College of Apothecaries of London 1829 (aged 21)

Fellow of the Royal College of Surgeons of England (exam) 1844 (aged 36)

Booth was highly regarded and, at the pinnacle of his career became the President of the British Medical Association in 1857. But before this he became a visiting surgeon and Proprietor of Broom House Private Asylum at Mansfield, described in White's 1853 Directory as 'being a spacious mansion, surrounded by gardens and pleasure grounds, fitted up with every convenience

and comfort for treatment, more especially
the cure of ladies of unsound mind superin-
tended by Booth Eddison Esq of Nottingham'.
Booth's nephew Robert William Eddison told
my grandfather, Francis Eddison that he was
always frightened that mad ladies might get
loose while he waited for his uncle.

At the age of twenty-nine Booth married
Miss Eliza Ellis of Mansfield in the Old Friends
Meeting House in Quaker Lane. In a silhouette of the young pair Eliza looks the taller,
her high poke bonnet towering over Booth's
top hat. Another silhouette [117] shows Booth in
a handsome high collar, with neat wispy hair
and just the tiniest of spectacles. A concurrent photograph shows his intense
expression, determined mouth and untidy hair.

Booth and Eliza Eddison

Booth Eddison, President of the BMA
1857 by Sir John Gilbert RA 1857

Eliza Eddison and her daughter Mary
by Sir John Gilbert RA 1857

117 The two silhouettes in the author's possession.

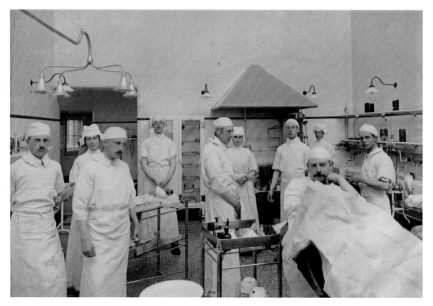

Edith Eddison had a sucessful nursing career. She is seen (centre) assisting
Sir George Makin in the operating theatre at St Thomas's Hospital in 1906

For the first three years of their marriage Booth and Eliza lived with her widowed mother, Sarah in Belvedere Street, Mansfield but later moved to Stoney Street, Nottingham. Six years later when Booth was a GP they lived at 29 High Pavement in Nottingham. The house, built in 1820, was said to have the finest brickwork in England; the bricks had been soaked for two weeks for damp-proofing and smoothed with sandpaper; the mortar passed through a hair sieve. Their last home in Nottingham was in The Park.

Booth and Eliza had four children in eight years, Sarah Anne, Alfred, Margaret and Mary. Booth's great-great grandson Aubrey Bowden, has portraits of Booth and Eliza, painted in 1857 by Sir John Gilbert RA, who later painted Edwin and Hannah Maria in 1861. In her portrait, Eliza Eddison is holding her daughter Mary who is wearing a white shawl over a plain black dress, pinned with a little spray of flowers and she is clutching her Dutch doll dressed in black and white in a Quakerly way.

Booth may have initiated the Eddison medical tradition. He would have been proud of his niece, Edith Eddison, a brave matron in a Dublin hospital during the Irish troubles, who was awarded the Royal Red Cross by Queen Alexandra and later met Florence Nightingale. Several other Eddisons qualified as doctors, although a few opted out of the profession. Two of these were

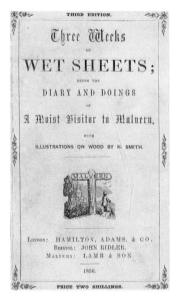

A humorous account of Joseph Leech's visit to Malvern for a water cure in 1853

Florence Nightingale, Charles Darwin and Booth Eddison were treated by Dr Gully

The notorious Dr Gully

Robert Eddison OBE opted out of the medical profession to become an actor

Robert as the Grail Knight in Indiana Jones and the Last Crusade

Martin and Sydney Eddison. Martin took up engineering after studying medicine at Cambridge

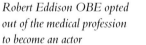

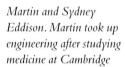

my uncle Martin Eddison (1920–2005) who became an engineer and a cousin, Robert Eddison OBE (1908–1991), who had a successful acting career.

Booth became ill shortly after becoming President of the BMA and from then on his health declined steadily. His obituary declares that 'though he was fit, temperate in his diet and an early riser, his illness was through his working too hard.' Desperate to get better he tried changes of scenery: first Devon, then Italy. He consulted experts, even going to see the notorious homoeo-path James Manby Gully who treated Charles Darwin, George Eliot, William Gladstone, Samuel Wilberforce and Florence Nightingale [118]. Gully's ridiculously simple treatment was to wake his patients at 5am, wrap them in wet sheets and then cover them in blankets. An hour later buckets of water were thrown over them; they then went for a five mile walk with an alpenstock and a flask of mineral water, stopping at wells to drink the local water. Much of the day was spent bathing and sometimes they wore a wet sheet called the 'Neptune Girdle' round their middle, removing it only at mealtimes which usually consisted of boiled mutton or fish, followed by a few hours in a dry bed. If they survived this without catching cold, the cure was deemed successful.

Back at Gateford, Booth's sisters huddle together reading Eliza's latest letter telling them that their brother is sinking fast and that Dr Lund thinks recovery is doubtful, which Booth has already guessed. Congestion of the kidneys has ended all hope. The swelling extends so much that he is unable to rise from his chair without help. A hair mattress is dragged into the garden where he can lie surrounded by the scent of flowers and birdsong. Sometimes he lies on the sofa in his soft 'wrapping gown'. He has little appetite and the letters unnecessarily describe distressing flatulence. He eats chicken jelly, light bread puddings, arrow root and on the very last day he has some chicken broth and a few spoonfuls of jelly with the juice of an orange. Kind Portuguese friends send delicacies: calves-foot jelly, strawberries, sweetmeats and proper turtle soup.

After several bad nights a tepid bath refreshes him but feeling that his end is near, he quietly says to his wife 'I think I find comfort in Jesus, I believe there is a mansion prepared for me in Heaven, but I do not like or wish to speak too

118 Writing to her cousin, Hilary Bonham Carter, in 1851 she describes Gully as a genius, and in one of her notebooks she writes 'The water-cure: a highly popular amusement amongst athletic invalids who have felt the *tedium vitae...*' *The Life of Florence Nightingale* by E.T.Cook 1914.

Booth's granddaughter Vera Whitaker,
who married Sir Harold Bowden
Painting by Denholm Davies

Vera painted her father-in-law Sir Frank
Bowden who turned a small firm in
Nottingham into the Raleigh Cycle Company

confidently, I hope we shall all meet there.' He finds it a blessing to have his family around him.

There is a vivid description of Booth's last day in Eliza's long letter. After a good night Booth begins to ramble and imagines he sees figures up at the top of the bed and indicates that he wants to be lifted up. 'Do lift me up. Don't you see them? I want to go. Oh help me up there, 'tis not far.' Then he quietly says 'Mother'. The children thought he saw her. Again he implores them to lift him up and he tries to raise himself calling out to his son, Alfred to come and help but falls back with exhaustion and soon his speech is unintelligible.

To ease his misery the children stand around the bed singing hymns. When they stop he urges them on again, his face beaming with peace. Then his breathing alters. His eyes become dull and he appears calmer. Eliza and the children can only tell that he has died by noticing the blood draining from his lips and the pallid change in his complexion. He dies at 4 o'clock on 7 March 1859 with a sweet peaceful expression on his face.

Dr Lund conducts a grim post mortem before the funeral which reveals general tubercular infiltration of both lungs with cavities in each, enlarge-

Booth Eddison's granddaughter Vera wrote a letter to Dr Francis Eddison just after the second World War, in which she describes going to Shireoaks Hall and fishing for crayfish in the lovely cascades that flowed into the lake in front of the Hall

ment of both kidneys and an oily liver. It was said that he died of phthisis (tuberculosis), the disease rife among the Booths. The funeral takes place two days later and Eliza, extremely distressed, is helped by two kind friends who arrange everything. They choose a plain coffin of chestnut with his initials and age on the lid.

There was an English cemetery nearby and as most of their friends were members of the 'Scotch Church' they decide to have a simple Presbyterian service. At a later service they gather up a number of friends, along with twelve of the principal British residents, the British Consul among them.

Almost inevitably in such a close family, tuberculosis spreads further. Two years later Booth's only son, nineteen year-old Alfred dies; two years after that his fifty-four year-old wife Eliza; then three years later, the daughters Margaret and Sarah Anne die within a month of each other, which their Uncle Edwin, nearing his own end, finds immensely distressing.

Booth's youngest daughter Mary escaped the scourge and lived until 1900. She married Joseph Whitaker, a well known naturalist and author in 1872 and

THE RALEIGH FACTORY

they lived at Rainworth Lodge near Blidworth, where Joseph bred and studied water-fowl.

Vera Whitaker, Booth's granddaughter, an amateur painter, ornithologist, fine horsewoman and an outstanding shot with gun, rifle and pistol, taught riding and shooting to Yeomanry recruits in 1914. She married Sir Harold Bowden in 1908, whose father the first baronet, Sir Frank Bowden, had gone to Hong Kong as a young lawyer where he amassed a considerable fortune. Retiring with a bad heart at the age of thirty-five, he went to live in France. His doctor advised him to take up bicycling for the sake of his health, which he did, and as well as buying his first bicycle he also bought a small firm in Nottingham where 12 men were producing three bicycles a week which he turned into the Raleigh Cycle Company. It became the biggest bicycle manufacturer in the world, employing 12,000 people in Nottingham and producing more than a million bicycles a year.

18

Two Weddings
and a Doctorate

Her parents held the Quaker rule,
Which doth the human feeling cool,
But she was trained in Nature's school,
Nature had blessed her.

Charles Lamb, *Hester*

After hurrying across the Atlantic in one of the new steam ships, twenty-one year-old Robert, Edwin's eldest son, writes home from America in 1856: 'I crossed the ocean safely and had a very pleasant passage of 12 days. There was nothing to attract attention except a few hundred porpoises and two or three whales…'

Edwin thought that after spending a few years articled to him, Robert was finding sedentary office work was not what he wanted to do, so it was arranged that Robert should spend a year travelling in the United States and Canada. He was to stay with his mother's cousin, Henry Billington Tatham who, with three of his brothers, had started a lead-pipe business in 1840 and who now owned a house in Brooklyn and a deserted island off the coast of Philadelphia.

That summer the Tathams are renting a house in the county where Robert shoots grouse, prairie chicken and rail, a bird like a corncrake, which lived in the sides of the river Delaware. After shooting seventy-one birds in twenty minutes, he says that it should be called murder rather than shooting. Six hundred birds were killed every day and still as many seemed to be left for more shooting. Young Robert likes the friendly, inquisitive, communicative Americans but finds the country grand and imposing and quite different from England. He writes: 'What they call cultivation we should call neglect.'

There is excitement about the Presidential election. Staunch Republicans, the Tathams fear that if their candidate, John Fremont fails to win there will be civil war. Fremont is beaten by James Buchanan and, as they thought, the

Civil War breaks out in 1861 and in the next four years 620,000 American lives will be lost.

Robert loves his visit although he finds the cousins are a bit young for him. The Tathams show him various sights leaving him to make a solitary trip to the Niagara Falls where, feeling bleak and insignificant, he longs to have someone with him 'to hear the wild noise of the water; to sense the danger and to watch the staggering spray.' Perhaps his thoughts are dwelling on the intelligent thirteen year-old Anna Paulina Tatham.

Robert is fascinated by American agricultural engineering and on returning home this burgeoning interest brings him into contact with the Quaker John Fowler (of steam plough fame) with whom he becomes close friend and collaborator, devoting the rest of his life to the growth of the Fowler Steam Plough Works in Leeds as a partner and director.

In 1860 the Tathams come to England and a happy jaunt to Scotland is arranged for Charles Billington Tatham, his wife and their children, Mary and Benjamin who are joined by Edwin's children, Hannah and John Edwin. In a red marbled notebook labelled, *Botanical Notes of a Journey in Scotland July 1860* Hannah has pasted some dried flowers and noted the places they visited. She may have secretly been in love with Charles Middleton, the man she will marry in 1862. On the last page, entered two years later, there is a sprig from her wedding cake. On the next page, presumably from the honeymoon in Flamborough Head, there is a dismal looking flower.

Hannah, Edwin's only daughter was difficult. Letters comment that 'she requires great care' and 'Hannah is very well for her'. Few of her letters were among the papers but an explosive letter written in 1865 reveals quite a bit about the problems in her marriage. Hannah had been tiresome in the years before her marriage. Her mother said that no illness could excuse her rudeness or the provocative things she said to her parents. A photograph portrays an attractive but obstinate young girl in a spotted silk dress with a feathered fan in her hand. Her large eyes are like those of her namesake grandmother, Hannah Baker; her hair is sleeked behind her ears from a central parting and her determined mouth is not quite smiling.

She may have given up all hope of marriage, but at the age of twenty-eight she fell in love with the thirty-four year-old curate, Charles Henry Middleton in Scarborough. This was scandalous as the pair had not been introduced and Hannah may even have made the first move. The Eddisons knew nothing about the Middleton family and hastily made enquiries about the curate.

*Hannah Eddison 'an attractive
but obstinate young girl'*

*The Rev. Charles Middleton
caused a family row*

Cuthbert Middleton aged six

*Cuthbert Dallas Middleton-Wake
died in Cornwall cared for by his butler*

Charles took offence at this and tensions boiled up, particularly over money matters.

The six Eddison brothers took an instant dislike to the man and one wonders why. His fine-boned face has a stern expression; his hair is combed over his brow and an impressive cascade of side-whiskers, known as Dundrearies, sprout around his jaw. He could well have been red haired and he may have been too intellectual for the Eddisons. The Middleton family came from the Durham area and Charles's father was vicar of Melbourne, Derbyshire, having previously been chaplain to the Duke of Devonshire.

The couple did not want their marriage to be delayed but Charles had not found a proper living and was a mere Chaplain to Armley Prison and the Leeds Infirmary. Later on his career would take an interesting turn. The wedding takes place in the rain at Adel Church in early June 1862. Nineteen year-old cousin, Anne Eddison (daughter of Uncle Benjamin of Shireoaks) writing to eighteen year-old Mary Radley [119] excitedly describes the cheerful family gatherings, walks, drives, tea parties and dances. The day before the wedding they all help to decorate the barn. The stage is decorated in 'grand style' with space for the musicians to play on a platform above. Brother Frank scrubs the stage with soft soap and white material is swathed on the walls. Cousin Libbie Dougill soaks armfuls of flowers in buckets of water while others work furiously till 1am. Up at 5am with still more to do, they race through breakfast, make up the bouquets and then rush off to dress. Meanwhile the parents of the bride and Miss Godby, one of the bridesmaids arrive. Cousin Anne Eddison dresses in her white bridesmaid outfit with its delicate transparent bodice and the hem of her skirt trimmed with pink. The finishing touches are a matching scarf and pink hawthorn pinned on her bonnet – the whole outfit 'engagingly tinged with pink' writes cousin Anne in her letter to Mary Radley.

There is a hush when the nervous bride arrives at the church in her white silk dress, the Honiton lace veil fastened to her hair by a pearl brooch. 'She did look nice – like an 'hangel' comments one admiring helper. It is unseasonably cold for June and the three bridesmaids, Anne, Libbie and Miss Godby shiver in their carriage waiting for the bride's carriage to appear. Hannah is exceptionally nervous: '*she is so delicate*' so her bridesmaids precede her down the aisle in a protective triangle as it is feared she might faint if she goes in front.

---

119 Mary Radley of Manor House, Beighton, Sheffield was the sister of Vessey Radley who married Robert Eddison of Shireoaks.

*Cousin Anne Eddison, whose album
turned up on the internet (see Chapter 4)*

The sky grows greyer, the rain pours down and the pink hawthorn sags. There
are no umbrellas at hand so they are all drenched walking down the long path
to Adel Church. After the service, eight or nine clattering carriages take sod-
den guests to the bride's home at Headingley for the reception. Anne's letter
captures the mood:

> *There was such a gabble in the drawing room and at last we all got to the dining
> room where the tables were covered with her presents – she has had quantities, dear
> creature. Then the breakfast was ready which was in a marquee in the garden, so
> off we popped in pairs through the French window and took our places, a fellow*

calling out Mr Schunck[120], and Miss Dougill, Mr Simpson and Miss A. Eddison,
Mr Frederick Eddison and Miss Godby and so on till all the company were gone.
The tables were arranged beautifully – the flowers were lovely. The bride had her
veil fastened back which looked like a Spanish head-dress. There was not much
speechifying. Mary Eddison, Frank, myself then set off to Adel. I took off my attire
and went with Frank into the barn and set to work to make some letters in spruce.
His name, her maiden name, a ring, his name and her name now. I put on my
wedding dress again, which I looped up with ribbon for the dancing (for we had
all ¼ yard train – they looked very pretty) The ladies were at a premium for there
were all Uncle's clerks from his office and gentlemen friends and his 6 sons. There
were nearly 200 men women and children We began with a country dance at about
9 o'clock when the place was lighted up, it was a pretty scene I assure you. After we
had been dancing, some of the Irish danced reels, sang comic songs and so passed
the time until shortly after 11 when our party departed to Headingley amidst
deafening cheers. We danced the Lancers, polkas, schottisches, waltz gallop and
Sir Roger de Coverley. I danced with a Mr Williams, Ottie, (Octavius Eddison)
Marshall, Ford (a slow coach) Fred, and Frank; Ottie is about Charlie's age and
he dances so nicely, he is a dear little fellow. Oh by the bye I danced with Mr
Schunck (pronounced Shoonk), then my man Simpson took his departure in the
afternoon and I was not sorry for I did not care for him much. He was a widower
with a little boy 7 years old. On arriving at Headingley aunt was poorly, Robert
William lame, Fred with a strained ankle and everybody dreadfully tired. Now
goodbye dear Mary, it's 11 pm so goodnight. I hear George snoring.

The honeymoon was spent at Flamborough Head where the previous year a
696 ton iron ship, *The Prince Alfred* had been wrecked, scattering the coast with
its cargo which included 150 casks of paraffin. It is a bleak spot, even in summer, and not a brilliant place to start a stormy marriage.

Maybe Charles knew he was marrying a difficult woman. He felt the Eddisons had money and probably thought he could cope with anything; Hannah
was evidently in love with him but the six Eddison brothers made Charles

---

120 Edward Baron von Schunck 1816–1861 a successful Yarn and Stuff
     Merchant who married Kate Lupton in 1867. He rented The Willows,
     Adel from the Eddisons,.

uneasy at family gatherings with their ironic Yorkshire jibes. Having been to Cambridge Charles was on a different plane.

Sixteen months after the wedding Hannah became pregnant with Cuthbert their only child. Two months before the birth, Charles, desperately worried about his wife's behaviour, had a meeting with his father-in-law, Edwin. He needs money and complains about the way he has been treated by the family and asks Edwin to leave his daughter the same amount (£2,000) that he is leaving to her brothers.

Edwin is speechless. Hannah Maria sits down to compose a long letter to Charles saying how grieved she is to hear of the interview with her husband. She says that it is very unlikely that Edwin said that he would leave each child £2,000 and points out that

> ...he only hoped to leave them that amount but he needs to leave provision for his wife and has too much knowledge of people richer than himself being unable to predict what they would leave at their death.

Charles writes back saying that he needs money now to furnish their house and they also need an income of £100 a year. Outrageously he suggests that the Eddisons can afford this as he thought Hannah Maria had brought Edwin a fortune on their marriage. Hannah Maria expostulates that he was never more mistaken and tells him that when they married she had a £70 legacy from her grandmother and a year later £50 was given to her by one of her uncles. With all the rest, plus birthday gifts, she was probably worth £500.

However, Hannah Maria admits that some years previously her mother had given Edwin the house at Headingley Hill and also, jointly with Aunt Eliza Tatham, her mother had given them the dog-cart. She says that £2,000 would not repay Edwin for the actual time and money he spent on legal matters for relations; he was an extremely busy man and relations often expected him to help them for nothing. She stresses that he has earned all his money through hard work and, except for a small sum, had spent his entire inherited fortune on his own education and made his own way in life.

Hannah Maria and Edwin are very upset. How dare Charles ask what he is going to inherit from them? They suspect he might be after Hannah's money because Hannah Maria points out in her letter that her daughter's health had been brought up before the wedding. It is quite possible that the girl had always had mental problems. Edwin had been worried that they had insisted on getting married before Charles had found a proper job and he is now alarmed

that Charles wants money paid directly to him. Hannah Maria says in her letter: 'One would think you were afraid that Hannah would not let you have it'.
Charles explains that it would be less of a gift when paid to Hannah than if it
was given to himself. Hannah Maria snorts:

> *Am I to understand that you would rather have £80 or £90 paid to yourself than*
> *£100 given to your wife? That appears to me to be the meaning of your remarks.*
> *As to any difference of feeling in the matter which it implies, I would give my*
> *daughter £100 with much more pleasure than I would give £20 to her husband.*

Charles replies that his wife complained that her father had taken off the
Income Tax. Hannah Maria is surprised at this but says Edwin had invested
£2,000 for her and would now send the exact sum. She writes more calmly:

> *You ought to feel very much complimented for I certainly never saw any one so*
> *completely under cupid's influence as she was, and believing that she would be*
> *happier with you, I was very glad for her to be married, and certainly to her own*
> *satisfaction, and moreover, after she accepted you, her own home and her family had*
> *only a small place in her thoughts.*

But this is followed by a further barb. Charles had been affronted when Edwin
tried to find out more about his prospective son-in-law 'as if he had been a
menial servant'. Hannah defends her husband, saying that if she had been a
widow, she would have done exactly the same and would have made even
more enquiries, 'not that she doubted him in the least.' She asks Charles

> *… if he would have been proud if his only daughter had married a man she had*
> *met at a watering place without the introduction of even a friend and of whose*
> *family he knew nothing?*

There is another mystifying point in her letter:

> *Mr Eddison says that he understood you to say that you had made great sacrifices*
> *to oblige us. I do not know what that means, unless with regard to the invitations*
> *to your father's wife.*

Did he not want his mother asked to the wedding? Was she not respectable or
too grand? Perhaps she was mad.

All this trouble could not have come at a worse time for Edwin. He is extremely busy and bouts of his pain flare up under the stress. Hannah Maria ends her long letter positively, saying that the only bright aspect of the whole affair is that Hannah had not been aware of what Charles was doing:

> It must affect her, but I am glad she did not take any part in it. Of course you will not name it to her at present, but I shall want to know sometime how she can account for the sudden change from smiles to tears. I am your affectionate mother, H. M. Eddison.

Hannah Maria evidently slept on the letter which she had written out in rough and adds a long postscript following a hasty note from Charles that arrived that morning. She seethes when Charles says:

> Don't forget my thinking about my letter that my only object in going to talk to Mr Eddison in the hope that he and I might understand each other better, and so gradually grow into better and more father and son like feeling.

Charles adds that Edwin has not acted fairly towards him in money matters and that his way of paying money is so offensive and unkind that his daughter had been in tears after receiving it. Hannah Maria insists that Hannah had kissed her father a few months before and thanked him with smiles. Charles's final complaint is that he was not treated properly by his father-in-law and his seven brother-in-laws. He says that Edwin has never invited him to anything nor had he called on them at their house. Hannah Maria, exhausted, replies that Edwin, who never had an unkind thought about him, had been almost paralysed by his letter and that he was always welcome at the house. She explains that her husband never sought the society of men, even those of his own age, and anyway Charles had many general invitations from his in-laws. Ending sadly, Hannah Maria writes:

> I am sorry, very sorry that this has happened because nothing can put us in the position towards each other as we were before you called, for it would be simply absurd to say that we can either of us ever forget it. And here I will leave this painful subject.

To the Eddisons' relief, soon after this heated exchange, Charles takes up the living in the idyllic parish of Lingen in Herefordshire where he probably came across the diarist, Reverend Francis Kilvert who had a nearby parish at Clyro and whose diaries give an enchanting picture of the people and the countryside. The area around Lingen was beautiful and Hannah and Charles flourished here away from the claustrophobia of Leeds and the Eddison relations.

At the age of fifty-two Charles's career changed when he inherited a considerable amount of money from his cousin Robert Wake and took the name Middleton-Wake. He was then appointed Assistant Chaplain to the Chapel Royal Savoy in London and in the same year got his Cambridge MA degree (he had been at Christs College). He then became a director of the Fitzwilliam Museum in Cambridge and while in London he catalogued and arranged the Rembrandt etchings in the National Gallery.[121] He was also Art Director of the South Kensington Museum and a Fellow of the Linnean Society.

It is not certain whether his nervy wife and child went with him to London where he lived at 2 South Villas, Campden Hill Road, but at some point Hannah and their son, Cuthbert went to live at The Manor, Adel and were joined by Charles, who died there aged eighty-seven.

Cuthbert was described as 'delicate' (his great niece, Rachel Mainwaring-Burton says he was decidedly odd). There are photographs of him aged six wearing a braided knickerbocker suit holding a straw hat. He has dark staring eyes and his great-grandmother, Hannah Baker calls him 'a fine boy'. In a later photograph when he is about nineteen, he is dressed in a stripy summer suit with a rose in his buttonhole. His hair, prematurely balding, is flicked either side of the middle parting and his wide moustache is capriciously waxed at the ends.

After his father's death he changed his name to Cuthbert Dallas Middleton-Wake and tried his hand at farming. To the horror of the family, he started a pork butcher's shop and a library at Cudworth in the West Riding. He also kept a pilot boat at Hull. Being rich after his parents died, he later lived in Cornwall at Dallas House, Flushing where he died in 1951 aged eighty eight, a bachelor cared for by his butler.

In August 1862 Robert Eddison, now a young engineer with John Fowler and Co. crossed the Atlantic for the second time, taking with him a Kitson

---

121 He wrote the *Catalogue of the Etched Work of Rembrandt* in 1877 and his 1897 lectures, *Invention of Printing* and the *Rembrandts at the National Gallery* were published by John Murray.

Robert William Eddison became a director
of John Fowler & Co. Leeds

Annie Tatham, who married Robert
William Eddison, was described by Anne
Eddison of Shireoaks as 'uncommonly
clever, she is moreover pretty.'

& Hewitson ploughing engine with the object of establishing new markets for steam cultivating machinery and securing patent protection for Fowler's various inventions. The mission was aborted as the Civil War was plunging the country into chaos and while he was there Robert was able to witness the Battle of Bull Run at first hand. It was during the trip that he fell in love with his seventeen year-old cousin, Anna Paulina Tatham whose father, Henry Billingham Tatham, a wealthy industrialist in Philadelphia, was to play a major role in Fowler's entry into the industries of heavy electrical engineering, electric lighting and lead covered cables. Old Hannah Baker was pleased by this marriage but sadly there are no letters about the wedding which took place in America the following year.

When Robert and Anna Paulina returned to England, the new bride was introduced to the relations. She impressed them all and Anne Eddison of Shireoaks described her as 'uncommonly clever – little- but a most beautiful figure so compactly made, and anything she does she does beautifully – she is moreover pretty.' The Eddison brothers chortled when her initials change to APE.

*Annie Eddison, the first woman to
be awarded an honorary doctorate by
Leeds University*

Annie, as she was called, was certainly bright and she soon joined a group of women from the leading families of Leeds who, inspired by a national campaign led by Emily Davies [122], were pressing for the improvement of women's education. Annie was a dynamic leader in the campaign to provide a girls' school in Leeds which could match the education of the Boys' Grammar School and was rewarded in 1912 when she became the first woman to be awarded an honorary doctorate by Leeds University. One of the eight houses at the Grammar School is named Eddison House in her honour. Another, Lupton House, is named after Francis Martineau Lupton who helped to establish the school and is the great-great grandfather of the Duchess of Cambridge. The Luptons, a philanthropic family, associated for many generations with the municipal and educational life of Leeds, lived near the Eddisons and are mentioned in the diaries from time to time. Edwin would have been delighted at Annie Eddison's success in the world of womens' education but, alas, he did not live long enough to see her receive her honorary doctorate.

122 The founding Principal of Girton College, Cambridge, 1869

19
Bank Crash

But little crime we see in Quakers
and least of all is found to be
'Mongst those engaged in carpentry.
                                          W. H. Auden

Newly retired, Edwin took a large sum of money to America for a three-month family holiday in mid-June 1866. He took £500 in credit and £50 in cash (roughly £25,000 and £2,500). The holiday was risky as his health was faltering but he wanted to visit the New Country and the Tatham relations before he died. He almost certainly banked with the Quaker bank Barclays, one of the seventeen banks in Leeds, and among his papers there are references to Overend and Gurney the Quaker discount bank which had just crashed with huge financial losses. The Overends were cousins and Edwin had probably heard rumours of the bank's difficulties and had been worried about his savings.

Overend and Gurney was the City of London's leading discount house, with a turnover second only to the Bank of England [123] and double all of its competitors combined. On Thursday 9 May 1866, the day before the disaster, a notice was pinned to the bank's door regretting that there had been a severe run on their deposits and all payments had been suspended. The public were horrified. This most respectable of banking houses was closed by noon the next day (Black Friday) and was besieged by a tumultuous crowd of desperate depositors.

The humiliating failure of Overend and Gurney Bank (thinly disguised as Grapnell & Co. in George Eliot's *Daniel Deronda*), caused a massive financial crisis in the City. The collapse quickly spread to other banks including the Bank of London, the Consolidated Bank, the British Bank of California, the Contract Corporation, Grant's Imperial Mercantile and the Agra and Master-

---

123 It was a discount bank used by the smaller banks as a safe place to deposit their short term surplus cash and for them to earn interest.

man's Bank. Firms including Peto & Betts, builders of Nelson's column and the Reform Club - all went into liquidation along with many shipbuilders and railway companies.

Banking had been a Quaker success story. In the days of highway robbery when banking was in its infancy, rather than carrying money, Quakers insisted on leaving their cash in the hands of Friends and soon others began to trust their money to Quaker banks, which in those days were still local or regional institutions such as the Aldams, Peases, Woodall Banks in the North East and the Gurneys Bank in Norwich. These local banks became swallowed up by larger ones and the great Quaker banking houses of Lloyds and Barclays emerged. Sampson Lloyd's business principle was succinct: 'We do nothing for nothing for nobody.'

Overends, as it was called, was a banker's bank. The suspension of all its payments in May 1866 caused a massive financial panic. Within three months more than two hundred other companies collapsed and Overend and Gurney itself had debts equivalent to GBP 1 billion at today's values. Investors were outraged, fortunes were lost and the horrified family of George Eliot's heroine, Gwendoline was made destitute overnight. Business was suspended in financial centres across the world and the City of London would never be the same.

The blue genealogical rolls found in the Bedale tin trunk produced a tightly knit mosaic of Quaker intermarriages which helped in linking Eddison connections to other Quaker banking families such as the Peases, Backhouses, Barclays, Gurneys, and Frys. The Overends first appear on the family tree in 1659 and in 1783 Richard Overend from Tatham in Lancashire married Martha Tatham. During Edwin's life the Overend cousins were in and out of Gateford House and the letters chatter with their activities. Edwin's 1826 list of measured relatives includes the weights and heights of Martha and Isabel Overend, daughters of Hall Overend, the Sheffield physician.

The Yorkshireman John Overend (uncle of Wilson, Martha and Isabel Overend) was an early partner in the ill-fated bank along with his brother-in-law, Thomas Richardson, a London bill broker's clerk who set up on his own in 1802. It helped that Richardson was related by marriage to the mining and railway-backing Peases and that the bank had invested heavily in the early railways. In 1807 John Overend joined the Gurney banking business, leaving shortly afterwards, but the disgrace hangs forever over his name.

The Gurneys were successful Quakers, their fortune coming from wool and then from banking. The wool industry was highly lucrative in the eighteenth century and Gurney's Bank, founded in Norwich in 1770 was a logical development. They were not the strictest of Quakers but were generous philanthropists, supporting the Norwich theatre and the Norwich Society of Artists founded by local water colourist, John Crome. In later years family members were part of the circle around Harriet Martineau, a writer on economics and an early campaigner for women's rights. Though the Gurneys had their roots in Norwich rather than the City, Bagehot's definition of the London private banker fitted them well: 'He was supposed to represent, and often did represent, a certain union of pecuniary sagacity and educated refinement which was scarcely to be found in any other part of society.'

Cobbett sneered at Quakers, referring to them as 'the Jew-like fraternity'. Regarding them as upstarts, he singled out Dick Gurney, a Norfolk brewer and member of the banking family, for an insult about his gaberdine, a loose cloak worn by Jews. The fact that he was a brewer caused further sneers, as it meant that he was one of those who lured the poor away from their home-brewed beer to drink the unwholesome and doctored concoctions dispensed by brewers.

The small firm in which the Gurneys invested, eight years before the Battle of Waterloo, dealt in bills and grew to become the foremost bill-broker in Europe, eventually emerging as the doomed discount house Overend, Gurney & Co. The success of the bank was largely due to the character and talents of Samuel Gurney, born in 1786, the second son of the banker, John Gurney of Norwich. In a backhanded compliment, Karl Marx referred to him as 'the first-rate expert, the esteemed, crafty Quaker', and writing years later Bagehot differentiated the patriarch from his MP son as 'Samuel Gurney the Great'. In the usual Quaker tradition, Samuel started work at the age of fourteen as an apprentice with his relatives the Frys.

Samuel Gurney did not look like the others who worked in the City. Instead of the usual black frock coat and glossy top hat, he wore a brown broadcloth coat, gaiters, squared-toed shoes and a low hat with a broad brim of white beaver. In the Quaker manner, he would irritatingly wear his hat inside as well as outside the office, re-

Samuel Gurney

An Overend share certificate, in the end not worth the paper it was printed on

moving it at home or in Friends' meetings 'in the sight of God'. He addressed his business letters to 'Esteemed Friend' or 'Respected Friend' – the former suggesting an inflexible decision was about to be expressed and the latter that there was some room for discussion. Samuel's sister Elizabeth, the prison reformer, was married to the unlucky banker Joseph Fry, whose bank collapsed in 1828.

Under Samuel's stewardship the bank weathered many storms. Bad debts and market crises led to a run on their deposits but he steered the bank through them all and the business flourished. By the 1850's it was discounting £70 million's worth of bills a year and after paying its senior partners handsome salaries, generated profits for its owners of around £200,000 a year.

Some argued that the firm began to slide even before Samuel Gurney died, tracing a hairline crack to a mere cargo of zinc ingots. Under his successor, his nephew, David Barclay Chapman, Overends discounted £200,000 of Bills for a metal-trading firm against the security of stocks of zinc together with tin, iron and cochineal. It was a routine banking deal, but it was serious money. The documents of title had been forged and the metal already pledged to another lender. Chapman discovered this too late, after the bank had parted with the money. He had two choices, to prosecute or to cover up and he made the wrong one. He gave the fraudsters a second chance to come up with genuine collateral and told them not to breathe a word about it. They laid their hands

Desperate depositors besieged the Overend and Gurney Bank
on Black Friday, 10 May 1866

on some genuine security at other creditors' expense and to the outside world everything seemed normal. It was a relationship the traders talked up to their great advantage as they went on duping other banks in what turned out to be an early version of a Ponzi scheme, in which new investors' money is used to pay high interest to earlier investors until, inevitably, everything collapses.

Some years earlier the bank had invested in an Irish shipping dream. Peter Daley, an aggressive self-promoting and entrepreneurial Roman Catholic parish priest had built up a large property portfolio, wanting to relieve suffering and poverty in Galway. He submitted a proposal to Whitehall to make Galway a transatlantic shipping terminal by designating it as an official packet station for mail between the British Isles and North America. His plans included a railway from Dublin to the heart of Galway and building there the biggest hotel in Ireland. This all made sense on paper as Galway had a magnificent natural harbour and was 300 miles nearer to North America than Liverpool. But Galway was inappropriate because the docks were not suitable and the ships of the Galway Line were too puny and unreliable for Atlantic crossings.

*The trial of the
Overend directors*

They were driven by paddle-wheels, powered by engines that gobbled coal and were backed up by sails which could be set ablaze by the hot embers. The Irish terminal could not compete with Liverpool. Overends had a complicated involvement in the scheme and could have cut their losses but instead they commissioned six new ships and increased their investment.

Several other bad investments caused further problems, but what made this particularly disgraceful was that on the 12 July 1865 Overends turned itself into a limited liability company and offered shares to outside investors. Investors paid £15 per share and further shares were to be issued or calls made on existing shares if the new company required more money in the years ahead. This was to become a nightmare for the investors who lost not only their original investment but also the further calls on their shares. The shocking part was that the partners had known that the newly acquired mass of loans might never be repaid.

After the crash, criminal proceedings were brought against the former partners who briefed the best QC of the day. The plaintiffs, having in effect lost all their money, were poorly represented and not able to compete. In his summing up, Lord Chief Justice Sir Alexander Cockburn told the jury they were not to decide whether there had been misrepresentation or concealment, but whether the six men had embarked on a 'deliberate design to deceive and cheat the public.' Cockburn was clear that they had not. The prospectus that had been accepted by the public did not reveal the truth. But Cockburn did castigate the former partners. 'Though turning aside from the safe settled path of business and going astray after vain phantoms and elusive dreams, embarking their capital in the wildest speculations and the rashest enterprises, led away by the spirit of greed and gain, we have seen them reduced to ruin, their lost fortunes scattered in the winds their reputations tattered and impaired, but they are not on trial for that.'

The partners were found not guilty. They were poorer but not destitute: one hopes they were sorry. The Quaker movement never recovered and its decline started around this time. The principles of the Society of hard work, caution, and plain honest dealing had been compromised.

There was one amusing incident on the day after the failure of the bank. The Fellows of an unnamed Cambridge college which had deposited a large amount of cash at Overends, clerics to a man, gathered in a panic waiting for their bursar, a layman, to tell them that the college was ruined. Not so. 'I am pleased to report, Master,' he declared, 'that the College's funds are secure … when I was in London last week, I happened to call on Messrs Overend and Gurney and looked in on the manager. I found him reading the Bible. So I at once withdrew our balances.'

The disaster probably hastened the death of old Samuel Gurney. Chapman lost his reputation for plain dealing over the cover-up and was forced out of the firm after two years but took with him his capital of £250,000. The active partners in the firm were Gurney's eldest son, Henry Gurney, Barclay Chapman's son David Ward Chapman and John Birkbeck, who was married to Henry Gurney's sister.

The collapse of the bank shocked England to the core, not just by its scale and suddenness but also because the bank's partners were prominent Quakers. Newspaper headlines screamed out:

'Terrible and disastrous Financial Panic in London'

'Failure of Many of the Largest Banking Houses in London'

'Almost Total Suspension of Business in London, Liverpool and Other Commercial Centres'

'Lombard Street Blockaded By A Tumultuous and Terror-Stricken Mob

'The Panic Without Parallel in the Financial History of England'.

What drove apparently sensible and honest men to behave, or misbehave, in the way they did? Was judgement distorted by greed, ambition or overweening self-confidence? The Directors were tried at the Old Bailey for the crime of making false statements in the share prospectus but were acquitted by the jury after the judge directed that they had committed a 'grave error' rather than a crime.

So just a few days after the crash, his wallet full of newly drawn notes from the bank and further cash stacked away in the trunks, Edwin studies the map of America and plans the routes of his trip. Presents for the Tatham relations have been bought, suitable clothes packed and the large trunks forced shut. The family's excitement is palpable as they are driven to Leeds station to catch the Liverpool train. The pain in Edwin's side is not too intense but now he is worried about his heart trouble. He could not have imagined what lay ahead.

20
Doomed Trip to America

You never know the value of your relations until they are dead.
Edwin Eddison to his sister Ann Eddison of Toothill

A few months before the American trip there were problems with Henry who was out of control. Staying with his sister, Mary Dougill at Thorpe House near Huddersfield he had shocked his niece Elizabeth with his behaviour. She wrote to her aunt:

> *I feel that our prospects just now are uncertain if Uncle Henry misbehaves himself in the way he did lately again. I think we cannot stay at Thorpe with him, and he must either be somewhere else or he must go altogether and some place quite out of the way, where he could not get what takes his senses from him.*

Henry is sixty three. He had let the family down by failing to cope at Gateford and is now drinking himself to death. Edwin was fond of his brother and notices that he is looking ghastly. Mary struggles on but it all becomes too difficult so Henry is packed off to Lightridge House, a nursing home at Fixby, quite near Thorpe House and Toothill Hall; here he lives till his death in 1874, paid for by his three sisters.

For the past few years Edwin had been involved with the management of Adel, the estate his mother-in-law inherited from her brother, George North Tatham. Farming was in Edwin's genes; he had known about his grandfather's friendship with the agriculturalist, Arthur Young and enthusiastically immersed himself in estate matters. He leased Adel Mill Farm which he later bought and then built the bailiff's cottage; he bought a two acre field on the south-east side of Adel Mill Bridge in 1852 and built two more cottages, one for the gamekeeper and the other for the craftsman, George Davison. Three substantial houses were built for members of the family and now he set about making the farm more efficient. In 1856 a large barn was erected at Adel Mill with a water mill to drive the machinery, and the Manor House and two more new cottages were built later that year. In 1860 a coach house and stable were built then two more large houses: The Willows, rented initially by the

A cottage at Adel. Watercolour by Thomas Sutcliffe c. 1850

Adel farmyard scene. Watercolour by Thomas Sutcliffe c. 1850

Hannah Middleton-Wake sitting by Adel Mill

wealthy stuff and yarn merchant, Edward Baron von Schunck (who danced with cousin Anne Eddison at Hannah's wedding) and Church Lane House for Edwin's mother-in-law, Hannah Baker.

Major alterations were done to Blackhill Farm: the house was rebuilt, the barn enlarged and a new stable and granary added. Next the Yorkgate, Smithy Mills, East Moor and Beck Farms were upgraded. The area swarmed with Eddisons. At various times the houses were occupied thus:

Edwin and Hannah Maria at Ashfield House,
Headingley Hill

Hannah and Rev Charles Middleton-Wake at
Adel Manor in 1910

John Edwin at The Lodge, Adel

Robert farmed at the Willows 1881, Adel Mill and 1891
at Adel Manor

Harold, Robert's son lived at Stairfoot House, Adel Mill, Adel Manor

Frederick lived at Adel Manor in 1878

Octavius lived in St. Helen's House, Adel

Hannah Baker lived at Church Lane House, Adel.

The March weather is terrible in 1866. Restless and bothered by heart trouble, Edwin decides to take a two month holiday to the South of England with his family. They travel first class to Weymouth the favourite seaside resort of George III of whom a story is told of his peevish encounter with a Jamaican planter whose coach was even more resplendent than his own. 'Sugar, eh?' the King was heard to exclaim loudly.

Edwin wrote to his sister, Elizabeth from Weymouth cheerfully describing the frost, snow and howling wind outside and sixteen year-old Octavius [124] rushing in, raw-faced, to persuade his twenty-four year-old brother Jack [125] to join him outside where they are having biological fun dissecting a seagull. Edwin cannot resist quoting Otty's exuberant remarks:

Come Jack! It will do you good. The tide is down and the wind is a whistler, the sailors say it is "half a gale" but I call it a whole one. It has blown the wind out of me as I turned the corners in coming from the Quay. It will be good Physic for your delicate limbs. It will make your juvenile whiskers grow rapidly and curl that moustache on your thin studious phiz. Oh just look at the waves ... splashing and roaring and showing their snowy leaping crests for nearly half a mile straight before us. Stretch up and face the wind like a Yorkshireman. Come along poor old Doctor! Bring your hammer and I'll carry the bag for your stones and shells and then we will have another grand dissecting.

124 Octavius Eddison, later a solicitor with the Leeds firm Nelson, Eddison, Lupton. His son E. R. Eddison, CB, CMG, (a childhood friend of Arthur Ransome who shared the Eddison's governess, Miss Glendinning) was a scholar of Icelandic literature and after retirement wrote works of high fantasy which influenced Tolkien. His early works drew strong praise from C. S. Lewis who invited him to Oxford to read his stories.
125 John Eddison later qualified as a doctor. He was a friend of Andrew Lang, the poet and author of fairy stories.

The Eddisons travel on to Exeter, Penzance, Newlyn, Mousehole, Lands End and back via Bristol, Glastonbury and Wells. But Edwin is a tricky travelling companion doing exactly what he wants to do and truculent if crossed. He describes his routine in a letter and his old enemy the Pain gets a mention:

> I rise at 7.15 to 8, lunch at 1 and dine at 6. I first tried dining in the middle of the day, but I find it seems to affect my pain more after eating my chief meal if I go out after it, so I have changed my hour and I think am better for it. I never feel any ailment and I think I have not done since I left home except (and it is indeed a very humiliating exception) the pain which I suppose is the pain in the stomach.

The holiday is not coming up to Edwin's expectations. His wife and niece Libbie Dougill cannot join them as Hannah Maria has a cold. He is quite glad but cannot stop them joining the party later. The letter ends with a description of the view from his window with the wind whistling and the waves smashing and crashing headlong over one another. He comforts himself with the thought that he will soon be beside a good hearty Yorkshire fireside and looks forward to a welcome from his sister Ann at Toothill.

There is time to reflect on the loss of his dear brother, Booth and most of Booth's family who have recently been wiped out by tuberculosis. He writes to his sister Ann, 'You never know the value of your relatives until they are dead' and imagines what life would be like if Booth was still alive and retired at Rainworth Lodge with him at Adel, both growing old together and reflecting on boyish days and their early struggles at Gateford. Edwin marvels that he has reached the age of sixty-two and remembers how often his mother used to say to him, 'I never expect to see thee twenty-one!'

Having recovered from her cold, Hannah Maria and her niece Libbie Dougill join the party at Ryde and Libbie writes to her mother: 'Uncle Edwin was much nicer today... railway travelling does not seem to hurt him'. They love being at Sandown but Edwin is fidgety and on the Portsmouth railway platform abruptly decides that he wants to go on to Penzance where he decides to stay for a week. Then he becomes anxious to get home. Hannah Maria would have liked to stay longer but her arguments make him more crotchety and she has no influence.

The April weather is glorious in Weston-super-Mare and they are in ecstasies about the primroses, violets and cowslips that are beginning to bloom. Edwin forgets his fractiousness and delights at the feathery hedges and clouds of white blossom and Libbie hears a cuckoo at the top of Torr Hill. They love this part of the country but Edwin, suddenly in a bad mood, says that his wife is 'the best hand in England for spending sight-seeing money on her companions and whirling about'. Hannah Maria, now marvellously well, forgets her asthma for the time being and carries on 'whirling about'.

A few weeks after this holiday, which has done them all a power of good, Edwin draws up many lists and makes final plans for the three month trip to visit his wife's Tatham relations in America. This was an interesting time to go as the four year-long Civil War had just ended and parts of America were in a battered state. Edwin may have hoped to find a suitable wife for his son, John Edwin (Jack) or a husband for his niece, Libbie Dougill. Ironically they married each other fifteen years later!

In mid-June 1866 the excited party set off from Liverpool in the steam ship Java. The group consists of Edwin, Hannah Maria, Edwin's twenty-four year old niece, Libbie Dougill, his twenty-five year-old son Jack, (now a qualified doctor), his three-months pregnant American daughter-in-law, Anna Paulina and her baby son Edwin (Teddy) who is only thirteen months old.

Libbie writes to her mother saying smugly that everyone except for her is seasick. She describes the tiny cabins with two berths, a sofa and table. Her American sister-in-law, Anna Paulina has her own cabin and the nurse, Mary Ellerby shares one with the baby Teddy. Uncle Edwin strides around the ship examining every corner while the others make themselves comfortable on the deck with rugs. Libbie is bubbling with young womanhood and meets a young merchant from London on board called Mr Briggs who is travelling with his brother. She finds the atmosphere of the ship thrilling, the beat of the sails, the whirr of paddle wheels and the rumble of the steam engine are music to her ears. They cannot wait to see America but do not know what is in store for them.

After a rough passage of eleven days with a headwind all the way from Liverpool, they arrive at the bay of New York on 27 June 1866. Coming up on deck they are hit by 'warm winds as if from a furnace' and the smells of the new country fill their nostrils. Edwin feels rather old and is quickly exhausted by the bustle and heat and has to sit down. He is given his little grandson Edwin to look after. The nursemaid does all the packing while the ladies are busy 'decorating themselves' for the meeting with friends and relations.

The bay of New York overwhelms them. It is the largest and finest they have ever seen and down on the pier they catch a glimpse of the elegant forms of James and Henry Tatham (Anna Paulina's brothers) and her uncle Charles Billington Tatham who are waiting with his carriage and pair to take them to

Edwin took his family to America after the Overend bank crash in 1866. The party included Hannah Maria, above left, Edwin, above right, his neice, Libbie Dougill, his son Jack, his daughter-in-law, Annie Paulina and his grandson Teddy

his house in Clinton Avenue, Brooklyn where they will stay for over a week. It is an area with many big houses which Libbie describes as:

pretty, but the roads are dreadful, full of holes you could put a pig in. Every main street has a car track – a railroad for horses drawing passengers down both sides of the road. The cars are large vehicles taking 30–60 people, with 2 or 3 horses going about 6 miles an hour from to and through the cities every 10 minutes with constant roars and ring of bells on the horses necks day and night.

Edwin is horrified by the pig-sized holes in the roads having being much involved with municipal aspects of Leeds. The only roads he can call decent are Broadway and Fifth Avenue; others are dirty with rubbish and evil smells of all kinds and he is shocked that even in the best streets barrels of rubbish are put outside each house where small boys are constantly seen grubbing around in them. Their first visit is to Barnum's Museum which had been burnt down the previous year, and they listen to stories of how the dangerous animals would appear round corners and startle pedestrians in New York streets.

Letters describe 'very grand' houses made of unpolished marble – some made grander still with polished granite pillars. The City Hall, banks and stores are 'imposing' but they feel the city has an unfinished look; the buildings are mixed up with poorer frailer houses which have 'so much rough woodwork that it looks as if a good strong wind would blow them all away'.

On a cool morning they set off very early in a wagon with a pair of horses to drive thirty-six miles up the Hudson River over dreadful roads to Mr Tatham's farm where he grows vines, Indian corn, wheat and potatoes. The woods on the banks of the river around the farm are lovely with houses dotted around and many varieties of ferns, flowers, humming birds and fire-flies.

Two days later they go to Philadelphia escorted by Hannah Maria's first cousin, William Penn Tatham who had started the lead-pipe business in 1840 with his brother, Henry. There were five Tatham brothers in the firm: two in New York and three in Philadelphia.

The Tatham business made a great amount of money. It was the largest lead-pipe maker in America with a factory in Philadelphia and a lead works and shot tower in New York. The American method of sizing lead shot was invented by the Tatham Brothers. Previously, gun shot had been made by pouring lead into wooden moulds but a faster method was to pour molten lead from the top of the shot tower through sieves with different sized holes for different sizes of shot into a large container of water. A great deal of shot was

The Tatham Brothers'
sheet lead rolling mill
and lead pipe factory in
Philadelphia, 1847

A Tatham lead ingot

William Penn Tatham
who started the lead
business in Philadelphia

needed for the Civil War and to give some idea of the intensity of the battles, bullets were found welded together in the scrap brought from the battlefields to the Tatham's Works. [126]

126 Report in the *Hartford Weekly Times*, 1879.

[241]

The Tatham's 50 ton Gothic Steam Engine, 1857 on display
at the Henry Ford Museum in Dearborn, Michigan

As involvement in wars was incompatible with Quaker pacifist principles, the Tathams may have found it difficult to deal with the ethics of manufacturing bullets. A firm with similar ethical problems was Samuel Galton's of Birmingham, owned by a successful Quaker businessman and scientific thinker who had inherited a gun-making firm from his father and, with the threat of revolution, found himself targeted for disownment from the Society. His defence was that he had inherited the business rather than built it and that gun making was valuable for the 'purpose of DEFENSIVE war, to the Support of the CIVIL POWER, to the PREVENTION OF WAR and to the PRESERVATION OF PEACE'.

The Billington family (Charles Tatham's mother was a Billington) made their money in Philadelphia out of army clothing [127], so it is likely that when she married James Tatham in Germantown, Pennsylvania in 1805 Mary Billington had a good dowry. The family may even have been related to John Billington who came over on the Mayflower and was hanged for murder. His son Francis, married Christian Penn, a cousin of the great Quaker William Penn, founder of Pennsylvania. There is no proof of a connection but it is significant that Charles Billington Tatham's brother was called William Penn Tatham.

Many early Quakers in America owned slaves but they changed their views in 1699 and worked hard for the total abolition of the slave trade. In 1775 they created a society to promote the emancipation of slaves and were much concerned with their welfare and education. The Tathams took Libby to visit a school for coloured children where she longed to take home a little Negro who was 'as black as coal'. She also visited a free school in Brooklyn and was impressed to see words such as 'recalcitrant, reciprocity, consideration' from dictation on the slates, no doubt due to the cult of spelling in the country dating back to Benjamin Franklin's proposal for a public spelling contest in 1750.

Edwin is impressed and asks if he can say a few words to the pupils in a mixed school of 1,500 children. He is fascinated to know what motivates Americans and in a letter writes 'we must educate our people to keep pace with the Americans in wealth'. He is staggered that the Gerard's College in Philadelphia, attended by all classes of orphans, was built of marble and the grounds covered 100 acres.

Edwin's eyes are opened wide by this trip. Everything impresses him: churches, chapels, schools, market houses, waterworks and drinking fountains. He is astonished not to have seen a drunken man or woman since his arrival and is also amazed by the rates of pay, hearing that the Tathams employ no one for less than $11 a week.

But not everything is perfect. On 9 July they are joined by George Tatham and move on to Washington where several things shock them. The American hotels are dustier and dirtier than English hotels and often spotted with gobbets of tobacco juice where men and women constantly fail to spit into the

127 Mary's father, Thomas Billington, a clothing tycoon had orders from the
     War Department for weekly supplies of 400 suits for the troops during the
     American War of Independence,

strategically placed spittoons. American customs are very strange to the Eddisons who are intrigued by the coloured people who wait on them attentively but are as clumsy as overgrown children. During meals they find the servants' habit of fanning guests with giant feather fans as irritating as the flies and the housekeeping routines surprise them as the women seem to do much of the work themselves while the quiet serving girls hardly do any dusting at all. The food is new to them and arranged in six different little dishes round their plates and with a great variety of vegetables and cakes. The kitchens are in the cellars and a rumbling hoist brings the food up into a small pantry at the end of the dining room. Breakfast is at 7am, lunch at 1pm and dinner at 4.30pm Libbie delights in the breakfasts and writes:

> *They have plates of small buns not made of bread I think, with shortening in which they call biscuits and eat instead of bread. The bread we have is often hot and always cut in thick slices and piled on a plate and then we have hot corn bread (Indian corn) and no end of cake of all kinds, some good and some I don't like. For breakfast we have had stewed kidneys chopped up into small pieces. Clam fritters, corn fritters, milk, beef steak, fried potatoes and hashes of various kinds done up with potatoes, and eggs boiled – they put them into glasses and make grand messes of them. At dinner we have a joint of some kind and lots of vegetables of various kinds and done in different ways and then fruit or cake.*

Libbie badly wants to look at the village for the freed slaves at Arlington, just outside Washington, but the others are reluctant to go fearing a depressing scene. Fugitive and liberated slaves from Virginia and elsewhere had recently poured into the city in search of work and shelter, so something had had to be done to help them. Freedmans' village was just a camp which had been established three years earlier in the grounds of the Custis and Lee estates where the slaves lived in a collection of fifty small houses, each divided in half in order to house two Negro families. There were schools, a hospital, a home for the aged, a laundry and churches neatly arranged round a central pond. The intention was to educate the slaves and train them as skilled labour – they were paid $10 a week but had to pay back half their salary for their keep. This all seemed praiseworthy but a disapproving Quaker group reported that the residents lived entirely under military discipline with military rations and there were stories of miserable blacks wandering the nearby roads begging for food.

Freed slave village at Arlington

The only source of water for the village was a well on what had been a swamp which still spread frequent outbreaks of scarlet fever, measles, whooping cough and smallpox. It was not an entirely happy place and residents were often glad to leave but the village served a useful purpose and lasted for over thirty years. Henry Billington Tatham employed two freed slaves Rachel and Martha Syphix whose unusual surnames appear in the history of the Arlington Freedman's village. A John Syphix, whose mother had been a slave in the camp, wrote to the Secretary of War in 1888 asserting that the freed persons from Arlington should be compensated for the improvements they had made to the property.

Libbie was irritated by her Aunt Hannah Maria who sweats and fusses in her hot garments and as she only has one travelling dress and desperately needs thinner clothes, Hannah Maria takes her niece shopping to buy expensive new outfits. She thinks it would be thrilling to take American clothes back home but Libbie, despite her enthusiasms for things American, is not so sure about this and, feeling homesick for England, tells her aunt that she 'would not live in America for anything'.

The American heat begins to cool down and the social life goes on with a party at the Tathams' house where the young have to sleep in the large airy billiard room. Libbie, a strong rosy-faced girl, notices that most American girls at the party are pale and delicate and is quite taken aback that they can tell at a glance that she is English.

The family dine with the wealthy political Quaker, Benjamin Tatham, in his fifteen bedroomed house, 36 Stuyvesant Street, New York. Benjamin enjoyed living in style, and was a prominent figure in the early municipal movement in Philadelphia. He was a responsible Indian Commissioner and tried to do as much as he could to improve the condition of Negroes and Indians. Conversation at dinner that evening about the rebels, rulers, the Civil Rights Act and the problem with the freed slaves was bitter and political.

Rebecca Tatham, Benjamin Tatham, Henry Tatham, Isabella Tatham

Benjamin Tatham looks wonderfully self assured in a full length silhouette portrait [128] with one hand resting on the small of his back, the other across his front. He is wearing a high collar, frock coat with narrow trousers tapering down to a pair of delicate feet. He is facing his wife, Rebecca [129] who wears her hair in a prim chignon and clasps a long necklace.

The Eddisons, eager to explore the rapidly developing city of New York, now visit the newly created Central Park, an area recreating the English Picturesque style by Olmsted and Vaux. Although it is in a raw state, they are bowled over by its magnificence. Six hundred acres of land were bought in 1853 for the new park in an area described by the board of commissioners as 'a suburb more filthy, squalid and disgusting can hardly be imagined'. It was six miles round and beautifully laid out with water, trees, hills, dales, good drives, riding paths, skating houses and bridges. Libbie suggested that in twenty years when the trees were fully grown, it would be even more beautiful than anything in England. But in an under-punctuated letter home she is a little critical of the carriages:

there were numbers of carriages of all kinds but they seem to enjoy themselves in quite a different way from our aristocratic and stately driving in Hyde Park. They

128 With the author.
129 Rebecca Collins, granddaughter of the Quaker printer and publisher, Isaac Collins, Royal Printer to George III, who printed the first newspaper of New Jersey and the first American Bible – far more error-free than most of its contemporaries.

Central Park, New York, 1860

*get a good pair of horses and a very light high carriage, the wheels look like cobwebs
and the people themselves don't dress so much and cram as many as they can
wedge into the vehicle and the master seems to drive in a great big ugly hat and a
loose duster coat and sits in the easiest position he can find, and both carriage and
horse and harness generally look dusty and not bright and spanking, like our Hyde
park turn outs.*

Americans seem very different to her and seeing some men in livery, she ex-
claims 'they do look comical' –

*They sit in a loose sort of way and not one article of their clothing seems to fit
and they look so serious and important all the time. There are a good many black
people about. They are in the cars and about the street and both men and women
seem to delight in wearing white garments. Mr Charles Tatham has a black man as
groom but he is very stupid about driving and scares Aunt greatly.*

There is rather a scene when one of their horses is kicked in the leg by another causing blood to gush but the nonchalant driver says it was nothing. People
come up and put their heads through the carriage window and offer help.
One bossy woman says 'your horse will bleed to death, get out your handkerchiefs and make bandages!' Then, to their embarrassment, people shout,
'there are ladies in there who will let the poor horse bleed to death rather than
soil their handkerchiefs!' The poor injured horse is sent home and another is
found to take them to Central Park. They have only driven down one street
when this animal falls grazing his skin in three places, so they go to the next
livery stables to get a new pair. Libbie writes 'American horses are made of

different stuff to English ones'. But she is much impressed by Charles Tatham's Arab beauties which she thinks are quite tough.

A notorious clergyman, the muscular, long-haired Henry Ward Beecher[130], a social reformer and abolitionist, happens to be preaching locally. At that time he was the most famous preacher in America even though his thickness of speech made it difficult to understand. He was close to a number of women and became involved in an adultery trial. Libbie was of course enchanted by him but found his sermon more of a lecture. She wrote with fascination:

The notorious Henry Ward Beecher with his sister Harriet Beecher Stowe who wrote 'Uncle Tom's Cabin'

we had several real currents of laughter interspersed and several times when you might have heard a pin drop. The people were so intensely interested and the church was crowded. They say hundreds go away not able to get in every Sunday. It seems so queer to see people all fanning themselves in church even the ministers do with large palm leaf fans. I find mine of great use. Mr Beecher said before he began his sermon that he had some flowers as he was always supplied with a bouquet by some of his congregation ... and he thought perhaps those who had been admitted into membership that day would like one to take away as a memento. He is a wonderfully eloquent man.

They visit the Navy yard and go round a turreted war ship, 'a dreadful looking thing', and see an iron clad torpedo boat. Hannah Maria's asthma is now better and Edwin is feeling quite good but is tired by all the sightseeing and can only walk very slowly.

The annoying fanning goes on everywhere, not only in churches. But for the Eddisons, the most wonderful thing of all is the iced water, which is always on hand, even in the railway cars and steam boats. Houses have a daily supply like milk deliveries in England. They revel in this luxury and marvel at the

130 Brother of Harriet Beecher Stowe, the author of *Uncle Tom's Cabin.*

View from Spruce Street, Philadelphia c. 1820, where Henry Tatham lived

two bathrooms in the Tathams' house, with hot and cold water available all day long.

It was a relief to leave the dusty New York hotels to go and stay with Henry Tatham at 1102 Spruce Street, Philadelphia. The heat intensifies and the family shift uncomfortably in their thick clothing. Staying at Willards Hotel, Washington, the haunt of Presidents and royalty, they visit George Washington's house at Mount Vernon, but are disappointed to find it in poor condition. They then steam up the Potomac river and visit the Senate and House of Representatives where they cannot hear a word of the speeches. When they return to Philadelphia, the heat reaches 104 degrees in the shade and fifty-seven year old Hannah Maria daringly buys a bathing dress. She does not care what she'll look like. Edwin is horrified.

The young shoot, fish, bathe and go on thrilling midnight walks. Jack and his cousin Harry Tatham disappear all night to the consternation of the others, returning in the early morning saying they had lost their way. Now Edwin starts to get ill and doctors are summoned. Writing to his sister Ann at Toothill, Edwin says that he is not satisfied with any of these American physicians:

It is not because they do not seem to understand what is matter with me but they do not explain the ailment as poor Thackrah of Leeds used to do. When Thackrah gave his descriptions I felt almost to see what was the matter.

He constantly analyses his symptoms and alarms himself:

Since I came here to Philadelphia, I have frequently at night had a difficulty in breathing, or perhaps I should say a noise or huskiness in my breathing. I cannot say that it keeps me awake. I think it arises partly from the heat of the weather. I imagine the thermometer at 104 degrees in the shade which it was in Philadelphia 10 days ago. In one week there were 700 persons dead and I think nearly 100 of sunstroke in one day.

They need to get out of the oppressive heat so the Tathams take them to a famous American bathing place called Cape May, about 60 miles south of Philadelphia, and then they visit the Seven Mile Island, a deserted island described

BATHING DRESSES. —(See Description, Fashion Department.)

Hannah Maria had to buy a bathing dress. Illustration from Godey's Lady's Magazine

in Libbie's letter as 'Juan Fernandez's' after Alexander Selkirk's [131] sparsely inhabited island off Chile. Amazingly, the Tathams owned this 3,000 acre island which had first been bought in 1772 for £72 by Aaron Leaming. At that time it was uninhabited apart from Algonquian and Lenni-Lenape Indians who came to fish and trap in the summer. The Tathams built the first buildings there, including a number of beach houses for early 'excursionists' who came for the day to picnic on the island.

It must have been a wild paradise for the Eddison party. They pile into the Tathams' carriage drawn by a pair of mules as big as Arabian horses which trot along the seven miles of sea shore. The beach is perfect but there are too many green-head flies and mosquitoes which cause the mules's legs to stream with blood. The bathing was 'quite equal to Scarborough' they thought – the only drawbacks being the bugs. Fifty-seven year old Hannah Maria marches into the sea in her new bathing suit. She is hot and does not care about Edwin's horror. The skirts of the bathing suit reach her knees, but her legs are decently covered by bloomers. She would also have worn a black hat, black stockings and shoes. At that time even gloves were worn for bathing to keep skin milky white.

Having bought the island for a song from Aaron Leaming, Henry Tatham sold it to his brother, George North Tatham in 1854. Henry's house on the island (now a hotel called Stockton Manor) was described by Libbie as 'not beautiful, but convenient and capacious'. Two towns have been built on the island: Avalon [132] and Stone Harbor, both now packed with holiday houses of the rich and famous.

George Tatham also owned Windmill Island in the middle of the Delaware river which was once a haven for pirates and is now known as Smith's Island. It had been reserved as the private property of the Quaker Penns but it was never surveyed for the Penns or for the Commonwealth so George Tatham applied and bought it in 1849.

The Tathams' 120 acre farm grew Indian corn and oats and bred 300 merino sheep that wandered anywhere. There were hundreds of acres of wild forests where cows sheltered under the shades of the trees to avoid the flies. This was a time to watch nature. Edwin could sit in the shade and forget his ail

---

131 Daniel Defoe almost certainly based his character Robinson Crusoe on the castaway, Alexander Selkirk 1676–1721.

132 The old Tatham farmhouse in Avalon was near 25th Street and Dune Drive.

Edwin's sisters, Elizabeth and Ann, lived together at Toothill Hall

Thomas Firth a Quaker philanthropist
who left the Toothill estate to Ann Eddison

ments for a while and be amused by a collection of beautiful chickens picking insects from the cows' legs. Libbie is intrigued by a huge black fly the size of a butterfly alighting on a reclining cow's back, followed by a tiny chicken who waits until the fly thrusts his proboscis into the cow's skin, then snaps him in two and gulps him down.

It is at this point that Edwin writes a curious letter to his elder sister, the fifty-nine year-old Ann who is living at Toothill Hall, near Huddersfield with the recently widowed seventy-seven year-old Thomas Firth. Edwin writes how sorry he is to hear that Mr Firth is ill and he sends Ann advice saying that she should keep things peaceful in the house. He advises that if Mr Firth is troubled, it might be a good idea for him to get anything that disturbs him off his mind and ends pointedly that he hopes Thomas Firth has made his peace with heaven.

Thomas Firth [133] was a Quaker philanthropist who had inherited the Toothill estate in 1828 from his rich uncle Robert Firth. Sir John Ramsden, a local landowner, wanted to buy the estate as he dearly wanted to be able to say 'we own Huddersfield' and Thomas Firth said he would consider selling if Sir John could cover the largest floor in Firth's warehouse with sovereigns standing on their edges – which of course was impossible. In 1866 Thomas Firth later bought more land from the Thornhill family who owned much of the land around Huddersfield.

For some reason, Edwin's sister Ann had gone to live at Toothill to help look after Thomas Firth's ailing wife Betsy, who died in 1864. There is a line in one of Thomas Firth's letters to Ann saying: 'Thou knows I tell thee if we could but borrow thee for a daughter how happy a circumstance it would be … Betsy is so low and poorly … Betsy desires her love and hopes to get to see thee. This is too selfish of us both.'

Ann was pretty and in a painting she is looking flirtatiously over her shoulder while pulling on a silk glove. She has a tiny waist but we know from Edwin's lists that at the age of twenty-four she weighed a healthy eight stone five pounds and was five foot four inches tall. She was religious and in her old age she exhausted her nieces by repeating her favourite verse: 'While place we seek or place we shun / The soul finds happiness in none / But if the Saviour lead the way / Tis equal joy to go or stay / Or will be so some future day'.

133 The Firths were related by marriage to the Eddisons.

After old Betsy Firth died, Ann Eddison, aged sixty, became engaged to the seventy-five year old Thomas Firth but he died during their engagement, leaving her the entire Toothill estate where she continued to live in a grand style with her unmarried sister, Elizabeth, who seems to have been too shy to have had much fun in life. Elizabeth's photograph was in a Machin album; she was dark-haired and good looking but there is quiet resignation in her face. She may have been too worthy to have had an admirer as in her will she left legacies to The London Missionary Society, The British and Foreign Bible Society and the Female Heathen Education Society.

Dying at 83, Ann outlived her siblings. She treated her servants well and kept their proud photographs carefully named in a box. She shared her wealth among her nephews and nieces and her will mentions the portraits of her Uncle Robert Booth, her mother and her brother Henry.[134]

Canada and the Fenians

For the next part of their trip an intrepid party of Eddisons and Tathams travel to Canada in August 1866 to visit an area that had recently been bruised by an extraordinary battle. A few weeks earlier a small army of Fenians had attempted to conquer Canada, intending to hold the country hostage in return for a liberated Ireland.

When the American Civil War ended nearly a million men found themselves unemployed, among whom the hardest hit were thousands of Irish-Americans. Some of them formed themselves into a battle-hardened group and swarmed into the city of Buffalo, watched by nervous Canadians from across the narrow Niagara River. On the last day of May 1866 the situation had become menacing enough for the Prime Minister to call out the Canadian militia. Because of Britain's support for the South in the Civil War, the Americans were not helpful.

The battle began in the early dawn of 1 June 1866 with 900 Canadian militia under Lt. Col. George Booker opposing the Fenians who had plenty of enthusiasm but not much military experience. At first the Canadian militia held their ground but were eventually defeated by the rebels after much confused fighting. Although victorious, the Fenians were afraid of being surrounded and retreated to Fort Erie and then moved on to the edge of the Niagara river,

---

134 All three paintings are owned by the author.

The extremely hot Eddisons and Tathams pose for a photograph by the Niagara Falls

In 1867 Fenians attempted to conqueror Canada at The Battle of Ridgeway

at which point their grand invasion plan fizzled out. Only nine Canadians had been killed and thirty-seven wounded. Fenian losses are unknown.

In the middle of the night, two months after this battle, the exhausted Eddison party arrive at the Catacall Hotel, Niagara, where at breakfast the next morning the staff recounted recent events. Edwin feels well after a good night's sleep so they visit the Canadian side of the Falls, not far from the site of the military skirmish, and pay four shillings to have their photograph taken. Edwin and Hannah Maria, sitting on chairs arranged precariously near the edge of the Falls, look extremely hot and uncomfortable in their plain clothes. Edwin's beard is bushy and long, and unbelievably he is wearing gloves. The Tatham brothers are wearing dark suits and waistcoats and Libbie leans against her aunt's knees looking jaded. Young Jack Eddison, not in a waistcoat, sits on the grass near his cousin Margaret Tatham who strategically looks away. Only the mens' straw hats give an indication of the intense heat.

The family go to visit Dr Mewburn (relation of their friend, Francis Mewburn, the 'Railway Solicitor') who lives at Stamford Village just by the Falls. He and his wife are in misery. They are mourning their only son, twenty-one year-old John Herriman Mewburn who was one of the nine Canadians killed by the Fenians. The Eddisons may have made this Canadian trip to share the Mewburns' grief.

Writing to his daughter, Hannah Middleton on 13 August 1866, Edwin describes the local atmosphere seething with Fenian rumours. He tells her that the 800 strong 10th Regiment of Infantry are bracing themselves to go to the frontier the very next day and explains the situation:

> I have only today been able to make out what the Fenians want. It is to conquer Ireland and make it independent and to make Canada a part of the United States. The US Gov. appear to be unwilling to do anything to affront England but the disbanded soldiers and the lower classes of the US appear to me to sanction the Fenians and to wish them well. But whether they will be able to make any way in their mischievous notions is doubtful. There are 3 Regiments here that seem loyal and ready to fight them. The 10th, 17th and 47th and as far as I can learn from them and others, they long to be 'up and at them'. The leaders of the Fenians as far as I can learn are discontented Irish, chiefly Catholics and the disbanded soldiers of the late North Army who want to be after mischief and are too idle to work... There are about 150 Fenian prisoners in the Gaol here, who were taken at the Raid at Ridgway when poor Herriman Mewburn was killed. There are 15 on the

Guard constantly and they are always prepared with loaded Muskets. When will war cease?

At this stage the Eddisons' travel plans and health start to fall apart. After the nerve-racking visit to Canada they leave the Falls by train but the drive shaft of the engine breaks so they have to continue their journey to Toronto by steamer arriving at their hotel late at night. Hannah Maria is laid low for the next four days with her asthma but recovers sufficiently for the party to travel on to Kingston. Bumping down the rapids seems to make Hannah Maria more cheerful, but now Edwin falls ill.

On the Quebec steamer from Montreal, Mary Tatham and Libbie collapse and travelling on to the Montmorency Falls, Mary becomes so much worse that a doctor has to be called. Her brother Ben watches over her at the hotel while the others manage an outing to inspect an Indian village.

It takes poor Mary a week to recover. Her worried father, Charles Billington Tatham arrives to take care of her, while the rest of the party travel to Montreal and stay at an uncomfortable hotel where they are horrified to find no fires and no breakfast before 8.15. From Montreal they trundle on to Caldwell by stagecoach and stay at the much smarter Fort William Henry Hotel. Three days later they are back in Henry Tatham's comfortable house in Spruce Street, Philadelphia, but once there Edwin is suddenly taken fearfully ill. The Tathams' doctor, the eminent Dr James Levick, is sent for and has grave forebodings. The next we know is that Hannah Maria is hastily telegraphing New York to change their booking to the iron-hulled ship the Persia, the largest and fastest steam-ship in the world, which will be sailing in five days' time. Edwin rallies and watches while the trunks are packed and then goodbyes are said to all the young Tathams. The party of Eddisons finally arrive at the docks; Edwin is wheeled on board in a bath chair with the four Tatham brothers and their sister Emily standing on the quay to wave them off. There are worries that Edwin may not survive the journey.

The wind is in their favour and the trip only takes nine days but Edwin finds the motion of the ship unbearable. Hannah Maria uses the new transatlantic telegraph cable, which had been completed six weeks earlier, to telegraph ahead to Frederick, now a partner in his father's firm, instructing him to get the house ready. Edwin's health is not mentioned but the telegraph says 'Come to the station alone'. The ship docks at Liverpool on 14 September and the subdued party catch the 4.00pm train arriving at Leeds at 7.00pm. to be met by the anxious Frederick.

Cunard's Persia, the largest and fastest steam-ship in the world

As soon as they arrive home Edwin is eased into bed in agony. The loyal Mr Teale is summoned, then William, Ann, and Benjamin gather at their brother's bedside, later to be joined by Mary and her husband John Dougill. Edwin lies still, his head swimming with the motion sickness of the journey: the effort to reach home alive has exhausted him. His appalling headaches, intense pain and the bad nights are all recorded by Hannah Maria in her dark green diary.

On 26 October brother Henry and sister Elizabeth arrive. During the evening celebrations for Walter's twenty-first birthday they are delighted to see Edwin edging down the stairs, clutching the bannister, the first time he has left his bed since arriving home. Slowly he seats himself at the head of the table and listens to the conversation. In her diary, Hannah Maria writes that it was 'the best night and day since he came home'. Two days later on 30 October, feeling even better, Edwin decides to go out for a drive.

The next week thunderous headaches return. Mr Arthur Cheatle, the Leeds ophthalmic and aural surgeon is sent for. Hannah Maria again records the fearful headaches and tries to remain cheerful for a series of three celebrations: her birthday on 16 November; their 36th wedding anniversary on 18 November (for which Edwin again drags himself out of bed); and on the 20th there is a sombre dinner without Edwin, to celebrate Hannah Baker's eighty-seventh birthday. On 23 November, Edwin's spirits soar when he realises that the violent pains in his side have vanished. But the joy is short-lived. The pains return the next day with a vengeance. The doctor realising that nothing can be done, orders a single palliative leech to be applied to his stomach that night which of course makes Edwin weaker and he feels worse the following day.

The widowed Hannah Maria Eddison

During the week before Christmas family spirits are lifted by Anna Paulina, who had been pregnant during the American trip, giving birth to a second son, Henry Baker Eddison. There are no comments about this child who dies fifteen months later.

Christmas is a dismal affair. Hannah Maria and her mother dine alone downstairs as Edwin cannot be left on his own. He does not want fuss or noise and the next three days are just about bearable. Two days into the new year things start to change and Hannah Maria telegraphs for Otty to come quickly as his father is 'very ill'. Mr Teale hovers around trying to soothe the pain with fresh tinctures but they are no use. Edwin's condition worsens and an uncomfortable makeshift bed is arranged on the floor of his bedroom for Hannah Maria, but she too is unwell as her asthma has become worse with all the strain.

[259]

Now the pain that had tormented Edwin all his life becomes unbearable. In her new damson-coloured diary Hannah records in faint blue ink that he is being given morphine. Before long the valiant Edwin Eddison starts to fade and on the icy cold morning of the 13 January 1867, he loses his hold on life.

Although devastated and exhausted, the family are relieved that his sufferings have ended. There are no more letters or diaries for a time but life goes on at Adel and the next generation of Eddisons take charge. Four years later, Hannah Baker dies at the age of ninety-two, then in 1872 the sixty-three year-old Hannah Maria dies only a year older than Edwin at his death.

Edwin had lived so much of his life in pain and perhaps this was why he dwelt so much on his own mortality and why he stored the simple, conscientious letters of his childhood and put the details of his adulthood in order. He lived intensively on the edge of life and perhaps, who knows, his deep feelings trapped within the attic papers were waiting for resuscitation to inform a present moment. The pages catch a pause in history and bring Edwin alive for a brilliant moment, like the flare of a sulphur match.

But now the Eddison voices fade. The gramophone winds down to a whisper and the portraits can relax. Not all of their secrets came out of the trunks.

Illustration Acknowledgements

I am most grateful to the following for permission to publish the following illustrations:

Aubrey Bowden for the portraits of Booth Eddison, his wife Eliza and daughter Mary by Sir John Gilbert RA, and also for the portrait of Booth's granddaughter Vera by Denholm Davies and the portrait of Sir Frank Bowden by Vera Bowden.

Christopher Eddison for the portrait of Hannah Maria Eddison by Sir John Gilbert RA.

John Machin for the print of Gateford House by Samuel Heironymous Grimm.

Guy Peppiatt Fine Art for the print of Barlborough Hall by Samuel Heironymous Grimm.

Bedale Hall for the print of Bedale *c.* 1820 by Ray Todd.

The Religious Society of Friends in Britain for Thomas Aldam by William Bell Scott.

The Company of Cutlers in Hallamshire for the portrait of Wilson Overend.

Elizabeth Adkins for the portraits of William Booth, and Ann Eddison of Toothill.

Professor Mary Fowler for the photograph of John Fowler.

Bibliography

Anderson, Verily, *Friends and Relations* (Hodder and Stoughton 1980)

Ashelford, Jane, *The Art of Dress, Clothes through History* (National Trust 1996)

Bailey, Brian, *The Luddite Rebellion* (Sutton Publishing 1998)

Baines, Edward, *Leeds Guide 1806*

Baldwin, Neil, Edison, *Inventing the Century* (Hyperion 1995)

Black, Maggie, *Food & Cooking in 19th Century Britain* (English Heritage 1985)

Booth, Abraham, *The Reign of Grace* 1812

Brandon, Piers, *The Spice of History* – lecture 2002

Briggs, Asa, *How They Lived* (Basil Blackwell 1969)

Buchan, William, *Buchan's Family Physician* 1802

Burney, Fanny, *Selected Letters and Journals* (Oxford University Press 1987)

Campbell, Mildred, *The English Yeoman* (The Merlin Press 1983)

Carpenter, Humphrey, *W. H. Auden, A Biography* (Faber and Faber 2010)

Clarkson, Thomas, *A Portrait of Quakerism*, 1806

Cobbett, William, *Rural Rides* (1830)

Cole, D., and Davison, F., *From a Family of Wheelwrights*

Cook, E. T., *The Life of Florence Nightingale* (Macmillan 1914)

Crompton, Val, *History of Adel, Yorkshire* (2009)

Davenport-Hines, *Richard, Auden* (William Heinemann 1995)

Defoe, Daniel, *Selected Writings of Daniel Defoe* (ed. J. Boulton Cambridge 1975)

Ditchfield, P. H., *The Old English Country Squire* (Methuen 1912)

Dyer, F. L., *Edison, His Life and Inventions* (Harper Brothers 1929)

Eddison, Edwin, *Worksop and Shirewood Forest* (Longman 1854)

Edgeworth, Maria and R. L., *Practical Education* 1801

Eidson, Wanda, *It's spelled E I D S O N* (Gregath Publishing Co.)

Elliott, Geoffrey, *The Mystery of Overend and Gurney* (Methuen 2006)

Flanders, Judith, *The Victorian House* (Harper Collins 2003)

Fox, George, *A Journal Vol. 1 and 2.* (Anthony Pickard 1836)

Girouard, Mark, *Robert Smythson & The ElizabethanCountry House* (Yale 1983)

Glendinning, Victoria, *A Suppressed Cry* (Routledge Kegan Paul 1969)

Granger, R. F., Notes

Grayling, A. C., *The Quarrel of the Age, The Life and Times of William Hazlitt* (Phoenix Press 2000)

Green, Daniel, *Great Cobbett* (Hodder and Stoughton 1983)

Gregory, Roy, *The Industrial Windmill in Britain* (Phillimore 2005)

Greville, C. C. F. *The Greville Memoirs* (B. T. Batsford 1963)

Hardman Moore, Susan, *Pilgrims* (Yale University Press 2007)

Hardyment, Christina, *Behind the Scenes* (Penguin 1992)

Hatfield, Mrs, *Letters on the Importance of The Female Sex* 1803

Haydon, Benjamin, *The Autobiography of Benjamin Haydon 1786–1846* (1853)

Haydon, Benjamin, *Autobiography*, published 1853

Haykin, M. A. G., *The Works of Abraham Booth* (ParticularBaptist Press 2007)

Heaton, John, *Walks through Leeds 1834*

Holroyd, Michael, *Works on Paper* (Little Brown 2002)

Hughes-Hallet, *The Immortal Dinner* (Viking 2000)

Israel, Paul, Edison, *A Life of Invention* (John Wiley 1998)

Josephson, Matthew, Edison, (John Wiley & Sons 1992)

Jukes, Edward, *Indigestion* 1831

Kennard, Mrs A., *Mrs Siddons, 1887*

Kennelly, A. E., *Thomas Alva Edison* (National Academy of Sciences 1932)

Kenyon, Edith C., *The Life of John Wesley* (J. B. Knapp, London 1891)

Lamb, Charles, *The Complete Works and Letters of Charles Lamb*, Modern Library 1935

Laird, Mr, *The County of Nottingham* (George Cowie 1820)

Leeds Directory 1822

Leeds Guide 1806 (Printed by Edward Baines)

Martineau, Harriet, *Autobiography, Volume 1* (1877)

McCall, H. B. *The Early History of Bedale* (Elliot Stock 1907)

McLelland, David, *The Achieving Society* (Van Nostrand 1961)

Miller, F. Trevelyan, *Thomas A. Edison* (Stanely Paul 1932)

Mitchell, W. R., *A History of Leeds* (Phillimore 2000)

Montague, Lady Mary Wortley, *Letters Written During her Travels in Europe, and Asia and Africa Vol 1,* Anthony Henricy, 1796

Neave Brayshaw, A. *The Quakers, their Story & Message* (The Ebor Press 1982)

New Jersey Historical Society Archives

Newsome, David, *The Victorian World Picture* (John Murray 1997)

Pearson, D. R., *Annesley through the Ages* (Denis R. Pearson 1995)

Pennant, Thomas, *A Tour in Wales 1778–1783*

Porter, Roy, *English Society 1714–1815* (Longman 1992)

Puckler-Muskau, Hermann von, *Touring England, Ireland and France in 1826*

Punshon, John, *Portrait in Grey. A short history of the Quakers* (QHS 1984)

Rae, Pamela, *Turtle at Mr Humble's.* (Smith Settle 1992)

Ransome, Arthur, *The Autobiography of Arthur Ransome* (Century Publishing 1976)

Reed, Michael, *Georgian Triumph 1700–1830* (Routledge & Kegan Paul 1983)

Reynolds, Simon, *A Chronicle of Bedale* (St Gregory's Publications 2001)

Riley-Smith, Tristram, *The Cracked Bell,* (Constable 2010)

Robertson, Una A., *The Illustrated History of the Housewife* (Sutton 1999)

Rochefoucau, Francois, Duc de la, *A Frenchman in England 1784*

Rodes, Sir John, *A Quaker Post-bag, letters to Sir John Rodes of Barlborough Hall*

Rule, John, *Albion's People,* (Routledge 1992)

Simond, Louis, *Journal of a Tour and residence in Great Britain during the Years 1810 and 1811,* 2 vols, (Edinburgh, 1817)

Simond, Louis, *An American in Regency England: The journal of a tour in 1810–1811*; (Maxwell)

Simonds, W. A., *Edison, His Life, His Work, His Genius* (Allen & Unwin 1935)

Swift, P. R., *From Sawbones to Keyholes* (Barny Books 2003)

Tatham, Richard E. *The Family of Tatham of Tatham* 1857

Thomas, Gill, *Diary of a Dairymaid* (Hanes Llangollen History 2007)

Thompson, F. M. L., (Ed) *The Cambridge Social History of Britain 1750–1950 Vol 2*

Thoresby, *Topography of Leeds, 1732*

Tomalin, Claire, *Samuel Pepys* (Penguin 2003)

Vipont, Elfrida, *The Story of Quakerism* (Bannisdale Press 1954)

Vipont, Elfrida, *George Fox and the Valiant Sixty* (Hamish Hamilton 1975)

Wesley, John, *Primitive Physic* Printed by R. Hawes 1774

White, Francis, *Nottinghamshire History 1853 and 1864*

White, Francis, *History, Directory and Gazetteer of Nottingham* 1853

White, Robert, *Worksop, The Dukery* 1875

White, Robert, *The Visitors Handbook to Worksop* 1853

Wilson, Ben, *Decency & Disorder 1789–1837* (Faber and Faber 2007)

Young, Arthur, *The Farmer's Tour Through the East of England 1771*

Young, Arthur, *The Farmer's Calendar* (Richard Phillips, 1809)

Index

Lucas, Samuel, 92
Lucas, William, 132
Luddites, 108
Ludlam, 108
Lunar Society, 88
Lund, Dr. 201, 209, 211
Lupton House, 224
Lupton, Nelson, Eddison, solicitors, 236
Luptons, 47, 224,
Lupton, Francis Martineau, 224
Lupton, Kate, 218n

Machins, 30, 33, 34, 37, 177, 196, 254
Machin, Henry, ix, 30, 32–34
Machin, Henry Vessey, 30, 32–3, 38, 168, 177
Machin, Judge John Vessey, 30, 34
Machin, John, 30
Mainwaring-Burton, Rachel, 73
Makins, Sir George, 88
Mann, Thomas, 9
Mansfield, 46, 83, 168, 206, 207
Martineau, Harriet, 182–3, 227, 263
Marx, Karl, 227
Mason, Elizabeth, 160
McClelland, David, 89
Melbourne, Lord, 182
Mewburn, Dr, 256
Mewburn, Emily, 81m 141
Mewburn, Francis, 126bm 141–3, 145
Mewburn, John Herriman, 256
Middleton-Wake, Cuthbert Dallas, 215, 222
Middleton-Wake, Hannah, (née Eddison), 162, 184, 186, 214–6, 219, 220–3, 235–6, 256
Middleton, Lord, 168
Middleton, Rev Charles, 214–6, 218–9, 220–2, 235
Montague, Lady Mary Wortley, 101, 102n
Moon, George Washington, 134
Moon, John, 132
Moore, Robert W., 74
Moore, Samuel, 74
Morris, John, 130
Morton, Mary, 41
Moseley, Constance, 36, 173

Murray, Matthew, 121, 121n
Musters, Jack, 167

Napoleon, 45
Naylor, James, 84
Nelson, Eddison, Lupton, solicitors, 236n
Nelson, Thomas, 32
Newcastle, Duke of, 43, 168
Niagara Falls, 254–6
Nightingale, Florence, 74, 207–9
Noble, Matthew, 191
Norfolk, Duke of, 23, 25
Northumbrian, 146
Nottingham, General Hospital, 205 130, 140, 148, 150, 158–9

Palmer, Fanny, 56
Parkin, Elizabeth, 109
Partridge, John, 155
Pashley, Sarah, 197
Pasteur, Louis, 158
Payne, John Arthington, 117
Payne, Richard Ecroyd, 60–1, 79, 115, 122, 125–6, 130, 140, 148, 150, 158–9
Payne, William, 123–6, 132
Paynes, 47, 79
Peacock, Thomas Love, 22
Peak Frean, 89
Pease, Edward, 126n, 141–5
Pease, Elizabeth Lucy, 144, 200
Pease, Joseph, 144–5, 200
Peases, 47, 79, 87, 144, 226
Peel, Sir Robert, 136
Peirse, Richard, 2
Pemberton, Rev Francis, 2
Penn, Christian, 243
Penn, William, 22, 24, 35, 71, 76, 81, 84, 86, 91, 93, 136, 243
Penn, Admiral Sir William, 94
Pennant, Thomas, 106
Penns, 251
Pepys, Samuel, 93, 159
Perceval, Spencer, 132
Peto & Betts, 226
Pevsner, Nikolaus, 22
Polam Hall, Darlington, 197, 198n
Pollard, Joseph, 204